FISHTANK | *SATYRICOÑO* | *TWO ROBERTS*

"Migdalia Cruz rips the American drama out of the bougie living room and affluent morality crisis, and puts it directly in the human body—the desirous, gorgeous, disgusting, sacred, and misunderstood flesh that our souls call home. She probes the many places where beauty and horror coexist in our lives. No one else writes or thinks like Cruz; her work changed me and expanded our genre, returning it to its humble, sacred, and impolite origins. Put more simply, Migdalia's vision as a writer is ravishing."

—Quiara Alegría Hudes, *Playwright/Screenwriter, Pulitzer Prize, Tony Award*

"This new volume reaffirms Migdalia Cruz as one of America's greatest playwrights, still working at the height of her powers. These plays reimagine history and conjure new worlds, through blazing theatricality, boundless imagination, and heart-wrenching joy. Cruz's groundbreaking and seminal work continues to define our new American canon."

—David Henry Hwang, *Playwright,* three time *Pulitzer Prize Finalist, Three Obie Awards, Professor at Columbia University*

"Creating new worlds in the liminal spaces between the living and the dead, imagining the excesses of classical Rome in the context of an ecologically doomed, dystopian future, and leaping across centuries to reveal the relationship between a Puerto Rican pirate in the seventeenth century and a seminal Mississippi blues musician in the early twentieth century, Migdalia defies all expectations by uniting us with the secret corners of our mortal understanding. She whisks us by virtue of her theatrical imagination into realms otherwise denied our everyday, rational minds. I dare this generation to match her courage and produce these magnificent plays!"

—Linda S. Chapman, *Artistic Director, New York Theatre Workshop*

"Through these three disparate worlds of Migdalia's imagination, we travel from the heart-breaking, to the obscene, to the utterly phantasmagorical, where the impossible is more than impossible: it is necessary. She is our finest architect of grief in all its glories, crafting connections between love, violence and redemption, which if it's not achieved in this world, then surely in the next."

—Octavio Solis, *Playwright/Mentor, Lydia, Santos & Santos, Man of the Flesh*

"Migdalia's work feels like a seance of theatrical proportions."

—Caridad De La Luz, aka spoken word artist *La Bruja, Emmy Award Winner, Executive Director of Nuyorican Poets Cafe*

Copyright © 2024 by Migdalia Cruz

The Impossible Plays of Migdalia Cruz is published by Tripwire Harlot Press, LLC.

All rights reserved. Except for brief passages quoted in newspaper, magazines, radio, or television reviews, no part of this book may be reproduced in any form or by any means, electronic or mechanical, including photocopying or recording, or by an information storage and retrieval system, without permission in writing from the publisher.

Professionals and amateurs are hereby warned that this material, being fully protected under the Copyright Laws of the United States of America, and all other countries of the Berne and Universal Copyright Conventions, is subject to a royalty. All rights, including but not limited to, professional and amateur stage productions, recording, recitation, lecturing, public reading, motion picture, radio and television broadcasting, and the rights of translation into foreign languages are expressly reserved. Particular emphasis is placed on the question of readings and all uses of this book by educational institutions, permissions for which must be secured from the author's representative: Peregrine Whittlesey pwwagy@aol.com

ISBN: 978-1-7341402-8-6 (print)

Dramaturgy and Creative Direction by Jacqueline Goldfinger
Book design and composition by Daniela Naranjo-Zarate
Cover and interior illustrations by Christian Potter Drury
Map of Migdalia's Beginnings by Migdalia Cruz
[*Commissioned by Playwrights Horizons* Almanac, *2024.*]

About the Visual Artist

Christian Potter Drury decided at age 13 to become an artist, and has been one ever since. Her work has shown at many galleries, and she has won numerous awards including The Newport Museum Annual Show. For many years she worked at *The Los Angeles Times* and *The Wall Street Journal* as Art Director. Today, she continues to paint and illustrate.

Production Histories

FISHTANK
2020: Commissioned by Clubbed Thumb with a NYSCA Grant, Maria Striar, Artistic Director; Michael Bulger, Producing Director
2021: First workshop directed by Edward Torres via Zoom produced by Clubbed Thumb with Zuleyma Guevara, Zabrina Guevara, Michael Frederic, Charles Browning, Erin Cherry, Blanca Camacho, José Antonio Melián, Andres Santiago Pina, Keith Jones.
2024: Twenty-nine-hour Workshop directed by Edward Torres at Clubbed Thumb featuring Zuleyma Guevara, Zabrina Guevara, Michael Frederic, Charles Browning, Erin Cherry, Susanna Guzman, Anthony Ruiz, Chad Vann, Evan Horwitz.

SATYRICOÑO
2014: Roundtable Reading directed by Daniel Jáquez at The LARK with José Antonio Melián, Teddy Canez, Bobby Plasensia, Maria Helan, Laura Butler, Orlando Rivera, Christin Cato, Portia, Bernardo Cubria, Heather Velazquez, Gabriel Sloyer, Omar Pérez.
2015: Workshop Production directed by Daniel Jáquez at INTAR with the Unit 52 ensemble; Nidia Medina, Producer; Mariana Carreño, Unit 52 Acting Coach; Jordana delaCruz, Stage Manager; Cristian Amigo, Composer/Sound Design; Stefan Martin, Costume/Prop Co-designer; Ana Andrade, Costume/Prop Co-designer; Lucrecia Briseño, Lighting Designer; Raul Abrego, Set Designer; Lou Moreno, INTAR Artistic Director; John McCormack, INTAR Executive Director.

Cast:
André Sguerra - JUNIOR
Annie Henk - PODEROSA
Annie Vargas - TULLIA & PARTY GUEST 1, 3
Bobby Plasencia - MAN & MALPUSO
Christin Cato - MINA the METEOROLOGIST
David Anzuelo - OCTAVIO
Heather Velazquez - FILOMENA
Jacqueline Guillén - LUJURIA
Ashley Marie Ortiz - OENOTHEA
Oscar Cabrera - ENCO
Txai Frota - CYLVIO
David Mila - GANDULES
Stefan Martin - ARROZ
Hara Zi - VITA & PARTY GUEST 2, 4

TWO ROBERTS: a pirate-blues project
2010: Roundtable Reading at the Lark Play Development Center, NY, directed by Cándido Tirado, with Stacy Okulfor, Jeffrey Joseph, Josh Torres, Marilyn Torres, Dominic Colon, Shirley Rumierk. Juan Villa, Armando Riesco.
2011: Bare Bones Production at the Lark Play Development Center, directed by Cándido Tirado with Stacy Okulfor, Jeffrey Joseph, Josh Torres, Marilyn Torres, Dominic Colon, Felix Solis, Bobby Plasensia, Anna LaMadrid.
2015: Roundtable Reading directed by Sol Crespo at Pregones Theater, the Bronx, NY, with Flaco Navaja, Adriana Sananes, Lori Elizabeth Parquet, Calvin Thompson, Joel Perez, Antonia Vargas, Michelle Guadalupe, Anna Rahn, Gerry Rodriguez, Chad Carstarphen, Yaraní Del Valle Piñero.

TABLE OF CONTENTS

Invoking the Impossible
an essay by Migdalia Cruz...............13

Badass in Limbo, or The Haunting of Migdalia Cruz
a foreword by Todd London...17

Migdalia's Flowers: Life and Legacy
a reflection by Morgan Jenness 27

FISHTANK..31
SATYRICOÑO...113
TWO ROBERTS..225

Building a Safe House when No Space is Safe:
Your Words are my Home
an afterword by Virginia Grise...335

Thanks from Migdalia...338

$\frac{1}{2}$ of $\underline{12}$ circles

$= \frac{1}{2} \cdot \underline{12} = 6$ circles

and the 7th circle
was light... all smalled
was a pinpoint to guide me.

My mother told me that there were no baby pictures of me,

because we were too poor to have a camera.

I know I was once a baby, but there is no definitive photographic proof.

(x) $15 \times \frac{3}{5} = 3 \times 3 = 9$

(ix) $13 \times \frac{1}{3} = \frac{13 \times 1}{3} = \frac{13}{3} = 4\frac{1}{3}$

nothing younger than 5. Or older than $\underline{12}$.

Early Hobo collar

Self-cut bangs...

the world

of 9 triangles

calm

And teach mathematics on the rails...

6a. $\frac{12u - 8u}{} = \underline{12}$

I imagined mostly that I would get out of the ghetto.

6b. $r + 10 = 9$

I was sure I would be a hobo or a mathematician.

Or a mathematician hobo.

And travel.

There was freedom in knowing that I was no one's baby.

No photos. No evidence. I could be anyone.... Still can be...

-Migdalia Cruz- 1/19/23

Invoking the Impossible
an essay by Migdalia Cruz

There was once a little girl who only knew she existed because of the notes she left behind.

Though she never expected them to be read or remembered, she knew they summed up her remedy-less life. A life without hope was not a sad life, but it was a practical one. Impossible only because feeling the spirit in one's words is impractical, illogical, and irredeemable.

In those words, we find what hope feeds on—slim chances handwritten in dark blue ink.

Notes about people she saw, people she wanted to be, secret ways to calculate how many of her words came first from her heart and then from her soul—depending on the season, the year, the positions in the sky of her ancestors.

How far back did they go, anyway?

It always seemed they were closer than they appeared in the mirror.

And in the mirror, she saw her great-grandfather's eyes and her mother's arms, her aunt's crooked smile, her father's sharp cheekbones. She planted herself in all the cultures and countries the ancestors had walked over, watched as her feet mingled at the roots with all the others.

The skin of this tree was the color of a half-burned lilac bush, sepia brown and water-damaged—but still fragrant, still hinting at who it always was and could once again be.

The little girl realized that for her, the past became the future, and her present contains all the dimensions of time, from first ancestor to last descendant.

I write about the impossible because I need to write about things that others cannot or will not imagine—that is where I find my voice. I strive with the help of my ancestors to make the wayward, the questionable, and the unseen, present and fully realized in my work. In FISHTANK, I created a ghost story about aging siblings and the necessities of putting their recently deceased, hoarding parents' house in order. It is also a play about political hope, poverty, and how things transform after death. In SATYRICOÑO, I jumped off the work of Nero's scribe, Petronius, from 61A.D. and Fellini's 1968 film to reimagine the present obscene dangers of fascism and how we are doomed to repeat our dark histories when we do not grow beyond our pasts to make room for the light. In TWO ROBERTS, I imagined a world where demons were tired of being demonic, and two men named Robert unrelentingly chased their dreams onto empires made of crumbling sand. Selling their souls to the devil lands them in a purgatory soon to be washed away by the tide, letting go of this life and leading them to the next. I write about worlds trying to heal themselves. And often, these dramatic ecosystems come to me in dreams.

In March 2024, my distorted right femoral head, direly lacking in cartilage and all connective tissue, was detached via small bone saw—along with the femoral neck measuring 2.5 cm, slightly flattened on the supero-lateral aspect to make room for my new titanium hip.

My doctor used the Star Method. Finally, I was going to be a star...

He made a star-shaped incision in my right hip to part the nerves, tendons, ligaments and muscle, cut the bone, and then inserted the titanium ball-and-socket joint with a plastic place holder into the hollow femur.

Soon the bone will grow around the artificial joint and it will act as if it were alive again.

I will dance and hike and maybe sleep comfortably on my right side while holding my partner's back.

I will ride my stationary bike up imagined mountains, and down trails left by fairies to new places that only I can see with my eyes closed.

That unusual day when the surgery happened, another doctor who wore beautiful gold and ebony hoop earrings, gave me a powerful cocktail of sedatives and soporifics.

Painkillers and sleep-enhancers forced my eyes closed, and I fell quickly under her spell into another dimension where I saw my best friend's mother, who invited me to sleep over at her house, because there just happened to be one narrow bed left for me.

I slipped onto that bed, with the smell of lilac and fuchsia and other purple flowers reminiscent of blood from a fresh wound filling my head. I rested snugly in that small space, wedged between two other beds placed tightly together like a game of human Jenga. One bed was placed perpendicular to my teeny bed and then another bed was placed parallel to my bed. I reached out one arm to my left and my sister, Nancy, took my arm and rested her own head in the crook of my elbow. I hadn't touched her since her death in 2014. It felt warm and familiar—like holding my own hand—but more comforting than that and less awkward. How I missed my Irish twin. We were born 11 months apart but were basically inseparable until disease intervened. And on the other side of my bed was my best friend, Ana, who crossed over at age 44. We had been friends since the age of 14, when we bonded over braided hair and subway passes to Stuyvesant H.S. in our sophomore year.

They were both so quiet. I could hear a kind of wind sweeping over this bedroom with too many beds. And I thought of all the ancestors I reached out to for help and healing, after every wound—emotional or actual, but why did I never think of these two? Especially not together.

That's when it became clear to me that we can't choose our ancestors—not when to see them, not who will intervene, nor who wants to help you. You take who comes and they are more than enough.

Nancy and Ana were watching over me that particular day. We lay there in silence, the sound of my steady breaths competing with the purple-flowered winds that filled that room.

Does the place between life and death smell like the best place you've ever been?

Like the best person you ever met? Is that space nearest death the space that a sister holds? A best friend?

I slept so well in that slim bed. It was a space I would have to fill someday, but today, I would have to awaken again. But for a time, I did not want to. I closed my eyes and just enjoyed the feeling of life that came from these women who helped define my life and left me too soon to understand all they meant to me.

Ana drew me up beside her and though she didn't speak, I knew she wanted me to leave. "It's time. You can't stay here," her eyes told me. I felt the warmth leave her again as she walked me to the door of that crowded bedroom. Her face turned to alabaster. Nancy's too. I was in the bedroom-museum of their souls and they had let me stay to be comforted until I had to go back and live. So, there are not only near-death experiences, but near-life ones which prepare you to return to the land of the living.

This is why I write Impossible Plays. Plays that others could never imagine, but are so much a part of me that they smell of lilac and hibiscus. Pink roses and white gardenias. Blood flowers and blood ancestors, thorny yet gentle when they graze across your arm or your mind or your heart. Made of everyone you have ever met and ever loved and with whom you shared blood or built a home. We have found families that give us a pulse, but we cannot choose who can heal us, who can lead us, who can free us.

Our ancestors are the ones who choose—and it is those we aren't expecting who may help us the most.

I write because I must remember to remember my kin to keep history from ending with me. An unacceptable outcome. An unfathomable result. Now that's impossible. My plays are just the cartilage that lubricates my soul and keeps me connected. It is good to know that the longer I live the more possibilities there are to rebuild it. Good as new.

Stronger than ever.

Badass in Limbo, or The Haunting of Migdalia Cruz
A Foreword by Todd London

What makes a play impossible? Is it impossible to stage or impossible to fathom? Is it too expensive or too demanding? Does it defy convention —the agreed-upon possible—or dare theaters to dare more than they dare to? Is the woman who writes such a play an impossible person or, in a word from Tripwire Harlot Press's log line, a *badass*? Maybe a play's impossible simply because it's written by a woman over 60 without a Pulitzer or six-figure public honor to her name, despite being an artistic beacon to many of her theater colleagues and students? All of the above?

And what makes a playwright *badass*? Refusing to make nice when writing about sex or empire or human-on-human violence? Refusing to give fucks that not-so-young-anymore writers become dramatists *personae non grata*, expected to go quietly into the long night of their artistic maturity without so much as a party hat?

However you define it, Migdalia Cruz qualifies: all-of-the-above Impossible and Badass. She eschews the merely possible and sets no limits on her wild, brutal, loving imagination. She won't write down to audiences or to the people who program for them. In late 2023, Migdalia earned the honor of Legacy Playwright, together with important and irascible badass Frank Chin, a founding father of Asian American theater. This honor was bestowed by the Legacy Playwright Initiative at the Dramatists Guild Foundation, a national, multiyear project to shine light on playwrights deserving attention or re-discovery in a field that too often shuttles later-life artists aside. (LPI was the brainchild of longtime Lincoln Center Theatre dramaturg Anne Cattaneo, who gathered colleagues from across the profession to make it real. I currently direct the initiative but, full disclosure, I don't nominate or select winners.)

Some dramatic impossibilities braved by Migdalia Cruz: Her plays are polymorphous; they cross time periods, genres, genders, and realities. She draws on myth, fairy tale, legend, and dream, as well as political, literary, and personal history, to extend the reach of her storytelling, sometimes all at once. A truism of pragmatic playwriting pedagogy holds that you can't mess with both form and content at the same time, but Migdalia must have cut class that day. She even presumes to slam together multiple stories in a single play—take that, American theater! No wonder Tripwire Harlot is publishing her in their *Sledgehammer* Series.

Many of Migdalia's plays, from the very early *Miriam's Flowers* to *Fishtank* and *Two Roberts* in this volume, live in limbo lands, the "where do I go now" purgatory of life just after death. She is our bard of the bardo and, like that other, earlier bard with his Hamlets and Macbeths, Migdalia loves a ghost. In her three impossible plays, I count at least eight of them, not including the ghost of her childhood in the Bronx and of Puerto Rico, where her people are from. Yes, place haunts you, too, just like history.

"When you bury someone, where are they really? *The* ground? The sky?" Anabella asks in *Fishtank*, as she and her older sister Juliana attempt to clear out the roach-ridden, hoarder-crammed, trash heap of a house they've just inherited from their parents, who died suddenly, one after another, in the pandemic. "Or are they still hanging around their house? Waiting to see if it sticks. Or if they can stick onto you?"

Of course Ma and Pop are still hanging around the house. There's work to be done, haunting their daughters and making sure they find the buried treasure of their inheritance and the buried secrets of their family. The dead linger nearby, or maybe they permeate our bodies. Juliana wonders about that: "Because of the disease. So many people had to be burned. I wonder if the smoke could have blown you into the wind and then into my lungs, and if it did, would I know if you were still inside me somewhere, I mean, whenever I took a breath?"

Theater is a physical, visceral art, and Migdalia's writing works in and on the body, a site inseparable from the mind. "When Art, History, and Time braid together in my world," she has written, "I feel it in my viscera. I feel a strength—in my convictions, my voice, my reason for being." When Amador, the father in *Fishtank*, speaks from the outskirts of life, I hear what it must be like for Migdalia to write as she does: "When I was trying to breathe, I was going to all different times and places. My mind is a piece of tumbled sea glass. I passed through so many waves. So many changes. That's what stories are: these word-waves that wash over me."

And lest you think that only family haunts the living, consider the other five characters in *Fishtank*, each of whom steps out of pictures the now-dead parents stuck up on the wall above the smelly family aquarium: Martin (as in Luther King, Jr.), Robert (F. Kennedy), Shirley (Chisholm), and two Jesuses, one white and one black. They hang around, chatting and arguing, playing games, trying to remember their own lost lives. (I don't want to spoil anything but there's also, between the Black Jesus and the White one, some licking.)

Two Jesuses licking or (almost) kissing ain't got nothing on the monstrous, psycho-sexual mayhem of Migdalia's *Satyricoño*, inspired by Petronius's writing (61 A.D.) and Fellini's 1968 film, orgiastic nightmares lit by the sputtering fires of imperial Rome. It's the "future-present" of 2058-2064 A.D. amid "the chaos of the Ignited Dominions of Amerika—what's left of what used to be the U.S.A." This time the ghosts of the past and future lurk.

We have moved from the literal worship of civil rights era and Christian icons to a dystopic future of now, fashioned by every dictator ever, specifically the lineup Migdalia had in mind when she began the play early last decade: Mussolini, Franco, Hitler, Trujillo, Castro, Bush. In *Satyricoño* her Emperor (the "Presidemperor") diddles himself while "the whole world explodes," so as our prophetic playwright foretold, the beat goes on. We enter not Mar-a-Lago but *La Perla*, a nightclub that has been "renovated and made magical. On one wall is a sea of genitalia, animatronic penises, vaginas, and breasts. Like an adult version of the

"It's a Small World" ride, there are patrons strewn about the club in gondolas, equipped with adult pleasuring devices and an intercom to order up pleasure partners or simply snack foods." Two members of the royal entourage sit in a gondola, "wiping off their hands and genitalia with a wet wipe."

We catch citizens of I. D. of A. in individual spotlights: "Each one is trying to kill him or herself—unsuccessfully—over and over again. One slits his throat. One hangs herself. Two take poison. Another one hits his head repeatedly with a dictionary. One holds her head in a deep basin of water until she can no longer breathe—comes up for air, and then tries again. One takes line after line of cocaine—he is covered in white powder. These vignettes are performed to the music of [Fellini's composer] Nino Rota." Pig Latin is spoken here. The citizenry appears as Bunraku puppets. "There are many of them and they are all very sad." And when the sister of the Presidemperor's bastard son fists her nymphomaniac lover, the royal astrologer, "Sparks come flying from between her legs." Yes, there will be dildos, French maid costumes, and hermaphrodites. No, it won't play in Florida. One entrance will be made in a "chariot of fire."

How many ways can you spell Impossible?

But why? We've seen dream plays before, sexual surrealism, political anarchy—I'm thinking Shakespeare, Goethe, Strindberg, Jarry, even Kushner our contemporary. (Oh, right, they're men.) And what about the art world? What are theatrical spaces that would make room for the installations of a Joan Jonas or the attic of a Louise Bourgeois? Where are our theater companies that would dedicate the years and resources necessary to cultivate audiences hungry enough to wander in such strange lands? Where, other than in that vague Everycity appellation "downtown" or in some romantic, experimental, Off-Off Broadway past, can we celebrate the recesses of such a sensibility or the reaches of such an fantasy? (Tripwire Harlot seems to be asking and having asked, answered.)

Migdalia's path was blazed by her great teacher and mentor, Maria Irene Fornés, and Migdalia has used her own fire to light that path for students and colleagues. She's part of a contemporaneous cluster of Fornés' Latine playwright progeny— including Eduardo Machado,

Milcha Sanchez-Scott, Edwin Sanchez, Nilo Cruz, Cherrie Moraga, Jose Rivera, Luis Alfaro, Caridad Svich, Nilo Cruz, Elaine Romero, Bernardo Solano, Octavio Solis, Anne Garcia-Romero, Oliver Mayer, Ana Marie Simo, Lisa Loomer, and so many more—that ranks as one of the most stellar, influential writer dynasties of the past fifty years.

For Fornés the impossible play was the opposite of what you might imagine. It was the one that tried to anticipate its audience, as she told *The Drama Review* in 1977: "I think it is impossible to aim at an audience when writing a play. I never do. I think that is why some commercial productions fail. They are trying to create a product that is going to create a reaction, and they cannot. If they could, every play on Broadway that is done for that purpose would be a great success."

Fornés' teaching, famously, begins in the body and subconscious. When characters enter the writer's imagination, she gives them a home and lets *them* tell *her* who they are, what they want, what they wish to do. Plays of the Fornés/Cruz variety feel to me precisely like dreams—worlds that could only be dreamt by this exact dreamer, built of her history and experience, possessing the idiosyncratic logic of her inner life, articulated in the unique, associative language of her personal tongue. "I wish I could write with my tongue," the character Cornelius says in *Two Roberts: A Pirate-Blues Project*, Migdalia's third impossible play. Based on *Soul Train*'s host/producer Don Cornelius, the character appears as a guide through the limbo of after-life along with a mythological figure named Epifani. "Tongues are more honest than fingers," Cornelius explains. "A slip of the tongue reveals the truth and a slip of the fingers is just a mistake."

Every human comes stocked with her own dense mysteries. The theater is one improbable (but rich) attempt to illuminate those mysteries for each other. We sit together in the theater and share our common stories. We glimpse the inner immensities that unite and divide us. I want both: the accessible commonalities and the mysterious distinctions, private visions, special language, and impossible interiority. I want the ungraspable mystery of the other person—*that which is always out of reach*.

Migdalia's characters often live in proximity to just that. It's true of the dead Ma and Pop and their daughters. It's true of the characters in her

1995 play *Fur*, in which Michael, the owner of Joe's Pet Shop keeps the object of his impossible love/obsession—a hirsute beauty-as-beast named Citrona—locked in a cage, where he can see her but never touch her heart. *Fur* is a fairy tale of the unreachable heart's desire or, better, "desire's heart-fire," a phrase Migdalia uses in a double Haiku she wrote for Fornés:

> In six lines or less—
> I must honor the teacher
> who gave me the moon.
> It was an honest,
> clear, yet savage light, poured from
> desire's heart-fire.

Two Roberts: A Pirate-Blues Project takes this limbo of desire even further—into purgatory. Here Migdalia sledgehammers together the stories of two men from different centuries who, legend has it, sold their souls to the devil to succeed at their chosen professions—piracy and music—and to "score with ladies." Roberto—a 19th Century pirate and Robin Hood-like legend from Cabo Rojo, the SW coast of Puerto Rico—outmaneuvered the Spanish & English Navies for many years, sharing his booty with his landsmen and, in another sense, sharing his booty with women everywhere. The other ambitious adventurer is based on 20th-Century Blues legend Robert Johnson, who likewise knew his way around the body of a guitar and that of a woman. (Speaking of an artist's private associations, I love the way Migdalia lets us know that a statue of pirate Roberto Cofresi in Boqueron Bay has a nose "strikingly similar to my mother's nose, also a native of Cabo Rojo.")

The two Roberts find themselves shipwrecked in the afterlife, sharing a deserted island and condemned to watch their sidekicks and lovers wait for their return. They are "floaters" who will never return because, though they don't yet know it, they're dead. What happens to men who, having sold their souls to the devil, die? A question for their purgatorial guides:

> EPIFANI: It took us a long time to come up with something
> that would really hurt.

CORNELIUS: Torturing the soul has very little to do with equipment anymore.

EPIFANI: No fiery treadmills to walk or gigantic burning noxious cogs to turn.

CORNELIUS: Eternal damnation is what happens when all you love is within arm's reach—but it no longer recognizes you.

EPIFANI: They're here for you, but they will never find you. You'll see them searching and searching.

CORNELIUS: You'll feel their hearts breaking.

EPIFANI: And they will never get to leave.

CORNELIUS: And you'll watch them tortured—for eternity. All because of love.

Hell, for the dead, is other people—the still-living ones. The only way out is to let them go.

ROBERTO: The end. The moment when your eyes close is the only moment when you see yourself clearly—

ROBERT: —when you let yourself mourn all the people you left behind and they go on.

ROBERTO: Without you.

ROBERT: That's it.

ROBERTO AND ROBERT: The end.

Endings are never final for Migdalia. Her prolific body of more than 60 works for stage, radio, tv, film, and podcast is haunted by love's burn, the waters of death, and all that remains out of reach. Her plays are also fueled by the need to move on, hope for continuance. These three impossible ones each conclude with the words, "End of Play For Now…"

Where does her hope come from? This is what she says: "As my plays got bigger—in casting, in world view, and in exploration of adaptations and translations—my chances for production shrank. So why do I continue to write? It is an act of hope, of belief in the future, and a world filled with impossible plays improbably produced and performed on unlikely stages—is my idea of utopia."

Welcome to Migdalia's utopia, impossible people!

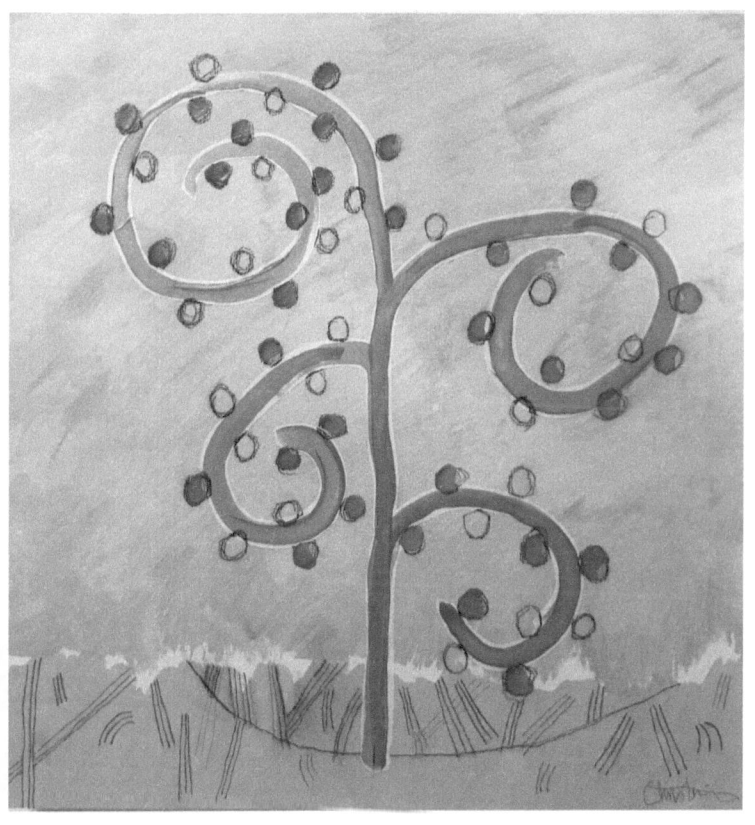

Migdalia's Flowers: Life and Legacy
a reflection by Morgan Jenness

Antonin Artaud said of actors that they should be like martyrs, still burning at the stake, signaling through the flames. This can also be true of writers... like Migdalia Cruz.

I first met the extraordinary Migdalia Cruz in the late 80s when she was part of a writing circle hosted by the impactful writer/teacher/then to be psychic Paul Selig at the 92nd St Y.

I vividly remember going around the circle asking the writers why they wrote plays. Many had smart, sometimes insightful, reasons but when it came to Migdalia's turn she simply said–"if I didn't write I would die" and burst into tears.

I was instantly smitten–and would become more so as I started to read her work.

I would see Migdalia Cruz burst into tears on many occasions in the years to come–on panels, in conversations about the world and her work, remembering her mentor, the great Maria Irene Fornés. It did become a bit of an affectionate bet: not *if* Migdalia would burst into tears on any given occasion but *when*.

I think we all respected her tears because Migdalia Cruz, in many profound ways, wrote not with metaphorical ink but with bodily fluids, tears, blood, sweat, spit, snot and vaginal secretions. And her characters–whether historical, in classical adaptations, or utterly original in the multi-translated 60-plus plays, operas and screenplays she has written–live their own viscous, visceral deep connections to it all. They also live their connections to the blood of history, and, like Lorca, to the earth itself and the other core elements of air, water and fire.

After our first encounter, I was determined to keep tabs on this writer of fire and fluids. This writer of often seemingly impossible yet utterly necessary plays. I continued to follow her work with great gratitude for her creative courage; from the young self-harming woman in MIRIAM'S FLOWERS, to a woman covered in hair kept in a box in FUR, to remarkable adaptations of classical writers from Shakespeare to Lorca (imagining what happens in ANOTHER PART OF THE HOUSE of Bernarda Alba) which look at the visceral (and fluid filled) lives of Anton Chekhov and Frida Kahlo (a perfect subject since many of us see Migdalia almost as a Frida Kahlo of the theater—hopefully without the literal surgeries). This is just a small sampling of her work, to which this volume of plays is a welcome addition.

In this volume, we see the impact on political and religious leaders of a Black Jesus, visit a Fellini/Cruzesque Satyricon of the future, and ourselves meet the devils which blues musician Robert Johnson encountered–as well as a Puerto Rican counterpart.

As mentioned above, a great impact and influence on, as well as mentor and nurturer of Migdalia's work, was the legendary Cuban writer María Irene Fornés. I would become a theatrical representative for, and friend of, Irene in later years after the passing of her long-term agent Helen Merrill, but I believe I must credit Migdalia for that relationship–as I really got to know Irene more through her many students whose work was so inspired by "La Reina"–particularly via Migdalia herself.

I think in those days Irene was a bit suspicious of me, and protective of "her" writers...and Migdalia was indeed one of her most beloved, and I truly think the one of whom Irene was most proud...and perhaps related to the most. Irene's work, as in her writing exercises, was sometimes cooler, more observational...asking writers to examine their emotions but then also see how they translated into language, images and intellectual ideas...exploring in some ways how the fluids could become mixed more with ink. I think this was a good exercise for Migdalia, finding a way to deliver the fluids without drowning in them...mixing them with ink the way Alfred Jarry mixed ink and absinthe...actually making what might seem more impossible utterly possible.

Migdalia also never never abandoned Irene personally during Irene's long illness. Migdalia also collected the sensory-based Fornés exercises and not only continued to use them herself but incorporated them into her own teaching to newer generations of writers. She still expands Irene's great legacy not only as a Latina writer of profound significance but as a teacher–and has already seen some of her students themselves become teachers...a potentially immortal continuance.

After Irene passed, her great friend and documentarian Michelle Memran (another great fan of Migdalia and her work) and I were going through Irene's possessions in the short time we had before they would all be thrown into a dumpster. I found a tiny box with Migdalia's name on it. Inside were several tiny religious charms (see page 30). When I gave them to Migdalia she was mystified but I think I understood. It was honoring an acolyte of a different religion, one of the theater, one who risked themselves while writing their characters and their stories.

Migdalia Cruz has dedication to bringing her characters to life that often feels like a calling–unlike Brecht's advice she weeps when they weep, has ecstasy when they do, and bleeds when they do.

I welcome you to take this remarkable journey though some more of the work of Migdalia Cruz.... La Nueva Reina.

María Irene's Gift to Migdalia

FISHTANK

FISHTANK

A NYSCA commission from Clubbed Thumb, Maria Striar, producing artistic director, Michael Bulger, producing director, Edward Torres, workshop director, 2023.

FISHTANK was commissioned and developed by Clubbed Thumb, made possible by the New York State Council on the Arts with the support of Governor Andrew Cuomo and the New York State Legislature.

For my sisters, Gloria, Nancy and Virginia.

> *"Absence is a house so vast that inside you will pass through its walls*
> *and hang pictures on the air."*
>
> —Pablo Neruda—
>
> *"Tragedy is a tool for the living to gain wisdom, not a guide by which to live."*
>
> —Robert F. Kennedy—
>
> *"The time is always right to do what's right. Hatred paralyzes life; love releases it."*
>
> —Martin Luther King, Jr.—
>
> *"Granny gave me strength, dignity, and love. I learned from an early age that I was somebody. I didn't need the black revolution to tell me that."*
>
> —Shirley Anita Chisholm—

CAST OF CHARACTERS:

JULIANA—(goes by Juli) a just about 55. Boricua. Multi-racial. Practical and pragmatic.

ANABELLA—(goes by Beebee) her sister, just about 45. Dreamy and romantic.

SHIRLEY—A once U.S. Presidential candidate. African-American.

ROBERT—A once U.S. Presidential candidate. Irish-American.

MARTIN—A once messiah-like leader. African-American.

CECILIA—JULIANA and ANABELLA's mother, 70s. She loves to listen to stories and dance.

AMADOR—Their father, 70s. He loves to tell stories.

WHITE JESUS and BLACK JESUS—About 33 years old, someone's messiah. Middle-Eastern.

TIME:

The day after a funeral. Late afternoon to night one Winter. 2020.

PLACE:

A townhouse in the Morrisania section of the Bronx newly belonging to two sisters, inherited from their parents, Amador and Cecilia Souchet-Acevedo.

And a graveyard.

PROLOGUE

A late afternoon in the Winter. A liminal space between the Souchet-Acevedo living room and the world to come.

CECILIA is mending the pockets of AMADOR's pants in the fading light by a window. SHE moves to look at two photos on the wall, one BLACK JESUS, the other WHITE JESUS, above her fish tank to silently ask for help threading her needle. She winks at one and then the other. AMADOR sits in his underwear reading the newspaper with a flashlight. The light in this space is not natural though it seems to be a real space.

AMADOR: There's nothing new going on.

CECILIA: That paper's two months old.

AMADOR: I guess no one brings us the paper anymore. I thought Juli was looking after the house.

CECILIA: Not for some time. She's got all in her head again.

(Holding up the pants.)
How's this?

(Pulls out the pockets that are sewn in not matching thread.)
I had to use navy blue thread. That's all we had left in the house. I used all the beige thread sewing on your shirt buttons.

AMADOR: Maybe its hiding in the darkness? Remember how you used to be so afraid of the dark?

CECILIA: Nooo...

AMADOR: I could come up behind you and— *(Pounding on the back of her chair.)*

CECILIA: That old trick does not work on me anymore, Doro. Juli was the one—

AMADOR: I know...I have to find new tricks, Ceci. New tricks for a new state of —what are we now?

CECILIA: Still ourselves. Just stuck here. Or back here. Like we never left.

AMADOR: Maybe we didn't?

CECILIA: Please put on your pants. We have to figure out what to tell our daughters. And I can't take you seriously in your boxer shorts. Who gave those ugly things to you anyway? With the shark mouth on it? Disgusting. Your brother?

AMADOR: Anabella. When she used to give us gifts.

CECILIA: Of course. And why is she speaking Italian now? She's never been to Italy. She left us a strange phone message...

AMADOR: That's her Spanish. It's just so bad it sounds like Italian.

CECILIA: That's really bad. We should have taught her better.

AMADOR: It's hard to teach children anything they don't want to learn. I wrote a story about it.

CECILIA: When did you find time to do that?

AMADOR: I make time.
(Meaning his head.)
Inside here. When I was trying to breathe, I was going to all different times and places. My mind is a piece of tumbled sea-glass. I passed through so many waves. So many changes. That's what stories are: these word-waves that wash over me.

CECILIA: Very pretty. My brain is much more practical, like a light switch, on and off. That's all.

AMADOR: Let me turn you on, honey! You're so hot I could cook a huevo on your fondillo.

(HE grabs CECILIA and dips her in a deep embrace. SHE slaps him gently away.)

CECILIA: Don't be so fresh!

AMADOR: Fresh? *(Pause)* Oh, okay. Once there was a town that smelled like fresh baked bread in the Spring driving the hungry to its borders. So many hungry, that one day that Summer, there was not enough bread for everybody because the wheat had dried up in the raging Sun, so the parents gave the children all the bread, as they let themselves slowly starve to death. And one Winter day there were only small children left alive in that town. Those children tried to awaken the withered grown-ups with water and poking and even kisses. Nothing moved them. They seemed gone forever. But that was too long a time for the children to bear, that they thought about the stalks of wheat and how sometimes they burned, but then grew back —when there was enough rain. The most practical of the children, little Ceci, told the others that if they buried the wasted bodies like fertile seeds wrapped in the dried stalks of wheat, that maybe the fertility Goddess Atabey *{ah-tah-bay}* would grow them back to shelter them from the Summer Sun before they could be claimed back too soon into the earth. Like the stalks of wheat. Like their parents who gave them life by giving theirs.

(There is an old record player that CECILIA moves to and plays a record, perhaps Gato Barbieri's "Caliente" album featuring the song "Europa." The music plays underneath their scene.)

So, then the children did as Ceci told them to, and wished for rain all through the rest of Winter and Spring, and it poured in blue sheets from the sky and grew trees in the shape of flowers so beautiful they hurt. And the town became a forest. And the forest became a jungle. And the jungle, a maze, and they followed that maze until it brought them back to their own hearts buried under the roots of giant flowers made of wheat and the blood and flesh of their ancestors. That was when their families came back to them, because now they remembered what beats underneath their feet. And so, history was born.

CECILIA: Te adoro, 'Doro.
(CECILIA puts out a hand to AMADOR and HE joins her in a slow dance, perhaps even a tango. The sound of a gunshot. CECILIA and AMADOR stop dancing for a moment and then begin to dance again.)

JULIANA: *(From upstairs. A loud whisper.)* That's not what I wished for...

(From behind the fish tank, the photos of SHIRLEY, MARTIN, ROBERT and two JESUSES—one black, one white begin to swirl rhythmically. THEY dance until we hear footsteps coming down the stairs, as JULIANA enters the living room from upstairs. As SHE enters, the dancing photographs crash into each other making the glass of their frames sing—like how water in glasses can sing/ring out when you circle the rim with your fingers. The photos seem to scream, a sound like glass about to shatter, or the highest note in a singing bowl.)

JULIANA: What the hell—?! HELLO!? You better get out of here!
(Waving her hand in her pocket like it's a gun.)
I have a gun in here!

CECILIA: *(Whispering)* She has a gun?!

AMADOR: *(Whispering back)* She has a pocket. She's just scared. I used to say that when I was scared.

(JULIANA walks in cautiously, turning on every light she can, but they are mostly burnt out. As SHE passes them, CECILIA pinches her and

AMADOR pushes her gently. JULIANA pulls out a real gun, looks at it, then puts it in her pocket and turns on the lights.)

SCENE ONE
Lights come up to further reveal the inside of the
Souchet-Acevedo townhouse in the Bronx.
Trash is strewn inside and out of the house.
The Sun has almost set.

> JULIANA: *(The sound of glass crunching as SHE walks around the living room cautiously.)* OUCH?! I bet there are ticks or something in here. Do ticks scream when they die?
>
> *(Sprays her arm with the bug spray she also uses on the furniture.)*
> Stay away from me, you little skitches.
>
> *(Scratches her arms furiously, as SHE surveys the state of the house.)*
> Looks even worse than I remembered—but that's what too much pride gets you. A house full of trash.

(JULIANA sifts through the broken TV remotes and old dust covered blankets and other accumulated items from her parents hoarding. Too many copies of old TV Guides, Reader's Digests, NY Daily Newspapers, unopened junk mail, old pay stubs. Boxes of VHS tapes and 8-track tapes, and other sundry useless stuff. SHE does this in silence as music plays in the background, the same music that segues into this scene from the prologue. Maybe SHE dances as SHE puts junk in a trash bag. A few things she tries to throw away get retrieved by either CECILIA or AMADOR who speak in whispers.)

> CECILIA: *(Hiding an old blanket behind the sofa.)* We raised a heathen!
>
> AMADOR: *(Pulling a copy of March 2020, Reader's Digest out of the garbage bag.)* Now, this is definitely not junk: "How Tragedy Couldn't Kill their Faith" and "Find A Doctor You Trust." What's wrong with her? I was saving this for her.

(As JULIANA keeps sorting through stuff, the lights cross to ANABELLA standing outside the front door. SHE carries cleaning supplies and a black and white feathered funeral wreath. She puts the wreath on the door, puts the cleaning supplies down, moves to get the keys out of her purse, but then suddenly thinks better of it.)

ANABELLA: Empty. I can't. Don't want to feel my voice echoing off the "they're not here anymore" walls of this place. When you bury someone, where are they really? The ground? The sky? Or are they still hanging around their house? Waiting to see if it sticks. Or if they can stick onto you?

(Something blows onto her head with a gust of wind.)
Ay! There's a reason I stopped coming home. I couldn't stand seeing how they let everything go. I just wish I could have moved them somewhere else before this. So they could—you know—go—in peace.

(Something hits her in the face)
Ok. Ok. So you haven't left yet.

(AMADOR and CECILIA move into the shadows as things continue to swirl around ANABELLA. JULIANA continues to sift through the rubble, things in the room seem to move. Small pieces of paper, a throw-blanket edge, a book on a shelf, shoes on a hook, anything that is hanging or suspended. The living room is separated from the front door by plastic beaded curtains in the foyer. The beads tinkle like something delicate is passing through them. Time passes. The record player turns itself on. JULIANA keeps checking her watch. It goes from late afternoon to evening. The music changes to something like Joe Cuba ["Tighten Up"] or La Lupe ["Fever"], maybe segueing into Harold Melvin and the Blue Notes ["Wake Up Everybody"] or Stevie Wonder ["Overjoyed"] or the Stylistics ["You make me Feel Brand New"] and then maybe Bad Bunny ["Vete"]. Finally, SHE finds what SHE wants to keep—a photo album. It is damaged by some animal chewing...but mostly intact. SHE sprays it with hydrogen peroxide [and maybe roach spray] and sanitizes her hands, then kills a roach that crawls out of it and has to spray it again.)

JULIANA: I did not bring enough Raid.
(ANABELLA struggles with the front door. SHE opens it and then it closes again.)
Ain't a roach alive that I can't kill. Alright now. I've been looking for this everywhere.

(JULIANA opens the book and studies each photograph. SHE speaks to a photo. The photos are projected on the walls and ceiling.)
There you are with Tío Feelee and Tío Tilo. You were so tiny, Pop. I remember the story you told me about why your feet were buried in the dirt. You didn't want anybody to see you had no shoes on. You and your brothers took turns on school days. Wasn't your day that day...not today either come to think of it. I asked the undertaker if people used shoes in coffins. But they burned you anyway. Because of the disease. So many people had to be burned. I wonder if the smoke could have blown you into the wind and then into my lungs, and if it did, would I know if you were still inside me somewhere, I mean, whenever I took a breath?

(Pause)
I love these. Here's one of all of us at Orchard Beach. Me in my favorite pink bathing suit. Well, my only bathing suit. I stopped going to the beach once I had to wear one of Ma's old ones that was 40 years out-of-date. With the hard-shell tits like—

(Making the pointy breast shapes with her fingers like they are guns.)
Fuwah! What a sweet photo with you looking at Ma with those dark brown—

JULIANA and AMADOR: *(in Unison)* "—love magnets!"
(CECILIA kisses AMADOR. The lights begin to blink. An electric blink.)

JULIANA: I guess that's what's still in this house—even without your bodies in it. A flicker of electricity where you once were. A house of magnets and magazines with crispy pages. It steals your energy for a minute and then things reset. Together. Isn't that what you always said, Pop? To the end, right? But not so much together anymore.

(AMADOR and CECILIA chuckle in the darkness. THEY begin to enjoy their daughters' confusion and invisible attacks by inanimate objects. CECILIA makes a box, filled with some clothes, tumble against the hall closet door with a bang or a bump.)

JULIANA: What the hell was that now?! Jesus!
(Crosses over to the closet and listens for a moment, her ear to the door.)
Just something falling. I'm such a boba sometimes.

(JULIANA tries to get into the closet which is blocked by so much stuff that SHE can't quite get it open. SHE begins to pull things one at a time out of the closet, a sweater, a hat, a glove, a house dress, a pair of pants, a very large doll, an umbrella, etc., as lights cross to ANABELLA, outside the front door.)

ANABELLA: To the end, right? Together. That's how family is. Always making me do dumb shit.
Can't we just hire someone to clean all their stuff up?
We are grown-ass ladies who do not need to get attacked by our parents' worldly possessions.
We're gonna find possums living in there. Or something worse —with sharp teeth.

(ANABELLA enters quietly and watches JULIANA for a moment.)
Why couldn't this wait, Juli?

JULIANA: Why should it wait, Beebee? I want to get it done and get the house sold A-sap.

ANABELLA: We just right now buried them. Isn't there a decency clause in your personal time clock?

JULIANA: Nope. And what took you so long? The funeral was yesterday. I've been here forever.

ANABELLA: Nobody says A-sap. Except on police and doctor shows.

JULIANA: Isn't this like TV? Our parents die hours apart from a disease no one understands. Fucking crazy.

ANABELLA: We shouldn't even be in here.

JULIANA: We won't catch it. They haven't been—they were in the hospital for six weeks.

ANABELLA: I know but it still gives me the heebie-jeebies.

JULIANA: Just go. I can finish this myself. Like I do.

ANABELLA: Nah…I'd never hear the end of it.

JULIANA: Uh, huh. And why are you still in your funeral clothes? Didn't make it past the first bar?

ANABELLA: I prefer cocktail lounges. And maybe I wasn't thinking about clothes.

(THEY put stuff into garbage bags in silence.)

JULIANA: What's that smell?

ANABELLA: Hmm…uhmhm! You've been living such a bougie life on Pelham Bay that you forgot the smell of rotting rodent.

JULIANA: You're the one upstate with all the other White folk. And that is definitely not mouse.

ANABELLA: Have you seen the dog?

JULIANA: That hound's been dead for two years already.

ANABELLA: I wonder how long it took them to notice. They got worse as they got older.

JULIANA: Pop was too sick to clean most of the time. And Ma...

ANABELLA: I mean this mess. The shit-piles piled up everywhere. I don't know why they kept this stuff. What did they expect to happen? That someone would buy it one day at an auction? Old copies of *Reader's Digest* do not bring in the big bucks.

JULIANA: I guess not. Doesn't make sense, but so little does.
(Pause; THEY keep bagging.)
Like how much Mami and Pop kept asking for you. I never got that since you never hardly came.

ANABELLA: Shit, maybe they loved me. You don't...get me and you've known me for 45 years.

JULIANA: Right. You're sooo mysterious.
(Pause)
Like how you making your money these days?

ANABELLA: Like what's that supposed to mean? Is it any of your business? I'm still working at a gallery.

JULIANA: Oh. Fun.
(Pause)
So, how'd you afford that new car you drove to the funeral?

ANABELLA: Rental. But again—it's still none of your business.

JULIANA: You're right, little sister. You're just like your mother.

ANABELLA and CECILIA: What's that supposed to mean?
(THEY move sheets off furniture and uncover a large fish tank. ANABELLA jumps away from it.)

ANABELLA: So that's what stinks. There's still water in here—green and black water. Ooey! And a half rotten bunch of goldfish. Ooh, and a dead mouse, I think. I am not cleaning that.

JULIANA: Wouldn't expect you to. But help me carry this out to the back porch, so I can hose it down, and then maybe you can sweep in here or something?

ANABELLA: Ok.
(THEY lift up the fish tank to bring it to the back porch to hose it out, but as THEY do five framed pictures fall to the floor.)
Oh shit! What the hell—?! Were they storing shit back there?

JULIANA: They always had things on top of the fish tank. Just like the TV. Anything with a top was a shelf to mom and dad. Remember how they stacked their little TV on top of the big TV? Weird.

ANABELLA: I don't remember anything on top there, except maybe fish food and a ratty old net.

JULIANA: It's La Colección. Mami's Colección. They were on top of the tank forever.

ANABELLA: La Colección sounds like a fashion show—who are these folks?

JULIANA: Look at them, Beebee. Famous people. Important people. People Mami thought they should have pictures of, I guess. Prob'ly just fell between the wall and the tank when they cleaned it last.

ANABELLA: Doesn't look like they cleaned in a long time.

JULIANA: Old people get like that. Too tired to clean. When they're sick all the time. I'm that way too sometimes. It's like I got something inside me, draining all my energy.

ANABELLA: Maybe you got a tapeworm. When's the last time you went to a doctor?

JULIANA: They don't know anything.

ANABELLA: Why were they so important to Mami? The photos?

JULIANA: She liked talking to them. I would hear her at night doing it.

ANABELLA: I don't remember that.

JULIANA: You don't remember much, do you? Lucky you were a sound sleeper.

ANABELLA: I don't feel lucky. *(to herself)* I feel lost.
(JULIANA and ANABELLA keep cleaning in silence.)

CECILIA: I collected them for them. I didn't want them to be lonely, but look at them, so alone still.

AMADOR: How could they know that? I didn't even know why you did that.

CECILIA: Nobody but me needed to know why. I wanted the girls to have people around to look up to.

AMADOR: Pretty idea. Pretty crazy. You're lucky I love you.

JULIANA: Ma didn't know how to talk to us.

ANABELLA: Did you like Ma and Dad? I loved them but they were not likeable people.
(A wind whips something onto ANABELLA's face. The parents enjoy this.)

JULIANA: I loved them, but—I never knew how much—or even if—they loved us back.

ANABELLA: That's why we weren't on the pesera. I mean photos of us. Not important enough.

JULIANA: Sounds about right.

ANABELLA: I remember those pictures up there. But I just thought we were related to them or something...

JULIANA: Seriously?! Look at them.

ANABELLA: *(Picking up the fallen framed photographs)* These aren't even really photos. Just cut-outs from newspapers and magazines. So faded you can't tell who they are anymore...ooh, wait, this one is Martin Luther King.

JULIANA: He's the only one you recognize?

ANABELLA: That guy looks like—was he a president?

JULIANA: Are you fucking kidding me?! Not a president. A president's brother.

ANABELLA: I liked MLK. He was fine. Even though he died seven years before I was even born. But this pasty ginger White guy...I'm stumped. And who is this woman?

JULIANA: Beebee. Look closely.

ANABELLA: I don't got a clue.

JULIANA: Ma and Dad wanted her to be president. They talked about her all the time. Like she could have made a world of difference to Black women and all us poor folk.
I guess you were too young to remember that.

(ANABELLA stares at her blankly.)
Damn, girl. Do you know nothing about politics?

ANABELLA: Current events yes. But that all sounds like way ancient history. I'm a need-to-know person. So, these are pictures of people who should have been president or were related to a president? What did Ma and Pop care about that? Weird. Ohh…wait…plus one Black and one White Jesus, but those are large, laminated postcards though. Look! Tilt them up and down and the eyes move!

JULIANA: Are you high?! Just how many important things have passed you by?

ANABELLA: You know nothing about me. Like I said.

JULIANA: I'll give you a hint. First woman to run for President of the United States.

ANABELLA: Oh, wait! Geraldine…

JULIANA: Ferraro. And no! That was a White woman. This one is Black.

ANABELLA: That picture is messed up. I can't tell anything…could be a picture of Abuela? I think I thought it <u>was</u> Abuela all this time. What does it matter, Juli?? Why are you interrogating me? These pictures have been here for like 50 years. Why do you care who they are? It's not like they're worth anything—like autographed or something. Just old crumply newspaper cutouts. Except for the Jesuses. They got creepy eyes. Look!

JULIANA: Abuela and Shirley did look a little alike, but no, stupid, it's not her.

ANABELLA: Our parents were so weird. Most people just have family photos.

JULIANA: *(Leaning the photos against the cart that holds the fish tank.)* Just pick up that end.

(The SISTERS pick up and begin to carry the tank onto the back porch through a broken screen door. It's a homemade back porch. THEY almost make it through the screen door.)

JULIANA: They almost never moved this tank. Too heavy. *(A sudden gust of wind makes the photos float around the room, and suddenly the photos smack into the wall and land behind the sofa making the SISTERS put the fish tank down.)* What the hell's happening now!?

ANABELLA: I'm leaving. When the house says "Get out" you go.

JULIANA: Nobody said anything. Anyway, people always stay in the movies.

ANABELLA: White people stay.

AMADOR: *(a whisper)* That's true.

JULIANA: Oh, right. Our people go. We outran the Spaniards into the mountains. Our *jibaro* blood tells that story. Smart and practical.

ANABELLA: I told you this was a bad idea. And you make it sound like we're running away from those bastards. It was about self-preservation. Live to fight another day. And those motherfuckers had horses. The Tainos were on foot.

(A sound at the door of something shaking loose and breaking off. The SISTERS grab each other close. THEY turn toward the door, which opens and closes two times.)

JULIANA: Did I tell you Pop's boots kept kicking me when I was walking past them this morning?

ANABELLA: The ones hanging from the pegs on the wall?

JULIANA: Yep.

ANABELLA: Just the wind. You said.

JULIANA: *(Shaking off the fear.)* Yeah. Sure. Wind. Let's get this tank out back so I can hose it down.

(THEY lift up the tank again. JULIANA's nose begins to bleed.) Did you hear that? *(Wipes her nose with her hand.)* Aw, shit!

ANABELLA: You're bleeding. *(Hands her a tissue)* And no, I didn't hear anything. What did you hear?

JULIANA: Like a whoosh and a sigh and a flap and like a bang.

ANABELLA: I heard something. It's really beginning to storm out. I'm glad we're not at the cemetery right now. We would have sunk right in the mud. If this rain were snow, we'd never dig out from under it. Why are you bleeding? Did you hit your face on something?

(JULIANA drops her end of the fish tank forcing ANABELLA to grab it before it falls to the ground. Then SHE places it on the ground. When SHE does so the SISTERS fall to their knees and into a memory.)

SCENE TWO
A memory. 1984. JULIANA and ANABELLA, at eighteen and eight, kneeling at a church-kneeler.

ANABELLA: *(Handing JULIANA a tissue.)* You bleed too much!

JULIANA: Allergies. The inside of my nose is a roadmap. Full of veins going nowhere.

ANABELLA: Shoot! I don't wanna take <u>that</u> trip up booger-boulevard!

JULIANA: Stupid. I can slap you till you bleed. Would you like that, pendeja?

ANABELLA: Oooh! You ain't supposed to call your own sister a "pendeja."

JULIANA: Shut up, Beebee, and pray please.

(THEY pray in silence. ANABELLA prays on a candy bracelet that she holds like a rosary. SHE bites pieces off the bracelet as SHE speaks.)

ANABELLA: What are you praying for, Juli? *(Bite.)* I'm going for big red sweater like Alvin on Alvin and the Chipmunks 'cept mines will have an "A" on it for Anabella—not Alvin. *(Bite.)*

JULIANA: Good thinking, Stupid. I'm praying that Philip Michael Thomas comes and marries me.

ANABELLA: That show's so boring. And he's so old. Like thirty. Don Johnson was kind of fine though.

JULIANA: What do you know about "fine??" Anyway, he's the same damn age as Philip Michael!
And I like a mature guy. More romantic. And so sexy—so powerful.

ANABELLA: He's just a cop in Miami. But... Mom and Pop would like that prob'ly.

JULIANA: Who cares?! It's my prayer, girl.

ANABELLA: That's true, girl.
(THEY close their eyes and pray.)
Can I get two wishes?

JULIANA: They ain't wishes. They're prayers, boba. And only one per customer. You'll dilute the connection to the deities.

ANABELLA: Who's that?

JULIANA: Everyone we pray to. Gods. Goddesses. Ancestors.

ANABELLA: Like our dead family? Like Abuela and Papabuelo? So, no one ever really lives forever?

JULIANA: Not really. That's what a soul is. Like the thing inside you, you used to be, that keeps being you after the outside rots away.

ANABELLA: Ohhh... Like old pieces of meat? My friend Aisha has a grandma who cuts off the rotten part of the fruit and still eats it. So, part rotten doesn't mean all rotten sometimes, I guess.

JULIANA: Finish your prayer. We gots to go.

ANABELLA: Ok, ok. You're so bossy.

JULIANA: *(Taking dissected frogs' legs out of her pocket.)* Look what I brought you!

ANABELLA: *(Taking them in her hands.)* What are these?

JULIANA: Frogs' legs. From biology class. We was cutting them up today. I thought they'd come in "handy." Even though they're "legs!" Get it?!

ANABELLA: *(Tossing them onto the ground.)* You're so mean!

JULIANA: Uh, huh. Jesus is not going to like having legs strewn about his house.

ANABELLA: I'm going to tell Mami.

JULIANA: She won't care. She does bad things too, Beebee.

ANABELLA: Shut up! In church?

JULIANA: Maybe.

ANABELLA: Shut up! Like where?

JULIANA: You don't need to know.

ANABELLA: Like what? Tell me, Juli!

JULIANA: She steals.

ANABELLA: No, she don't.

JULIANA: Yes, she do. From the store.

ANABELLA: Stop lying. A lightning will strike you dead in the head, girl!

JULIANA: Stockings. She steals stockings. And she stole a veil for your first communion.

ANABELLA: Uhuhn. No, I saw her take it out of a bag from Alexander's.

JULIANA: She puts it in a bag from Alexander's on the street and then comes in the house and takes it out. Bam. No questions asked.

ANABELLA: At least she does it smart. With the bag and everything.

JULIANA: Yeah, she's so smart, she's going to jail one day and leave you motherless.

ANABELLA: Just me?

JULIANA: I don't need her like you do, Tiny. I'm going to college soon.

ANABELLA: But I have Pop. I'd be ok.

JULIANA: Maybe. Are you done wishing?

(ANABELLA and JULIANA close their eyes and freeze as a rushing sound travels through the back porch, like an elevated subway train is going by.)

SCENE THREE

The record player plays a song like Cream's *"Sunshine of Your Love."* The five icons, SHIRLEY, MARTIN, ROBERT, WHITE JESUS and BLACK JESUS, rise dancing from behind the cart where the fish tank rested. AMADOR and CECILIA go to them. BLACK JESUS stands behind MARTIN, and WHITE JESUS stands behind SHIRLEY. Then they reverse. Then THEY reverse back.

SHIRLEY: I have such a sore neck.
(WHITE JESUS goes to massage her neck—but...)
No. I want the other one.

(BLACK JESUS then begins to massage SHIRLEY's neck.)
Ooh, you know just how to touch a lady, Jesus.

CECILIA: Ah, hah! I knew you could talk.

AMADOR: How come you never talked to us before?

SHIRLEY: You weren't dead yet.

CECILIA: But you weren't either—when we put you up top there.

AMADOR: The men were though.

BLACK JESUS: I'm dead in all pictures.

WHITE JESUS: Me too. But my eyes stay lively...are you supposed to be me?

BLACK JESUS: You got that reversed. You're imaginary. I'm real.

AMADOR: Not at the last supper. Or the stations of the cross.

WHITE JESUS: But I'm almost dead. On my way out.

BLACK JESUS: Or my way in. Or up. Depends on how you see it.

(BLACK JESUS and WHITE JESUS nod at one another.)

AMADOR: But you two ain't the real Jesus.

BLACK JESUS: One of us could be.

WHITE JESUS: But you kept us both up there, so how do you know who the real one is?

CECILIA: Every day, I pick the other one. And then pum and then pum. Back and forth. Cha-cha-cha-cha. You're both real to me.

SHIRLEY: And what about the rest of us?

AMADOR: In her mind. She used to talk to you and I thought she was crazy, but now I see you too.

MARTIN: Am I who I used to be?

CECILIA: Not at all.

AMADOR: You're a man trapped in a newspaper article that's only about half true. It says you're a communist. But you weren't.

CECILIA: When you died, I did too. My hope. That the world was changing. But it didn't change, Dr. Martin. It almost never changes.

ROBERT: Not for the better anyway. I died two months after you did, Dr. Martin. According to this article: "Speculation: Did the same people shoot MLK and RFK? Different men paid for the crime, but who made them do it?" Do the truly guilty truly pay when the truth is hidden so well...
I thought about the truth behind these murky fish tank waters, and what I learned was from listening in the dark to you, Mrs. Shirley. Speaking truth is hard for a Catholic, we hide so much.

SHIRLEY: You're kinder than I remember. And just so you know, I died of natural causes, having survived three assassination attempts. Strong Caribbean stock. But when some men found me threatening, they united against me. The one thing both white and black men fear are the mouths of women. I was a truth-teller and a faithful public servant—always. Even George Wallace couldn't keep hating me. I led with respect. And I never did reach that highest office I deserved.

AMADOR: I think she's trapped in an Op-Ed.

CECILIA: Yes. I wanted a poster, but they got all painted over around here.

SHIRLEY: Men didn't like a woman doing anything that might mean she didn't need men to do what she needed to do.

CECILIA: So... we really are dead.

AMADOR: I knew it.

MARTIN: Oh, yes. When I stepped on to that balcony and then I knew, in that last moment, as my head spun back into the concrete, that my last wish was to be home. Home to paradise or home with my family? I didn't know. I just knew I lost track of time as I saw my own demise. A bullet hit me in the right cheek, shattering my jaw, several vertebrae and severing my spinal cord. I was rushed to St. Joseph's Hospital, where I was pronounced dead at 7:05 p.m.

ROBERT: And two months later, it happened to me—but at 12:02 a.m., Pacific Standard Time.
(Trying to emulate the orating style of MLK, but more drama than divine inspiration.)
Let me set the scene: Los Angeles, the Ambassador Hotel. I had just won that crucial California primary. And then a bullet caught me in the neck...and then the brain. A simple, honest busboy, Juan Romero, perhaps an angel sent to console me—

(The JESUSes and AMADOR nod "No." CECILIA nods "Yes" and makes the sign of the cross.)
—held my hand as I struggled for breath. Life Magazine said "Kennedy had almost found his voice. In six years, we have lost two Kennedys and one King." Ethel leaned over and whispered in my ear...but I didn't die until the next day—also at a hospital —Good Samaritan.

SHIRLEY: Interesting how you bring it back to you always. There are men who are taken by surprise by the inevitable. Like you were. You thought you were safe that day, even though the universe already took your brother. Maybe it's the Catholic in you that feeds your ego. That church has so many rituals. I was Baptist myself. Simple, clear, and Christian.

CECILIA: I love rituals. Important things need to be wrapped and buried with prayers and love.

AMADOR: I liked that he was Catholic, like us.

CECILIA: Yeah, but not like us. Those people were loaded.

AMADOR: So, if we're dead and they're dead, what's next?

CECILIA: I don't know. My mother told me that when you're dying everybody thinks you need to let go, but it's the other way around. Everybody needs to let you go. "Don't let those sinvergüenzas keep you, Ceci, when it's your time to dream."

CECILIA and ANABELLA: I lost track of time.

(The SISTERS transition out of their memory into the present.)

JULIANA: Yeah. Just—these things happen. When people you love—when you lose the things that ground you. You get thrown out of time. I read about it in the *New Yorker*.

ANABELLA: You so fancy.

JULIANA: You know it.

ANABELLA: Should we bring it back in the house after you rinse it?

JULIANA: Nah. We'll leave it out here for the junk men who are coming tomorrow. They'll take everything away so we can do a deep clean and try to sell the house. I just wanted to take the important papers and photos—stuff like that. The real scrubbing they can do.

ANABELLA: Great. So you don't need me here. This place creeps me out.

JULIANA: You better not leave me here alone again. They're your parents too.

ANABELLA: I loved how Dad called this crummy backyard his *finca*. His deep South Bronx plantation. Growing feed corn and eggplants to nourish the best fed rats ever.

JULIANA: You are so dark, Beebee.

ANABELLA: I'm dark??? *(Slight pause; that was too real.)* Who wants a drink?

JULIANA and ANABELLA: *(In unison)* Me.

(The sky opens up and we hear pounding rain.)

ANABELLA: What was it that Ma used to say about the rain?

ANABELLA and CECILIA: "The angels are sad for us today."

JULIANA: And then Pop would say:

JULIANA and AMADOR: "More like the angels are laughing so hard at us, they got tears streaming down, clogging the streets with wet juicy laughter."

ANABELLA: Yep. They have to have a little rum in this house.

(JULIANA and ANABELLA walk back into the house. ANABELLA searches for something to drink as JULIANA puts a record on the stereo. CECILIA and AMADOR dance to the music. Lights cross to the icons.)

SCENE FOUR
The icons think about things THEY miss.

> MARTIN: Friends, do you think they have any Sister Rosetta on that player?

(The five people from the photos appear as the record player begins to play a rock'n'roll spiritual like "Didn't It Rain" sung by Sister Rosetta Tharpe. THEY sway to the music. BLACK JESUS sings along. WHITE JESUS tries to.)

> SHIRLEY: I was hoping she'd sing at my inauguration.

> ROBERT: Me, too. At mine, I mean. Makes me sad to think about it. Is it a wrong to be sad about dying?

> MARTIN: When I was fighting with Johnson about giving us the vote, I would listen to her music. She freed my soul. I felt loved when she sang.

> BLACK JESUS: The love of God is in her voice.

> WHITE JESUS: Or does her voice sound like God's love?!

> BLACK JESUS: That's the same thing, Fake Jesus.

> WHITE JESUS: I don't tan as well as you—but that doesn't make me fake.

> MARTIN: And that guitar! She played like an angel waging war with a demon.

> SHIRLEY: I'm sure she had demons. But she also had dignity and talent.

> ROBERT: Hmmm…maybe we can move in a different direction.

(The record player begins to play a song like "A Fine Romance" sung by Marilyn Monroe.)

SHIRLEY: Famous last words, Robert?

MARTIN: This is why I never trusted you.

SHIRLEY: Is that why? You both suffered from the hunger for a woman's love.
(ROBERT dances by himself, mouthing the words to Marilyn's song.)

MARTIN: I suppose we can take turns choosing the music.

SHIRLEY: Oh, she certainly knew how to sell a song. But she couldn't saaang. Like Ella for instance.

ROBERT: I always loved that story about how Marilyn told the owner of the Mocambo nightclub in Hollywood she'd sit at a table by the stage— bringing in the audience and the press—just so he'd let Ella be the headline singer in a white club.

(A song like "(I love You for) Sentimental Reasons" sung by Ella Fitzgerald plays. BLACK JESUS and WHITE JESUS sing along.)

MARTIN: So brave. And just.

SHIRLEY: Was that true? I know people said that, but was it really true? I'm not sure I believe it. *(To the two JESUSes)* Why are you two always so quiet? Shouldn't you be preaching about something? Quoting the bible or scriptures?

(The two JESUSes look at each other, then BLACK JESUS speaks.)

BLACK JESUS: I dream sometimes.

WHITE JESUS: Me too...I mean probably not as much as you do...

BLACK JESUS: Why do you say that?

WHITE JESUS: I think you have more to dream about. I just dream about coming back. My story ends there.

BLACK JESUS: I dream about trips to places I've never been that are not the places I was meant to be in and then I can't find my way out of those places—because I don't know where those places are. But I walk and walk and just end up where I began.

WHITE JESUS: Classic.

BLACK JESUS: Why do you say that??

WHITE JESUS: Some things just really are just classic. I was thinking about this priest I once knew. He had soft hands that felt like a blessing. Gentle and light. And he thought that his hands proved that he was worthy of God. That's a classic thought from a well-meaning priest, who really doesn't know my Father that well. Father likes rough things.

BLACK JESUS: I never believe your stories.

MARTIN: The most important thing is not the story but how it's told. Tell it well enough and people will believe. That's how lies become truths.

SHIRLEY: Stop talking like your newspaper article. You don't have to anymore. We're independent now. Free-floating individuals. I'm feeling parched from all that time over a fish tank. Always kept the water too cold and the house too warm. I was always in a cold sweat.
(Pause)
Stuck in that reductive story. It wasn't miraculous. It was time. About time a woman—a Black woman—tried to hold an important position in such a man-boy government.

ROBERT: I wouldn't mind a drink either.

MARTIN: I don't think I drink much.

ROBERT: Really? Maybe you drink in this story? Maybe you need to drink in this story. I do...

MARTIN: A little cognac could feel good on the tongue...

SHIRLEY: Men are always so thirsty. Women pour the drink of knowledge. But a little wine might be nice. We were trapped back there a long time.

MARTIN: We were hibernating.

ROBERT: Those fish were tragic. Like lemmings being picked off by the rodents. I didn't know rodents could swim like that— and jump. Jumped in a perfect arc in and then out of the tank, holding a half-dead-anyway fish in its mouth.

SHIRLEY: Don't rodents jump in Massachusetts, Senator?

ROBERT: I haven't been there in a long time. I'm only the mirror of what I was on faded yellow paper.

SHIRLEY: We've all been trapped in newsprint from 1968... What a year that was. Makes my rear end clench up to think of it.

MARTIN: I was right, wasn't I? The night before I died, when I said: "...I've seen the promised land. I may not get there with you. But I want you to know tonight, that we, as a people will get to the promised land. And I'm happy tonight. I'm not worried about anything." And then those devils shot me. Maybe I should have been worried, but I think my real self really went to that place. And this paper me, will crumple up and blow away on the next burst of wind.

ROBERT: After you died, I said: "Surely, we can learn, at least, to look at those around us as fellow men and surely we can begin to work a little harder to bind up the wounds among us and to become in our hearts brothers and countrymen once again." And those frickin' chowdaheads kilt me.

SHIRLEY: That's nineteen sixty-eight for you...Nixon. Vietnam. Change coming the hard way. Our country sure learned how to mourn that year. Maybe that's why we're here. That's why I ran for Congress that year and then later for president. Somebody had to try and do something.

MARTIN: But we just ended up on top of a fish tank.

ROBERT: A lot of fish tanks. In a lot of houses. People believed in what we stood for.

SHIRLEY: Yes. We were in quite a few homes. For a time. Until we weren't. It's a bit like dying—to be famous and then disappear like the ink on faded newsprint.

(Lights cross to the cemetery.)

SCENE FIVE
The cemetery at dusk.
An imagined eulogy.
The SISTERS speak to two cremation urns.
At first, they cannot hear each other speak,
and then when indicated in the text, they can.
They cannot hear their parents speak.

ANABELLA: I'm trying to remember the things you gave me.

JULIANA: It was mainly despair. You were always so sad, Ma. And you, Pop, so resigned.

ANABELLA and JULIANA: And I'm not angry about this anymore.

ANABELLA: I used to be so resentful of what you gave Juli. You gave her so much that nothing was left.

JULIANA: Was that your idea, Pop?

ANABELLA and JULIANA: Why didn't you just drown me?

JULIANA: You weren't warm so I was warm for you. I greeted the neighbors and brought them food when they lost their jobs. And took their children to school. And listened to their problems. Like I was you. But I wasn't. I wasn't the woman of the house. But they saw me like I was.

ANABELLA: I never saw myself in you. Would I go blind if I ever saw myself in your eyes?

JULIANA: Was I your favorite?

ANABELLA: Was she your favorite?

JULIANA: I was the maid and the plant-waterer. Never your daughter. I always felt lost.

ANABELLA: There was no room in that house for me. That's why I left and never looked back. It was Juli I missed. Not you. I wondered if I should break into your house and save her. But she was supposed to save me, my big sister. She had that little apartment, but she didn't really stay there. You pulled her back. I don't know why she went, but I wasn't going with her. *(THEY turn toward each other and begin to talk to one another.)*

JULIANA: Hear that? Flying into the trees.

ANABELLA: Bats.

JULIANA: Lucky. To be able to fly.

ANABELLA: Where would you go?

JULIANA: Into the sea.

ANABELLA: Suicide...Or fishing?

JULIANA: I like the idea of fishing! Pulling living things out of the ocean with my beak.

ANABELLA: Ripping out their lives with your teeth.

JULIANA: Why are you still so angry, Sis?

ANABELLA: You were angry first. I learned it from you.

(THEY begin to speak to their parents' urns again and cannot hear one another.)

JULIANA: I didn't think it would hurt so much.

ANABELLA: When I was little, I'd crawl into bed with you, so I could wake up with your smile. But it always washed away when you saw me.

JULIANA: I reminded you of everything you never got to do.

ANABELLA: Your closed eyes were like caterpillars crawling over dead apple cores in the garden.

JULIANA: Your closed eyes didn't judge me.

ANABELLA: Were you thinking of how you wanted your life to be?

JULIANA: Why did you marry Pop?

(The daughters cannot hear the parents, but they wish they could.)

CECILIA: He tasted of salty French bread.

AMADOR: I did? You're more like *pan dulce*, my love. Eggy and sweet and soft.

ANABELLA: Why did you marry her, Pa?

AMADOR: It seemed like she was waiting for me, to take her someplace new. So I took her somewhere.
(Looking around the living room.) It was prettier in my head. But it was ours.

JULIANA: When did you know you loved him?

CECILIA: When I took his hand that last time and knew I was going to follow right behind him.
That's when I knew. He was a bobo, but he was my bobo.

AMADOR: Took you long enough.

CECILIA: I was afraid to lose God—my love for you was so deep.

AMADOR: And I found God when I fell in love with you.

CECILIA: I don't like our daughters' good-bye speeches. They still have too many questions.

AMADOR: We never should have had children. Think of all the parties we could have had. All the dancing we could have done.

CECILIA: I'm trembling.

(AMADOR pulls CECILIA to him in a tight embrace. The daughters can hear one another again.)

JULIANA: Not again!
(Her nose begins to bleed.)
I'm so tired of this bleeding.

(ANABELLA hands JULIANA a tissue and SHE pinches her nose with it.)

ANABELLA: Damn, girl! You should really keep a pack around. Or a handkerchief. Or a transfusion.

JULIANA: I do. But I run out so fast. And a handkerchief gets all hard and keeps that copper smell on it. Makes me gag.

ANABELLA: I would have thought you'd be used to it by now.

JULIANA: One more day would have been good.

ANABELLA: I keep imagining that too—that we had one more day to ask them everything. But that's still not enough time.

JULIANA: You were the Mayor of your block, Pop.

ANABELLA: And she was the Queen. Isn't that true, Ma?

JULIANA: You know what I did? When they wouldn't let us come say good-bye? I sat in my car in the hospital parking lot and held my own hand-and just watched the clock. And listened to podcasts.

ANABELLA: Me too. Funny ones. But I was in my house. Riding my exercise bike and waiting for a phone call from the hospital.

AMADOR: What's a podcast?

CECILIA: A radio thing. Where you listen in. And people talk about things.

AMADOR: How do you know that?

CECILIA: I listened too. When I could still stand to listen to voices from my phone.

AMADOR: I couldn't imagine listening to anything except my own breath.

(Pause)

CECILIA: You think we should have told them?

AMADOR: No. Families need their secrets. Otherwise, they get bored with just the truth all the time.

CECILIA: You're right. Juliana was too fragile, and Anabella was just a kid. Anyway, they'll find out soon enough…

AMADOR: Time takes more than breath away.

(JULIANA and ANABELLA kiss the urns, first one and then the other. Lights cross to the ICONS.)

SCENE SIX
SHIRLEY, MARTIN, ROBERT, AMADOR and CECILIA play *Parcheesi*. BLACK JESUS and WHITE JESUS kibitz.

MARTIN: Roll the dice and make it nice. *(ROBERT rolls the dice.)* Double ones. Snake eyes. But no blockades to break up so just a little ole two. Can't move out on that. HA! My turn!

ROBERT: How can you be so far ahead of me?? I'm going to jump you and send you back to your nest.

SHIRLEY: I don't think so! Roll a five to stay alive.

CECILIA: *(Rolls the dice; it's a double five.)* ESO!! Pin para-ping-pang-poom!

MARTIN: Double five, Madam! You're a lucky lady. Move two tokens out.

AMADOR: How'd you do that so easy, Ceci??! Tramposa!
(CECILIA shrug her shoulders mischievously.)
Give me some of that!

(AMADOR kisses her.)

ROBERT: I don't think it works that way. Kisses never saved me.

SHIRLEY: Don't hate the winner, Gentlemen. It never feels good in the end—like jumping off a tall building—at first you feel like you're flying and then you end up a bloody mess.

ROBERT: I don't like these dice. I can't roll a five to save my life.

SHIRLEY: Not your game, Senator Bobby. Try a two and a three. I dream in many parts now. Time is in many parts. There are no more straight lines or pointed destinations.

AMADOR: You have to blow on the dice and think about something beautiful you'd like five of.

(ROBERT blows on the dice.)

ROBERT: Bobby needs a new pair of shoes!
(HE throws the dice.)
Finally a five and a two! At least I'm on the board. And I can move forward two spaces.

MARTIN: Double fives and sixes are the new elixirs.

CECILIA: You're so rhythmic, Doctor Martin.

AMADOR: I can do that too. "Roll it now—oh, wow!"

SHIRLEY: That almost rhymes, Doctor Martin. Ha. Another five. I'm all out.

MARTIN: You're good at this, Mrs. Shirley.

ROBERT: I used to be good at this too.

SHIRLEY: Your Parchessi playing is as good as your grip on democracy, Senator Bobby.

ROBERT: Discord, tyranny, greed. All a roll of the dice. Can democracy combat all of that? Can government regulate it?

MARTIN: Rousseau's dilemma. In the Social Contract, the people decide on the government they want, the government does not decide what government to give them.

ROBERT: What will the painting of this world look like if government is made in the likeness of its people? Is it a drawing in charcoal, stark and full of gentle shadows or is it a watercolor palette of primary colors?

AMADOR: I like the shadows. Then you can imagine anything you want.

ROBERT: Yes, in those folds between dark and light.

CECILIA: But the watercolors give us life.

MARTIN: I can't imagine what this world wants now. But I wasn't surprised when my time came up. When you choose a path covered in years of moss, you have to expect there might be snakes on it.

SHIRLEY: All my tokens can start heading home again.
(Pause)
I'm going to win this game, gentlemen.

CECILIA: You're amazing, Mrs. Shirley. If I could be anyone else, I would be you. You know how to be yourself and survive.

MARTIN: I suspect you're a survivor too, Mrs. Cecilia.

ROBERT: Women always win the long game.

SHIRLEY: You say that now.

ROBERT: I've learned a lot on top of this aquarium.

MARTIN and SHIRLEY: Mmmhmm...

WHITE JESUS and CECILIA: Like what?

MARTIN: Fish will eat other fish when they are hungry. And they are always hungry.

BLACK JESUS and AMADOR: Sometimes they eat their own children. Hunger is like a war for them.

WHITE JESUS: Blessed are you who are hungry now, for you will be filled...

BLACK JESUS: Luke liked speaking to the poorest of the flock.

SHIRLEY: But John said it best: "Whoever comes to me, will never go hungry..."

BLACK JESUS: In Heaven. In Heaven, you never go hungry, but here on Earth—

WHITE JESUS: People die.

SHIRLEY: I never realized how sad you are, Jesus. Both of you.

BLACK JESUS: Crucifixion gave me a lot to think about.

WHITE JESUS: I thought mainly about keeping my father happy.

BLACK JESUS: And I thought about why my father had to kill me off to save everybody else.

MARTIN: Sacrifice for the greater good is the greatest gift.

ROBERT: My brother used to say that all the time...

AMADOR: My brothers made me do all the sacrificing. Is that a gift? I worry about what I gave our daughters—

CECILIA: We gave them everything they said they needed.

AMADOR: But what did they really need? Juliana was—

CECILIA: She's fine now. It was just a few times. She just needed to stop thinking for a while.

AMADOR: More than a few times, Ceci. If she only read more *Reader's Digests*...they always cheer me up.

(AMADOR, CECILIA, SHIRLEY, ROBERT, MARTIN, BLACK JESUS, and WHITE JESUS, share a look. Lights cross to the dining room table.)

SCENE SEVEN
The dining room.
ANABELLA and JULIANA sit with
an open bottle of Olive Oil and two glasses.

> ANABELLA: Of course, it was in an old olive oil bottle. Pop always hid his rum from his brothers.
> *(Pause)*
> Why are we really here?
>
> JULIANA: You know. We have to find the will and their deed. And then you never have to come here again.

ANABELLA: You can have it all, Juliana. I don't want anything of theirs.

JULIANA: Me neither. We just have to show the deed to sell the house. That's what the real estate agent said. Then at least we'll have money for a stone for Ma and Pa, and maybe a place beside them for me and you.

ANABELLA: No thanks! Scatter me into the sea. I wanna be fish food.

JULIANA: That sounds useful.
(Pause)
What happened to you, Beebee? You used to be kinda pleasant.

ANABELLA: There was nothing specific. But around them, I always got the feeling that I was in the way. And I wished I wasn't. I want to start breathing on my own. I couldn't before. Always felt wrong. Or guilty. Or ugly. The way they made me feel, I never want my children to feel. That's why I never had any.

JULIANA: They were just that way. About everyone. *(Pause)*
When we finish our drinks, let's get back to it. I don't want to stay here too late. It's feeling like Winter in here. It never felt like this before. I was never afraid to spend the night or go upstairs. But now I look at their empty bed. Our old bedrooms. It feels cold. Like gone. Like the warmth is gone from inside here. And I don't know if it's because they've passed on or because some part of me has passed on with them.
Feel my hands.

ANABELLA: They're ice cold, Juli! Let's go and come back tomorrow morning. There's no rush.

JULIANA: Yeah, there is! I have to lift them out of me, Anabella.

ANABELLA: That's beginning to sound like crazy talk...

JULIANA: Yeah. I know. I go in and out of all my feelings. Like I think I'm fine and thinking about such good memories and then I feel a strange fist around my heart. So, I can't breathe. Like the blood is being squeezed out of my chest.

ANABELLA: Or your nose.

JULIANA: That's not funny.

ANABELLA: Not even a little? OK. Let's get back to it then. *(ANABELLA impulsively hugs JULIANA, who pushes her away.)*
You're shivering, girl.

JULIANA: No. Please don't—I don't want anyone to touch me right now.

ANABELLA: *(Changing the subject)*
So where should we look? I remember they had a metal box they said contained the "just-in-case" papers. Let's look for that.

JULIANA: Too obvious. You think they'd be so clear? We just had rum out of an olive oil bottle.
Maybe we should look inside the rooster.

ANABELLA: It was a duck. Good idea! First we find the ceramic pato. Mami and Papi kept a lot of their financial records in there. A lot of important papers were in that duck. That piece of pottery was Mom and Dad's pride and joy. It used to be on top of the fridge, but it's not there anymore.

JULIANA: Did you check the kitchen cabinets? I thought it just had checks and things in it.

ANABELLA: True dat. So where to begin...

(Looks around at the mess)
Hmmm...How about I start in this corner and you over there?

(Noticing that the screen for the back porch is swinging open.)
Better latch that door. The wind's so strong.

(ANABELLA sits down suddenly.)
I can't believe we got here, Juli. To this place. That this thing that happened to so many families, happened to us. Remind me why.

(JULIANA sits down next to her.)

JULIANA: Capitalism?

(THEY laugh.)

ANABELLA: So the government did this?

(The Icons all turn away from their Parcheesi game and look at the daughters.)

JULIANA: Yeah. Think about it. If people were worried about other people more than they're worried about themselves, these things wouldn't happen. Not the way it's happening now. Not so many people dying...

(The ICONs speak, but the daughters still cannot hear them. ANABELLA picks up the photographs and straightens out the paper. Puts them in a neat pile by her side.)

ANABELLA: I guess that's why those folks were on the fish tank. Ma and Pop needed hope in here. It was hard to feel that hope when so much was happening all the time that made you feel hopeless.

MARTIN: That's what I always said.

SHIRLEY: Yes. So many times. And over and over again. "Shirley, why do you keep defending the ignorant?" Because they needed to be understood, heard, and then when they knew it took nothing from them to give out some love and empathy— Only added so much—Until they knew that—nothing ever was going to change.

ROBERT: You did say it. I tried to say it too. But they weren't ready to listen.

MARTIN: To remind them of the possibility that equality, freedom, dignity could be theirs. No matter how poor, or dark, or what language they spoke.

JULIANA: I remember Ma cutting those pictures out. She thought she was talking directly to them.

ANABELLA: And I never even looked at them until now.

JULIANA: Do you feel it now? A cold tightness in your chest?

ANABELLA: How could she frame news clippings and never put-up pictures of us? That's fucked up.

JULIANA: We weren't important, Anabella.

ANABELLA: You're important to me.
(Pause)
Even they were important to me. But I hated the secrets. They whispered and laughed behind their hands sometimes when I asked them questions. It was weird and unsettling. People think children don't understand, but we know when we're being lied to.

JULIANA: You're so dramatic.

ANABELLA: Am I? Let's find that shitty piece of paper and get the hell out of here.

(JULIANA searches the shelves against the walls and ANABELLA checks inside a closet stuffed with stuff, sweeping and rifling though the papers and boxes there. BLACK JESUS puts his hands on JULIANA's shoulders. WHITE JESUS puts his hands on BLACK JESUS' shoulders.)

(Lights cross to CECILIA and AMADOR hiding behind the sofa, holding a metal lock box.)

SCENE EIGHT
AMADOR and CECILIA sorting through the stuff in the lock box.

CECILIA: The perfect place really…

AMADOR: I remember when we started collecting those photos from the newspapers. And you framed them.

CECILIA: Of course. Those are important people. They deserve a frame. It gave them context. And then they could stand guard over my fish.

JULIANA: You know how you have to pick out a Saint's card or a picture card for the funeral home? But since it's just me and you, we didn't go to the funeral home. Didn't have a funeral, just ashes, just this dust to bury. But I would have chosen St. Cecilia for Mami, of course. You're right, Beebee. I'm not very creative.
(Reading from the "Miniature Book of Saints: Book Two.")
"Cecilia was a lovely Roman girl. She loved Jesus with all her heart. But a young Roman wanted to marry her, but she told him she belonged to Our Lord alone.
But when the young man walked toward Cecilia, to force her into marriage, he saw her strong, beautiful Guardian Angel standing at her side."

ANABELLA: That reminds me of the time the bathroom ceiling fell on my head and Pop had to dig me out of the rubble with his bare hands.

JULIANA: What?! That makes no sense. I remember the ceiling coming down—but not on your head.

ANABELLA: You were at school doing something.

JULIANA: Why do you remember all the bad things that happened but none of the good??

ANABELLA: I was sitting on the toilet. It was so embarrassing. And so wet! All this stale water and plaster came down on top of me in a disgusting whoosh. Freezing cold water—and it was cold—like the waiting room at the local ER—the kind of cold from a place you expect to die in.
It left me trembling. And wood. Pieces of wood from the ceiling foundation. What's that called? The cross boards. Foundation? Slats of wood...*fuwahcatah* on my head. And little 8-year-old me on the toilet. Filled with shame. Maybe that's when I first understood that word.
Still haven't gotten it out of my system.
Shame is my default emotion.
What was it in the walls? Now on my skin?
Will it leave a mark? A scar?
I shook and cried that raggedy cry that I still do sometimes—like at the cemetery yesterday.
Lasted till Ma got home from her job at the hospital. I wondered "did I just die?" Is this what happens when you die? You get covered with shit and then your father comes through the fallen walls and ceiling to save you. I was lucky the firemen said, because if the tub had fallen on top of me, I'd of been dead. Those old iron tubs weighed a ton. But then when I looked up after it all came down, I saw the upstairs tub balanced on the cross boards of the ceiling.

JULIANA: They're called joists.

ANABELLA: I never knew their name. I don't know the name of any foundations—just that they hold things up and keep them from caving in.

JULIANA: Like Mom and Pop.

ANABELLA: Uhuhn. Like you and me.

(The record player starts playing "Lately" by Stevie Wonder. ANABELLA and JULIANA dance to it.)

JULIANA: You're so warm, Beebee. I could cook an egg on your ass.

ANABELLA: That's Pop's favorite expression.

JULIANA: Yeah, it was...

ANABELLA: When did they get that fish tank anyway?
JULIANA: It was here before we were even born.

ANABELLA: Maybe it came with the house. *(Pause)* Do you remember when they got me that albino hamster? I think it was a mouse though.

JULIANA: How do you figure?

ANABELLA: Angry. Hamsters don't get angry. Mice are always angry. They get fed to things.

JULIANA: I remember when it got loose and disappeared for a few days and then came back, covered in grease, not happy to be caged anymore even though Pop had bought him a new toy for his cage.

ANABELLA: Yeah. That's when you left the house. Moved in with that church guy.

JULIANA: I didn't know you knew about him. It was temporary. I thought he was going to save me.

ANABELLA: Of course, I knew. I could smell him on you. Cigarettes and stale beer. Some church guy.
But when you came back you had sad eyes. And Mom and Pop looked at you with sad eyes.

JULIANA: When they could bear to look at me at all. I don't think they could ever see me again.
I barely saw myself after I came home.

ANABELLA: Ma said he raped you.

JULIANA: She told you that?!

ANABELLA: Yeah. But I figured she was lying.

JULIANA: She wasn't.

ANABELLA: It was a cautionary tale.

JULIANA: Yes. For both of us. How come I'm 55 years old and I still remember how he smelled that day? How his fingers felt pulling me back by my hair? When do bad things go away from your mind?

ANABELLA and EVERYONE except JULIANA: Never.

JULIANA: I didn't think those feelings would last forever. I wonder if I had turned him in, if I would have felt better? I didn't want to have to tell people what happened. I didn't think anyone would believe me. He was so handsome. And he was a church deacon. I always think about it at this time of day—that moment when the sky goes from light to dark.

ANABELLA: Ma used to call it "Violet Time." I thought she was saying "Violent time." Why the hell would she tell us that? When I finally figured out what she was saying, it was time to leave home.

CECILIA and ANABELLA: My favorite time of day.

(ANABELLA and JULIANA move into a memory. The day JULIANA left home.)

ANABELLA: Why do you have to go, Juli?

JULIANA: I need to grow up, Beebee. I need to find my own way.

(ANABELLA gives JULIANA a teeny, little globe. It's a pencil sharpener.)

ANABELLA: You spin this and find your way home to me okay? Why you crying, boba?

JULIANA: It's the best gift you ever gave me, Beebee. But how're you gonna sharpen your pencils now?

ANABELLA: I'm gonna take one of Pa's knives and scrape out those points. I'm a survivor, girl! How are you gonna protect yourself without me?

(JULIANA pulls ANABELLA into a tight hug.)
Let me go! I have to get ready for my Daughters of Mary meeting. I hate the way the nuns smell, but I like how you have to make a big "M" with your Virgin Mary medal. It feels like a superhero—like Superman or something. Super-Mary.

(SHE hands JULIANA something else.)
Don't tell Mami I gave it to you.

JULIANA: It's your communion rosary though, Beebee! You gotta keep that.

ANABELLA: Uhn uh. No. You're the one needs it. To remember me. *(SHE touches her heart.)*
I keep us in here. I don't need no freakin' jewels.

JULIANA: I love you, Sis.

ANABELLA: Corny. You're too skinny to leave home. Better take some snacks. I recommend the coconut snowball in the fridge. I ate half, but you can have the other half.

JULIANA: I mean it, Anabella. I love you.

ANABELLA: Then why are you leaving me here?

JULIANA: It's just time...for me to go.

(ANABELLA grabs JULIANA around her legs.)

ANABELLA: Ha! Try and leave now.

(JULIANA tries. THEY both laugh as JULIANA drags ANABELLA across the floor. AMADOR and CECILIA watch them.)

AMADOR: Why didn't I stop her—make her just stay home? She had the pata caliente. Always running off somewhere.

CECILIA: We couldn't stop her. I asked God to stop her and he didn't do it, so how could we?

JULIANA: *(To herself)* How many souls are wandering without their bodies?
Hot feet moving over ice-covered soil, melting beneath them, sinking deep.
My landscape—soiled—dark painted stripes, encaging me,
Shadows passing through the Sun—like my heart—
Lost never to be found. A violent kiss through clenched teeth—
And my essence gone. Swallowed whole—a swallowed soul.
With my screams, night fills my mouth.
I choke on the sound of my sex being ripped apart.
Words like wet cloths filled with blood and mucus.
My shame, a disease turning in on itself—
becoming one with a world without Gods.

There is no hope when names are lost through the holes of memory,
Where self-love disappears through the torn viscera of violence.

ANABELLA:
(To JULIANA but SHE can't hear her.)
That's what I knew with you. Silence and forgiving.
Wrongs constant.
Life under the weight of your tears. Liquid pounding my heart
—a restless knowledge,
constant motion of emotion. Let me into your darkness, sister.
The black void of you tastes like me. Dancing to the irregular rhythms of your heartbeat.
Quick, quick, slow. Quick, slow, slow. So slow. Simple and singular love.
Honest love—a torture of the flesh.
A yearning that burns into your eyes. Just like mine. But I can't see it alone.
Your passion always blinds me.

(JULIANA and ANABELLA pull away from one another and sit on opposite sides of the couch, as the lights cross to BLACK JESUS and WHITE JESUS.)

SCENE NINE

BLACK JESUS and WHITE JESUS sit back-to-back as if THEY are in a confession booth in a church.

BLACK JESUS: What does it mean to be a protector?

WHITE JESUS: Who are we protecting?

BLACK JESUS: Them. All of them.

WHITE JESUS: Even the ones who don't believe in us?

BLACK JESUS: Why not?

WHITE JESUS: Seems like we could be doing something more constructive.

BLACK JESUS: I make myself useful. I hear confessions.

WHITE JESUS: Do you forgive?

BLACK JESUS: I do. But I don't forget.

(JULIANA confesses something to BLACK JESUS, when ANABELLA closes her eyes.)

JULIANA: When they gave me those calm-down pills, I would take them every other day, just to see how many I could save. It was a savings plan for life, I thought, but I just did it for a couple of years. Just to see if anyone would notice. Then I took them all and all it did was make me vomit. And kept me in a space like I was dead anyway. Like I couldn't move forward.

BLACK JESUS: I noticed.

JULIANA: So why didn't you stop me? Heal me? Make me feel like I didn't need to run away all the time?

BLACK JESUS: Prayer is just a wish. You have to do the doing.

JULIANA: Then what's the point. All these years trying to pray away the pain. Like all those crazy evangelists. Isn't that what they do? Lay on hands and heal people? What does our Jesus do?
Maybe that's why ma put the two of you up on the wall. Hedging her bets. Can you bet on healing? My money's on pain to place, win and show.

WHITE JESUS: I think the bet goes: Win, place or show.

JULIANA: Is that all you got for me? OTB corrections? Anyway, I was talking to him.

WHITE JESUS: People always talk to him. But it's me they pray to.

(JULIANA goes to ANABELLA and tries to put her hand on ANABELLA's heart.)

ANABELLA: Don't.

JULIANA: Let me feel your heart.

ANABELLA: You can't. It's on the inside.

JULIANA: I mean the beating of it, stupid.

ANABELLA: I don't like your creepy fingers on me. Like little wet spiders.

JULIANA: Why don't you let me love you?

ANABELLA: You're my sister. That's weird. Your fingers are strange and long and menacing. You're a creeper, sis.

JULIANA: I do have spidery fingers. I always feel like there is something sharp and sticky at the ends of my fingers. Don't spiders feel sticky? I mean at the end of their legs. And they make spider webs, so they must be sticky to make things stick to the webs. Right?

ANABELLA: Where are you going with this?

JULIANA: I see why you're alone. You never give anything away.

ANABELLA: So now that Mom and Pop are dead, you want to love me?
Can't you do it without all that finger bullshit?

JULIANA: You stayed away for so long. I mean even when you did show up. You had to find a way of keeping yourself apart from us. Are you afraid of my spit?

ANABELLA: What?

JULIANA: *(something half-heard)*
Are you afraid my spit would poison you? Are you afraid of tasting my sadness—because it's the same as yours?

ANABELLA: You always had that talent—of jumping to the right conclusions.

JULIANA: There was no jumping. I spent a lifetime thinking about you. I was there when you were born. When Ma had you in the fire station, because we couldn't make it to the hospital. It was just me and Ma and then you came.

ANABELLA: What about Pop?

JULIANA: He worked all the time. At the factory. The four to midnight shift. I'd wait up for him sometimes.

ANABELLA: You would?

JULIANA: Yeah. I never went to sleep until he came home. I imagined him walking from his car with a homemade knife in his hand—

ANABELLA: You're making that shit up! Was he coming from prison? Carrying a shiv? Stupid!

JULIANA: Nooo. But he used to make knives from the scraps of steel he would salvage from the machines at the factory. He'd sharpen them—then Voilá! A weapon...to walk home with. He needed it. You were too young to remember that old neighborhood—before the projects. The projects were luxury compared. And then the casita got built and it was even better. Like rich people. With a yard. That was like heaven.

CECILIA: You think we'll go there?

AMADOR: Not sure there is any there there. Maybe this is it. Roaming around for eternity in places we once lived and listening to how people we knew are still living.

CECILIA: That's a jodienda, 'Doro! I wanted a bigger garden at least.

AMADOR: Maybe you don't get to choose.

SHIRLEY: Maybe you're not quite all the way dead. I had a neighbor once, in Barbados, that came back from the dead. She was in a sugar coma. And she was just staring, eyes wide open at nothing for hours. The priest declared her dead—but she just needed a little orange juice—and to remember to breathe. It was as if she had forgotten how to do that. And this little girl went up to her and poked her with a stick in the place where her heart might be. That lady opened her eyes wide then. I told myself: always remember to breathe. *(Meaning MARTIN and ROBERT)*
Maybe that's why I outlived the two of you.

MARTIN: That could have something to do with it. I never remembered the basic rules of living. Rule One: Believe yourself worthy and always watch your back and your front.

ROBERT: You survived because you were a woman. People didn't think you could ever change society.

SHIRLEY: Society being led by short-sighted men, probably not.

ROBERT: Know any other table games?

MARTIN: How about a game of Gin?

SHIRLEY: What is that game where you put a celebrity's name on your forehead? You stick it to the middle of your forehead with your spit and the others give you clues about who it is? And you have to guess? What about that one?

MARTIN: I'll give it a try.

ROBERT: What do you think is worse? Dying? Or getting stuck in a yellowed piece of newspaper? We're barely recognizable anymore. Look how the lines in our faces have all faded—we are becoming blanks.

MARTIN: Isn't that all of history?

SHIRLEY: I don't mind fading—as long as someone better—well, stronger—comes along.
Someone who can win this time.

(ANABELLA puts the evening news on the TV.)

ANABELLA: I can't believe this TV still works.

SHIRLEY: We've all been replaced by mediocrity. Bad writers, self-concerned leaders. Seems like we keep moving backwards.

(JULIANA pulls out the remote and shakes roaches out of it.)

JULIANA: Oooh! Look at those roaches run!

ANABELLA: That's what the evil cop said to the peaceful protestors.

JULIANA: That's no joke.

ANABELLA: It's hard to make good jokes about bad cops.

(Long pause. The SISTERS continue to search through the rubble.)

SHIRLEY: Hmmmm...hm...hm...hmm...
(The sounds from the television are the sounds of disaster. Sirens. Police shootings. Politicians lying. Untrustworthy government workers making up stories.)
You see? It's not better.

MARTIN: Not yet.

ROBERT: *(Pointing to CECILIA and AMADOR)*
Maybe not in their lifetime.

MARTIN: Those folks are dead, Robert.

ROBERT: How about them? *(Pointing at the Two JESUSes.)*

WHITE JESUS *(with a laugh)*: Oh, us?

BLACK JESUS: Uhm, no. Not exactly.

(THEY tickle each other. BLACK JESUS goes too far.)

WHITE JESUS: Stop it. My skin is thin.

BLACK JESUS: No kidding.
(Pause.)
I don't even like you. I see what you turned humanity into. This horrible place.

AMADOR: Wooah! It's not that bad. Just needs some paint. And somebody to live here again. Who can still climb stairs...and doesn't get stuck halfway up and shits themselves.

CECILIA: Amador! Don't tell them that!

BLACK JESUS and WHITE JESUS: We already know.

SHIRLEY: We do too.

AMADOR: Some things you can't hide.

CECILIA: Some things you should hide.

SHIRLEY: That's debatable.

ROBERT: Why in confession booths can you see the priest through the mesh? If it's supposed to be anonymous? If you're supposed to be hiding your sins from the prying eyes of God, shouldn't it be blank—like looking at an empty blackboard?

BLACK JESUS: Where you can write all your sins?

CECILIA: That's pretty.

WHITE JESUS: Writing with your tongue.

(CECILIA blushes.)

AMADOR: You've always been in love with them.

CECILIA: It's true. You're supposed to love Jesus.

AMADOR: Not that way. That's nasty, Ceci.

CECILIA: But real. I've always been such a romantic. I yearn for all things beautiful beside me.
Jesus is so handsome. Always has been in every color.

AMADOR: I like the Black one. He looks more like me.

CECILIA: In my dreams!

(CECILIA and AMADOR kiss. BLACK JESUS and WHITE JESUS almost kiss.)

WHITE JESUS: That was close.

BLACK JESUS: Get away from me. You're too much. Too close. You're stealing my essence. I can feel it.

WHITE JESUS: I didn't know you could feel it…it's just that you are so perfect. It's intimidating.
I keep wishing I was just like you.

(SHIRLEY has created her own version of the Headbanz game. SHE has the name of a celebrity taped to her forehead. The celebrity is God.)

SHIRLEY: Feed me clues and I guess who's on my head. Who wants to play?

(WHITE JESUS and BLACK JESUS raise their hands. The other ICONS look away.)

WHITE JESUS: Someone everyone says has a special, magical power over them.

BLACK JESUS: Somebody who smells like fresh bread.

SHIRLEY: Is it a baby? They always smell so delicious. I wanted children but fate had other plans.

(AMADOR embraces CECILIA. Lights brighten on ANABELLA and JULIANA sifting through the living room looking for anything of value or importance in the piles of worthless stuff strewn all over the room. JULIANA pulls a plastic Hawaiian Lei from behind a dead plant in the windowsill.)

JULIANA: Look, Bee-bee, from your 8th birthday party. I think they were using it to decorate their windows.
Cheap plastic nonsense. Maybe to keep the outside air from getting in.

ANABELLA: This house could use some air. *(Pause)*
What else is trapped in this house? Do you think they wanted to keep all the memories shoved into the corners? Every space filled with a piece of the past.

JULIANA: Here's something Tío Cheo left us. A piece of broken glass from that bottle of Old Spice he gave Papi two Christmases ago. Remember? They got into a fight after finishing that bottle of 151 and *fahwahcata* he smashed it into the mirror over the sofa.

ANABELLA: Our dad was a pretty good dad, but he had horrible brothers. They beat him up all the time until he grew to be the tallest. Then they left him alone. He told me that one time his brother Cheo shit in his shoes—the only pair he had back then. That's why pop never wanted to go back.
He didn't have good memories.

JULIANA: Shit in shoes is never a good memory. It's almost funny until you're the one that steps in it.
Like he always told us: "Then you keep stepping in it, since it's your only pair of shoes." If Pop had been born somewhere different, he could have written one of those self-help books like "I Learned Everything I Needed to Know in Kindergarten" books that people love. He had so much common sense to impart.

ANABELLA: So true. Like that fish one.
(THEY laugh. AMADOR and CECILIA speak from behind the sofa.)

AMADOR: *(Incredulously)* I could have written books?

CECILIA: Sure. What's that other one you always like to tell the girls—the one about fish?

AMADOR: "Fish only take your breath away because they live in places where you can't breathe."

JULIANA: I was so stupid. I never understood it exactly. Like why would we think about fish and breathing and living. But other things took my breath. Shook me to my core. You were probably too young to remember that time, Tío Cheo came to our door. Banging on it. And so drunk he had pissed himself. I was so scared. But Mami wouldn't let him in.

I thought he was gonna come in and pull us out by our feet. Mami tried to talk him into going away, but he tried to break the door in. We had one of those police locks on the door though, so he couldn't get far. But I thought about his dirty fingers grabbing us and pulling us through that door. I still can't sleep without having my feet all covered up and my knees bent up to my chest with my fingers curled into my hands.

ANABELLA: I know. I don't know how you sleep like that. I always think you're gonna make a sound like an accordion when you wake up and uncurl yourself. And your fingers smelt like old oatmeal en-crustilated inside there.

JULIANA: Why the mother-fuck were you smelling my fingers?? You were the strangest child, you know that, Bee-bee? You slept like you were dead, on your back, with your arms neatly folded across your chest. So fucking perfect.

ANABELLA: Uhm, no. I don't remember ever sleeping perfect. I rest most of the time, but I don't sleep. Do you still eat oatmeal for dinner?

JULIANA: Sometimes.
(Madonna's "Isla Bonita" plays.)
And I still like Madonna.

ANABELLA: Holy shit! What's your problem, sister? Rich White people are buying up "La Isla Bonita" now.
Like that weird bitcoin guy? People throw things at his gate to scare him off, but he stays and stays. Says he's gonna buy the whole island. Says it already belongs mostly to him and all the

other rich investors. Conquer baby, conquer. There goes the Motherland.
(Pause)
Were you ever alone with Ma?

JULIANA: Huh? Why do you ask that?

ANABELLA: Just curious. I don't remember a time when it wasn't the three of us, so there must have been a time when the two of you were alone.

JULIANA: There was a time alright. I was so mad when you came along. Once you were there, you were always there. I was never alone with Mami again. The best time was when Ma took a bath with me. I was little—like three, but it's so clear. She was on her back in the tub and I sat on her belly and she washed my hair and my back. But she never let me wash her. And one day I noticed that she was wearing underwear. In the tub. That was weird. So I pulled on the elastic of her panties and she slapped me. Last time we ever bathed together.

ANABELLA: That's why you're so sexually repressed.

JULIANA: There was something so wrong about that. Why was she ashamed for her little girl to be naked with her? Or was that just how good girls—good women were? Always keep your underwear on until the last minute in case you die in the tub or slip and break your head and the ambulance has to come take you away.

ANABELLA: You're as freaky as mom, Sis.

CECILIA: She is. Because she has a good heart and good hearts are freaky because there isn't so many of them. And I'm just practical. You don't want to be naked in an ambulance, do you?

AMADOR: If you're in an ambulance, maybe it doesn't matter.

CECILIA: That's just not true.
(CECILIA blows into JULIANA's ear.)
That's a mother's love.

(JULIANA gasps.)

ANABELLA: What?

JULIANA: A cold air went right through me.

ANABELLA: There's nothing but cold air in here.

(Silence.)

JULIANA: What are you dreaming about these days?

ANABELLA: Taxis. That don't know how to get anywhere, and I can't tell them where to go, because I don't know where I am. I just need to get to an airport.

JULIANA: I have that one too. But in my dream the taxi driver can't get to where he wants to go because all the street signs have changed and the streets suddenly go in the wrong direction.

ANABELLA: Is it always a man who's driving?

JULIANA: Yes.

ANABELLA: There's also one where I get in a shared ride car but it's an abnormally big car with about six rows of seats. And then it joins a parade.

JULIANA: People. You miss them.

ANABELLA: Yes.

JULIANA: I wrote you a poem.

ANABELLA: You did? Why? That's freaking weird.

JULIANA: You wanna hear it?

ANABELLA: Not really.

JULIANA: It goes like this:
I found my suitcase empty.
It used to hold my desire—now the contents—stolen—but the shell still there.
A hard, leathery shell with blood no longer flowing.
It wasn't supposed to be a man.
I never thought a man would be able to steal my blood.
Never met one like him before.
Never met one who took my heart inside his mouth with his eyes. His lashes beat furiously against my beige skin.
It was then I knew how I despised his desire.
I used to love only my sister, but when I knew you wanted me, the world crashed like a falling star between my thighs.

ANABELLA: In all the books I read from ages four through eleven, people lived in mansions or palaces or places where the Sun always seemed to shine. There were dogs and lawns and porches. Spending money and new dresses for your birthday. Little girls wore coats made of wool or cotton or other natural fibers—and they always had hats to match. And hard-shell purses.
I read these books in Juliana's polyester pants and stretchy top outfits that she outgrew nine years before. I was so out of fashion, I felt out of time. In the wrong time. That was the only place I belonged, where no one else ever was.

(Lights come down on the SISTERS as SHIRLEY and the other Icons speak.)

SHIRLEY: Juliana's like a piece of tissue someone blew into and then tore into pieces.

MARTIN: I see that. Something that was clean and pure and then got dirty and as a result got split into so many parts that she can't even understand who she is anymore.

ROBERT: And what are we?

MARTIN: Different. We worked through some of our trauma. Politicians have to. But they haven't. People burned our pictures, but the things we stood for and did—that can't be erased. Right?

SHIRLEY: Not all politicians work it out, some of them keep living out their shame and disillusions in office. They use their power to manifest their pain onto others.

ROBERT: I read that issue too. *Reader's Digest* is under-valued.

CECILIA: Don't talk about my daughters like that—like a fix-up project or something. They do just fine.

AMADOR: Maybe they're right. Maybe we didn't give them the motor to keep moving forward.
Maybe they're just chassis with no engine. You try to do your best, but it doesn't always work. I mean, I wasn't always there. To protect you ladies.

CECILIA: Ladies have to learn to protect themselves...

SHIRLEY: That's the truth of it.

BLACK JESUS: People have to make things complicated. As if to say: If you have nothing to undo/correct/or reverse, why live? You live because eventually you won't. And that's when you finally realize what was worth dying for.

WHITE JESUS: Let me see your tongue.

BLACK JESUS: That's more than you need to see.

WHITE JESUS: It's just a tongue. Look at mine.
(HE sticks out his tongue as far as it will go, then speaks still with his tongue out.)
See? Not scary. Not scary at all.

BLACK JESUS: Disgusting. Pink. Sharp. I never would have pegged you for someone with such a tongue. I would have thought something redder, flatter, with bits of brown tobacco stuck to the ends of it.

WHITE JESUS: I don't smoke anymore. Show me.
(BLACK JESUS sticks out his tongue.)
Ooey. You definitely smoke. Gray and purple.

BLACK JESUS: Is that bad?

WHITE JESUS: Just interesting. Strange. And interesting.

BLACK JESUS: So you just want to suck on me?

WHITE JESUS: No. I just want to lick you.

(BLACK JESUS puts out his hand. WHITE JESUS licks it. BLACK JESUS yanks it away like he's been burned.)

BLACK JESUS: Your tongue is hot.

WHITE JESUS: You're just afraid.

BLACK JESUS: I hated that.

WHITE JESUS: We aren't allowed to hate.

BLACK JESUS: We definitely had different fathers.

WHITE JESUS: My father lives in a dark tunnel, soft walls like the inside of a mouth. There's moisture all around him. And the sound of dripping. It smells like a place where rodents live and raise their rodent families. And then they die. But he doesn't know that. Everything he believes in is dying in his mouth— Is stifled by his breath. He thinks he's still giving birth to things, but his faith is an apartment with all the windows sealed shut by old white leaded paint. Poison. To everyone but him. He thinks I still believe in him.

BLACK JESUS: There's no one you believe in then?
(Pause)
My father lives on a rooftop. He breeds pigeons I think, for fun. There's a coop there anyway. It's a place filled with sunlight. He's sensitive to the sun though, so he always smears his skin with lotion. Every noise makes him jump because he knows how alone he is—so any sound might mean that the end is coming closer. The air is too sweet, like its purpose is to cover the dead smell coming from other places. His hands are dry and rough from too much washing and wringing. He sleeps on a bed of freshly baked bricks blanched in rainwater.
Everything he has is clean and crisp. But cold—like a sun-filled snow-covered Winter day.

WHITE JESUS: My father could punch your father in the nose and make him bleed.

BLACK JESUS: No. He couldn't. You're the only one he gets to punch in the nose.

(WHITE JESUS's nose begins to bleed. BLACK JESUS hands him a handkerchief. JULIANA's nose begins to bleed. ANABELLA hands her a tissue.)

BLACK JESUS and ANABELLA: Pinch.

(The sound of hissing static fills the room as the lights cross to ANABELLA and JULIANA with a box of VHS tapes.)

SCENE TEN
Home Movie
ANABELLA and JULIANA find a box
filled with home movies.

> JULIANA: Wow! I thought these were left behind in West Farms when Ma and Pa moved.
>
> ANABELLA: I wonder if they'd still play?
>
> JULIANA: They're probably too old and crackly by now. Filled with insect eggs and crawly things.
>
> ANABELLA: Pop did love his video camera.
> *(Rifles through the box of tapes and other cords and things.)*
> Here's the cord. Let's hook it up.
>
> JULIANA: I don't want to.
>
> ANABELLA: What do you mean?
>
> JULIANA: I'm tired of the past, Bee-bee.
>
> ANABELLA: But it's all right here. Like they wanted us to find it and play something.
>
> JULIANA: Like they...Whatever.

(ANABELLA hooks the video tape recorder to the TV and puts in a tape at random. THEY sit in front of the TV cross-legged on the floor. Behind them CECILIA and AMADOR sit, and behind them sit SHIRLEY, MARTIN and ROBERT, and the two JESUSes.)

> ANABELLA: I wish I had popcorn.
> *(The JESUSes conjure up popcorn and pass the bucket to the Icons and the parents.)*
>
> JULIANA: Or Junior Mints. I love me some Junior Mints.

ANABELLA: I was a *Sno-Cap* girl.
(*ANABELLA presses the play button, and it is a black and white movie of shadows and static. THEY watch for a while in silence, then we hear the voices of CECILIA and AMADOR. THEY seem to be burying something wrapped in light-colored cloth. THEY cover it with flowers, pour Florida Water on top it, and say a silent prayer over it.*)

CECILIA: Why can't we tell anybody?

AMADOR: Because they wouldn't understand.

CECILIA: My mother would. She buried so many babies...

AMADOR: This one was different. When babies are born dead like that then you have to bury them quickly.
When babies are different like that, it's better to throw the dirt on them yourselves before the doctors get a hold of them and cut them up. If they cut them up, then they don't get into Heaven.

CECILIA: We can't let them take him. But what do we say now? I mean to God? And to Juli...? Shouldn't she be here?

AMADOR: We don't have to say anything.
(*The shadows grow deeper. The static gets more electric.*)
Feel that?

CECILIA: It's making my hair stand up on my arms.

AMADOR: That means God is here to take him home.

CECILIA: Will the animals eat him?

AMADOR: Not the important parts. Not his soul.

(*ANABELLA and JULIANA look at each other for a moment and then turn back to the screen. The static is changing now. It comes into focus and seems to look like a dark and empty yard. In the yard, there appears a fish tank—like the one they just moved to the backyard. The fish tank begins to fill with water. The water begins to overflow and flow into the ground. The tank becomes a waterfall. The waterfall becomes a river and the river widens into a sea. We hear the water flowing. The image grows shadowy again and then the static returns. The film ends.)*

JULIANA: Huh.

ANABELLA: Was that...?

JULIANA: I thought I dreamt that. There's a dream I had over and over where I drowned. First it was fresh water and then it was dirty, and I saw a baby dying. And then he was flying. It was bad and then good, death and then life. It made me hope it was true.

ANABELLA: Juli, why didn't you tell me? The church guy...?

JULIANA: You were a kid and I was so afraid. And WHO were they?

ANABELLA: Who knows? I'm just thinking about all else our parents must have hidden from us.

JULIANA: Yeah, well, I told you to watch out for the past. I want to know less of it.

(JULIANA takes all the rest of the tapes and dumps them into the garbage bag.)

ANABELLA: I knew all of you kept things from me. I hated that. There's gotta be so much more to learn in those tapes.

JULIANA: There's not though. Anything important we already know and if we don't, we don't need to.

ANABELLA: What are you afraid of?

JULIANA: Somewhere on those tapes, there's proof.

ANABELLA: Of what?

JULIANA: That they didn't love me. Or you.

ANABELLA: How old are you, loca? They did love you. They just didn't show it.

JULIANA: Look at the things they kept: the records they loved, the photos of themselves, their old clothes.
Nothing to do with us, sister. Not a single thing.

ANABELLA: So? We haven't been around.

JULIANA: You haven't been around. Me? I never left...And is that—buried in the back yard?

ANABELLA: I bet there's some stuff upstairs. Of ours, I mean.

JULIANA: It's a mess up there. You can barely walk across their bedroom.

ANABELLA: What about ours? They still have our old bunk beds?

JULIANA: You know they do. They can't throw anything out.

ANABELLA: I'm going to go look.

JULIANA: Don't. It's not pretty. You won't like it. You don't like messy things, Bee-bee. Remember that one time you spilled chocolate milk on your tights at the counter in Chock Full o'Nuts? You cried for hours as I yanked you around Third Avenue. I hated you that day. You looked like you had shit yourself.

ANABELLA: I was so embarrassed. I never ordered chocolate milk again. And that was—

ANABELLA and JULIANA *(in unison)*: —my/your favorite.

ANABELLA: Yep.
(Pause)
You know what? I love you, Sis.

JULIANA: I know you do...I—
(ANABELLA moves to the staircase.)

ANABELLA: I know there's something of ours up there. Just wait. I'll bring down your prom dress or something!

JULIANA: Please don't.

(ANABELLA runs up the stairs. WE hear her footsteps from overhead. JULIANA watches the sound of her footsteps. WE hear a wail. A lament. ANABELLA comes down the stairs holding a child's baptismal gown. There is old, dried blood on it. SHE holds it as if SHE was holding a bleeding person. The sound of static. The lights flicker like a movie.)

ANABELLA: Is this your blood?

JULIANA: I found that gown upstairs. They had a whole box filled with old baby stuff. Not ours. So, then I knew. It wasn't just a dream. I'm not for long.

(ANABELLA pulls up JULIANA's sleeve. There are slashes on her wrists.)

ANABELLA: Jesus, Juliana! Why do you keep doing this?

JULIANA: Why not? I found all of Pop's weapons inside his duck. He wanted me to find them. All those homemade knives...

AMADOR: NO I DIDN'T!

CECILIA: What did you do, Amador?

AMADOR: Just for protection. Trying to protect my girls... *(CECILIA smacks him on his head.)*

ANABELLA: So you're trying to kill me?

JULIANA: No...

ANABELLA: But I love you, you stupid, selfish bitch.

JULIANA: I know. But—Today is a day when I just didn't think I could see the sunset again.

ANABELLA: That's so selfish and dramatic, Juli. Why don't you wait a little? How many dead people do you think I can handle in one month?

JULIANA: I was doing it for me. I keep trying to look forward, see things in front of me, but everything stopped today, Anabella. Everything stopped for me and I didn't know how to make it start again.
(Pause)
You were the one who was good at that. Like that time we were on that Ferris wheel that got stuck in the air next to Claremont Park.

ANABELLA: That wasn't at Claremont Park. It was at the "Playa de los Mojones"—down by Soundview.
Where Pop took us to teach us how to drive—

JULIANA: And illegally change his oil and dumped it into water over there.

ANABELLA: Everybody did that, so he wasn't alone. The City dumped our dumps in there too. Sewage treatment plants are always full of lawlessness and shit. If your shit floats, use it as lifeboats.

JULIANA: You know it's too late to make me laugh.
(Takes out the gun SHE had in her pocket.)

ANABELLA: I know.

JULIANA: You know?

ANABELLA: When I came in. I could smell it. But I just thought you were sick again.

JULIANA: Do I have to explain it?

ANABELLA: Nah. Your sadness runs deep, Juliana. Always in your footsteps—the way your feet dragged a little to the right and made me tired just to look at you. So lonely. Always acting left out or put down, but there was never anything going on. But you believed the cracking spaces in your mind that filled with everything you thought you would never have. I saw it. Let me help you. You can come live with me. I have a nice spare room—with a picture of you and me on the wall.

JULIANA: It's hard to spackle minds. What do you fill it with? Those cracks are too big, too long—they just break more under the weight of —

(JULIANA walks away from ANABELLA. ANABELLA watches her. CECILIA and AMADOR hum a lullaby. JULIANA lays on the couch between CECILIA and AMADOR. One strokes her head and the other strokes her feet. ANABELLA leans her back against the couch.)

ANABELLA: Why? Just when we were remembering each other?!
Remembering that we loved each other—All this time you weren't even here!
Do you even care about me?

(Beginning to cry softly)

My big sister, you were always the Moon. I felt you all around me, but mostly at night. But then like some days when the Moon rises before the Sun sets, you'd be out there, taking care of anything—anyone other than yourself. You told me how empty you felt, but I thought you were just being dramatic.

(The Icons disappear into the darkness of the corners of the room. CECILIA places the five photos which once lived on top of the fish tank into ANABELLA's lap and ANABELLA turns them over. Behind one is the deed to the house, and keys are taped to the back of the other photos. And behind the two JESUS postcards are pics of the other Jesus.)

Oh. I never would have looked behind those photos.

CECILIA: I told you it was a good hiding place—la Colección.

AMADOR: It kept everything safe.

CECILIA: For our daughters.

AMADOR: We don't have to stay anymore.

JULIANA: Oh my God, are you gonna go without me?! I thought we could put it all to rest.

ANABELLA: Who are you talking to?

CECILIA: Don't worry. La Colección will always watch out for you. It's just our time to dream.

(AMADOR offers CECILIA his arm as THEY exit the house. JULIANA sees them exit.)

JULIANA: Don't leave without me.

(ANABELLA takes JULIANA into her arms and rocks her gently.)

ANABELLA: You used to do this to me, remember?

JULIANA: I remember.

ANABELLA: I think the storm is moving away.

(SHE takes the gun away from JULIANA and moves to the back door looking out at the night sky. The room becomes immersed in starlight for a moment. Then we hear the sound of the sea and the room seems like it is underwater. Fish swim by against the walls. ANABELLA flings the gun out the back door and it lands in some imaginary sea with a splash...)
That will slow you down.

JULIANA: You think so?

(SHIRLEY, MARTIN and ROBERT move to the fish tank.)

ROBERT: I didn't see that coming. Women are still so complicated. Time did not make them easier to understand.

MARTIN: Did you ever take a close look into a mirror and get afraid of what you saw there?
Maybe the future was right in front of you?

SHIRLEY: That never scared me. What scared me was that as hard as I tried, I couldn't see myself in it. Not in the way I wanted to see it and be remembered. But I had a good life trying to imagine it.

WHITE JESUS: What's the true sin? Living a lie or living to die?

BLACK JESUS: Maybe the best journey is the one you take only one foot at a time.

SHIRLEY: How about a friendly game of poker, Gentlemen?

ROBERT: Until some other family finds itself underwater.

MARTIN: If you see your life in the waves of the sea, can you learn to ride out the storm?

WHITE JESUS: Hope is—

BLACK JESUS: — like water.

(The ICONS and the JESUSes move to a table and play their imaginary Poker until THEY are in total darkness. JULIANA moves to ANABELLA's side and takes her sister's hand.)

JULIANA: Yeah. Okay.

ANABELLA: What! Okay what?

JULIANA: I see the sunset. Pieces of all of us are buried inside it.

ANABELLA: That's what makes it beautiful. *(Pause)* Not tonight, okay?

(JULIANA holds ANABELLA's hand even tighter.)
(The space fills with stars and darkness. Things begin to swirl. The outside comes in and it is like a disco ball of stars. Or maybe the Northern Lights. Music plays. Perhaps it is the theme from the TV show "Miami Vice.")

(Blackout.)

END OF PLAY FOR NOW...

Fishtank

SATYRICOÑO

SATYRICOÑO

Inspired by Petronius' *Satyricon*, circa 61 A.D. and Fellini's *Satyricon*, 1968 A.D.

First workshop during the New Works Lab@INTAR, June 2015, directed by Daniel Jáquez, with actors from INTAR's UNIT 52, and with music by Cristian Amigo.

First reading at INTAR, October 2011, Lou Moreno, artistic director, Daniel Jáquez, director.

Developed at the Lark's Meeting of the Minds, 2013-14, with roundtables @the Lark 2014 and 2015.

Includes words inspired by the sayings of Pol Pot and the book of ancient Sumerian proverbs "*The Gecko Wears a Tiara*" compiled by Mark Saltveit.

Sect,74, *"She will not spit in her bosom for luck."*

—Petronius, A.D. 60, Satyricon—

"The excrement of the King stinks like everyone else's."

—The Sayings of Pol Pot—

CAST OF CHARACTERS

OCTAVIO—The Presidemperor of the Ignited Dominions of Amerika (I.D.A.), elected in 2040, he has served his republic for 24 years or six consecutive terms.

FILOMENA—Octavio's wife, First-Lady of the Republic. A hermaphrodite.

ENCO—The Presidemperor's scribe and speechwriter, in love with his servant-assistant, Junior.

CYLVIO—Enco's best friend, also in love with Junior.

MALPUSO—The Poet-Laureate for Octavio.

JUNIOR (his real name is Constantino) a.k.a TINO—the bastard son of the Presidemperor of the Ignited Dominions of Amerika. A servant for now, but his star is rising. A Master of reggaeton, rap and hip-hop. Musically and sexually, he does it all.

PODEROSA—Junior's mother, a matriarch with big ambitions, takes only younger lovers.

LUJURIA—Junior's sister, in charge of the Presidemperor's security.

OENOTHEA—Lujuria's woman, in charge of the Presidemperor's astrology, a nymphomaniac.

MINA the METEOROLOGIST—a seductive and dangerous voice from the radio.

ARROZ con GANDULES—Poderosa's lovers, and JUNIOR's back-up. Also Palace Dancers. Arroz is hard. Gandules is soft.

A CHORUS of EUNUCHS and DOLPHIN-SKINNED

WOMEN—The people.

PARTY GUESTS—Just there for the free food...

TULLIA and VITA—The housemaids...

A MAN—Yanqui Owner of the Bar Batey in Old San Juan, loves children, often drunk.

TIME:

2064 A.D.

PLACE:

IGNITED DOMINIONS OF THE AMERIKAS

PROLOGUE:
2058 A.D.

Notes from La Perla, P.R.
The evolution of JUNIOR. JUNIOR is 10. Perhaps JUNIOR manipulates a YOUNGER JUNIOR puppet.
A time, some time ago, but still in the future.
PODEROSA and JUNIOR at El Batey Bar across from Hotel El Convento in Old San Juan, P.R.
Billie Holliday singing "Just One of Those Things" plays on the jukebox. A MAN sits at the end of the bar, smoking and drinking, a bottle of Ron Del Barrilito in front of him.

>PODEROSA: Couple—three hours at the most.

>JUNIOR: Ma—

>PODEROSA: Don't worry. I told that nice blanquito with the hat to keep an eye on you and that I'd get his tab when I come back.

>JUNIOR: Ma—

>PODEROSA: We need this, Junior.

>JUNIOR: But, ma, I need to practice.

>PODEROSA: Do it here. Drunks don't care. Put on any kind of show you want. You're a native. They'll think it's what we simple, happy people do. Tourists are always dum-dums. I gotta go.

>JUNIOR: I don't like you.

>PODEROSA: I don't care. I love you.

>JUNIOR: You fuck too much.

PODEROSA: Not possible. Not when it pays.

JUNIOR: Not always.

PODEROSA: A girl has to have some fun. Some hope—some hope of fun. Even moms.

(*PODEROSA exits. The MAN with the hat, seated at the end of the bar turns to JUNIOR.*)

MAN: Come sit by me, young man.

(*JUNIOR stares at him.*)
Don't you speak English?

(*Tapping the stool next to him*)
Ven acá.

JUNIOR: Go fuck yourself, old perv.

MAN: You speak very well.
(*Pause*)
What if I told you I was famous?

JUNIOR: I'd say, "Go fuck yourself harder."

MAN: You don't have to be afraid of me.

JUNIOR: Afraid? I can jack you up and spit you out through the holes in your skull. I can suck your eyes out of their sockets, chew them up, and shit them into your mouth.

MAN: The eye sucking part sounds good but…just trying to be friendly, kid.

JUNIOR: I'm not friendly. Embarrassing people are friendly.

MAN: She's not so bad. My own mother was a lot like her.

(*JUNIOR moves to sit by the MAN.*)

JUNIOR: Yeah?

MAN: I spent most of my childhood on a bar stool.
(*Pointing to a pair of lips and a signature in what appears to be lipstick on the wall behind the bar.*)
That's her signature right there—on the wall. Liked it so much they filled it in with red paint. Looks more like blood now...

JUNIOR: You're Puerto Rican?

MAN: I was born somewhere else, but I've lived here most of my life. I feel Puerto Rican.

(*HE puts out his hand for JUNIOR to feel it. JUNIOR slaps it away.*)

JUNIOR: Keep those to yourself.

MAN: You're tall for your age.

JUNIOR: How would you know?

MAN: I'd know.

JUNIOR: I need new shoes.

MAN: I can see that. Salt water kills the leather.

JUNIOR: You live around here?
(*The jukebox changes to a Janis Joplin song "Kozmic Blues."*)

MAN: Upstairs.

JUNIOR: You own this bar?

MAN: Maybe.

JUNIOR: You have a TV?

MAN: No.

JUNIOR: No?! Who doesn't have a TV, perv?

MAN: Me. I listen to music.

JUNIOR: What kind of music?

MAN: All kinds.

JUNIOR: You want to hear my music?

MAN: Maybe. What do you play?

JUNIOR: I sing.

MAN: Oh, ok then, what do you sing?

JUNIOR: Spider's webs. Venus Fly traps. Jaws of a praying mantis.

MAN: So I get you like insects, kid. Good for you. So few people do.
(*Pause*)
Want to go upstairs?

JUNIOR: Not without a TV.

MAN: This place has the best jukebox.

JUNIOR: Is that why you bought it?

MAN: Who says I bought it?

JUNIOR: You seem like a man who owns things.

MAN: Still a good jukebox, whether I own it or not.

JUNIOR: What did you want to be? When you were young? A bar owner? That's a fucked up life goal. Pervy alcoholic.

MAN: I wanted to be president.

JUNIOR: Me too. So I can declare war on my mother's ass.

MAN: Talk about fucked up life goals.
(*Pause*)
Can I buy you a coke?

JUNIOR: With some rum in it.

MAN: Alright.

(*HE puts a splash of rum in JUNIOR's coke.*)

JUNIOR: You don't give a shit, do you?

MAN: A little rum is better than a little crack.

JUNIOR: How would you know?

MAN: Some things you can just assume.

JUNIOR: Crack gives me stomach aches.

MAN: Really? Heroin makes my teeth hurt.

JUNIOR: You don't believe me?

MAN: Sure. Why not? You are a big crackhead.

JUNIOR: Will you buy me shoes?

MAN: What size are you?

JUNIOR: 9.

MAN: Same as me.

JUNIOR: What a coincidence.

MAN: You want these?

JUNIOR: Nah, they have your foot funk in them.

MAN: (*taking one leather sandal off and putting it on the bar*) I've never sweated much.

JUNIOR:
(*Sniffing his shoe*) Yeah…not bad.
(*MAN hands him both sandals, JUNIOR puts them on.*)
Huh…not bad…

MAN: Huh…not bad at all.

JUNIOR: Thanks.

MAN: No problem.

JUNIOR: You must have lots of shoes.

MAN: A man like me has to have a lot of shoes.

JUNIOR: A man like you…you accept things.

MAN: Yes. And now you have accepted my shoes.

JUNIOR: Who did you used to be?

MAN: I'm not anybody.

JUNIOR: You're famous. Isn't that what you said?

MAN: To be famous doesn't make you anybody, it just means other people make you somebody. But the you that's inside, doesn't ever really know. Because no one does.

JUNIOR: That's right. No one does.
(Pause)
I'm going to be famous.

MAN: Yes.

(JUNIOR kills the MAN with a garrote.)

JUNIOR: That's a nice hat.
(HE takes his hat, puts it on.)
A real nice hat. I don't deserve such a beautiful hat.

(HE puts it back on the MAN. Pause)
There are some things people wear that only belong on that person. It's funny how clothes do make a man.

(Pause; he speak-sings; a sort of rap)
"When you meet a spider, never touch its face.
Roll it gently on your flesh—in a warm embrace
Of crisscrossing spit kissed by lace.
It won't pretend to love you.
It don't know how.
It'll fool you—then school you fast—
Then fuck you in your big white"

(PODEROSA enters, pauses to take in the scene, then moves to the cash register.)

PODEROSA: Took you long enough.

JUNIOR: I didn't think you were coming back.

PODEROSA: I'll always come back for my boy.

(*SHE puts her hand out, HE takes it.*)
We almost have enough to buy our plane tickets. Your sister's waiting for us in Capitol City. She says a handsome boy like you can easily find work. Today, our life begins.

JUNIOR: I have a sister??

PODEROSA: Of course.

(*Lights cross to the chaos of the Ignited Dominions of Amerika—what's left of what used to be the U.S.A. Caught in individual spotlights are the men and women of the Ignited Dominions of Amerika.*
Each one is trying to kill him or herself—unsuccessfully—over and over again.
One slits his throat. One hangs herself. Two take poison. Another one hits his head repeatedly with a dictionary. One holds her head in a deep basin of water until she can no longer breathe—
comes up for air, and then tries again.
One takes line after line of cocaine—he is covered in white powder. These vignettes are performed to the music of Nino Rota. Suddenly there is a blackout, and the music stops abruptly with it. We hear the sound of running water. Slowly the lights return to reveal ENCO's bath.)

SCENE ONE

Six years later. The future-present, 2064 A.D.
ENCO lies naked in a Plexiglas tub. The water is pink—some blood has been spilled into it—but not too much. HE is inspecting his arms. HE has a line of straight razors balanced along the edge of his tub. CYLVIO washes his hair as JUNIOR bandages ENCO's slit wrists. JUNIOR wears a turban with ***ENCO'S*** written on it. It is part of JUNIOR's uniform, which is the turban and a pair of orange silk MC Hammer pants—strategically torn, so his fishnet stockings show through. He is topless. The walls around them are covered in raw orange silk that has been torn to shreds as if by giant bloody claws. Behind the shreds, we see a delicate web-like structure made of thin rope—as if the shreds are the skin and the ropes are the veins of ENCO's house.

ENCO: You would do the same.

CYLVIO: I doubt that. I wouldn't stop something I started. Why the bandages? Why not follow through all at once with this madness?

ENCO: If I die too quickly, I'll miss the party. Everyone's coming over in a few minutes. A farewell party. Isn't that right, Junior?

JUNIOR: That's right. I called everyone on your VIP list and sent an eblast to your "friends" in the book. They'll come. I said there'd be food and such.

ENCO: Smart. That draws them in—whether they care or not. Did you say it was my last day on Earth? Did you tell them of my persecution? Did you tell them how brave I'm being? Did you tell them that I'm on the list? That the chief of style and speechwriting is being prepped for elimination?

JUNIOR: No. I—

ENCO (*Splashing blood water on JUNIOR*): I told you to tell them. You're my assistant and that means you do everything I say.

JUNIOR: Is that what it means? I have no free choice? Is that why I'm dressed like a genie?! Just another member of the proletariat.

ENCO: You have a choice—stay—or go and starve.

CYLVIO: That's a choice?

JUNIOR: I get less hungry every day.

ENCO: I am simply trying to take matters into my own hands —and throw a fabulous party at the same time. Please.
(*Pointing with his chin toward JUNIOR*)
You'll care for him?

CYLVIO: Yes.

ENCO: I mean in a fatherly way.

CYLVIO: Uncle-ly.

ENCO: If you prefer.

CYLVIO: Yes.

ENCO and CYLVIO: Of course.

(*Long pause*)

ENCO: I'm glad I'm not related to you.

CYLVIO: Are you trying to hurt my feelings?

ENCO: Could I?

CYLVIO: Perhaps.

JUNIOR: Should I shave you, oh dying one?

ENCO: Yes.
(*JUNIOR uses one of the razors from the edge of the tub to shave ENCO's legs.*)
Why do we need hair on our toes? We humans?

CYLVIO: Do you think apes need it?

ENCO: Probably not. Just a trick then.

JUNIOR: Keeps them warm. Us, too.

CYLVIO: Yes. You're so bright, Junior. And delicious...
Don't you want to come live with Uncle Cylvio?

ENCO: Junior would never leave me. He knows how much I love him.

CYLVIO: Dip.
(*ENCO dips his head back into the water as CYLVIO rinses out the soap from ENCO's hair.*)
There. All clean. Ready for a new day of self-mutilation and self-pity.

ENCO: Mustn't forget the self-pity.
(*Pause*)
You're my best friend, you know.

CYLVIO: Don't. I won't do it.

ENCO: Even if I close my eyes and beg.

CYLVIO: Even.

ENCO: I don't think I'm brave enough to do it.

CYLVIO: You're braver than me.

ENCO: You're bigger than me.

CYLVIO: You're sweeter.

JUNIOR (*sarcastically*): Ahhh. Such good friends...

(*ENCO and CYLVIO kiss. JUNIOR begins to shave ENCO's toes.*)

CYLVIO: What if you didn't follow his orders?

ENCO: I'll be tortured—and then killed anyway. He's taking all of us.

CYLVIO: Not me. I'm no artist.

ENCO: You're an artist's associate. Didn't you read yesterday's memo: "When you pull out weeds, you must pull out all their roots. Artists—and their Friends—are like diarrhea—their theories flow from their mouths to their ankles without meaning."

CYLVIO: What in the world—? Octavio must have some form of mental—

JUNIOR: It's always dangerous not to pay attention—
to servants, women and other malformations.

ENCO: My Junior's so damn cute, isn't he?

CYLVIO: Mmmhmmm. I still don't understand how killing yourself makes things any better. Better to die fighting for something—than to do it avoiding something, pussycat.

ENCO: I would never be a cat—more like cattle—from the Highlands.
How are those toes coming along?

JUNIOR: You've got to be patient with these dense digits.
I can almost see the knuckles now.

ENCO: Toes have knuckles?

CYLVIO: Of course.

ENCO: I never thought about the knuckles of my toes before.

CYLVIO: No. They're not easy to think about.
There are so many bones and things on the feet.

ENCO: Complicated.

CYLVIO: Completely.

ENCO: Will you come to my funeral?

CYLVIO: What do you call this?

ENCO: I mean the official one.

CYLVIO: You think there'll be an official one?

ENCO: Oh, yes. It's all planned.
(*To JUNIOR*)
Get the plans.

(*JUNIOR gets the plans and brings them to CYLVIO. CYLVIO unfurls the scroll and reads.*)

CYLVIO: "Now I have taken my final ride.
Keep my picture by your side.
Never try to eat my heart.
If you do, we'll never part."

ENCO: I want that on all the place cards. For the dinner.

CYLVIO: I see. Here's the menu: Sweetbreads with figs and Stilton. Delicious. And honey wine. How African. Ancient. Nice touch.

ENCO: Rituals require the right atmosphere.

CYLVIO: Yes. And speaking of—three accordions? And a bagpipe? Awfully screechy, don't you think? Hurts the ears just thinking about it...

ENCO: I like that.

CYLVIO: And blue candles everywhere. Don't you think we'll all be sad enough?

ENCO: Blue is calming. I was thinking about your sadness.

CYLVIO: Oh. It's a great plan.

JUNIOR: Mr.Enco hooked it up.

CYLVIO: Yes.

(*The Party Crowd enters. The PARTY CROWD could be TULLIA and VITA, holding Bunraku puppets of the masses. THEY are dressed all in red and white.*)

ENCO: Welcome, dear friends. Thank you for coming to bid me farewell.

GUEST ONE: Where does he think he's going?

GUEST TWO: Same place. Different time.

CYLVIO: These are your friends? I've never met them before.

ENCO: I posted my suicide party: The Red and White Ball, on MyBook. Open call.

CYLVIO: And they showed up. How moving. A room full of people who really care.

ENCO: I don't need people to care. I need people to celebrate my life. Who know how to party.

GUEST THREE: True that.

GUEST FOUR: Are there snacks up in here? I'm feeling a bit squiblish...

GUEST THREE: True that.

ENCO: Oh, my manners! Of course! Junior, serve my guests— and use the good silver.

(*JUNIOR flinging his pedicure tools on the floor.*)

> JUNIOR (*an aside-rap*):
> I've had about all I can take of this shit—
> a dying whore and his Biblical fit.
> Thou shalt not take your own life in vain—
> who cares about him with the world so insane?
> Just like the story of Abel and Cain,
> my brother's bleeding but who'll heal my pain?
> No one cares about us—here on the down low.
> It's them and theirs and that's the show.

(*JUNIOR lights a match. The walls begin to burn.*)

> JUNIOR: Fire!! Everyone out!

(*The GUESTS flee screaming and taking snacks and drinks with them.*)

> ENCO: I'm not going anywhere.

> CYLVIO: This won't count. You won't even burn in that tub.

> ENCO: It's the smoke that gets you.

> CYLVIO (*Pulling ENCO from the tub*): This will have to wait.

(*CYLVIO puts ENCO over his shoulder and they run out of the house. Lights cross to just outside the threshold of ENCO's house. ENCO watches his house burn. JUNIOR holds a blanket around ENCO. CYLVIO throws rocks at the house. The GUESTS eat the snacks and watch too.*)

> ENCO: Fire not good enough for you?!

> CYLVIO: Do you think rocks can melt?

> ENCO: Yes. See how the flames get bigger when you throw those rocks into the fire?

CYLVIO: Is that from melting? Rather hard to tell really. Rocks. And fire. Put them together. Something unexpected.

ENCO: Like our dear presidemperor? He thinks I'm dying tonight. He suggested it. "More personal if you do it, Enco. We don't have time to be slow and nostalgic."

CYLVIO: It could still happen. You could run into the flames.

ENCO: So melty. I don't even eat fondue, Cyl.

CYLVIO: You're not really going through with it, are you?

ENCO: He'll have me killed unless I do it myself.
At least then maybe I can control the timing—and the pain.

CYLVIO: You never should have guffawed at the State brunch.

ENCO: Brunch is funny.

CYLVIO: You weren't laughing at the food.

ENCO: He was ridiculous.

CYLVIO: All his speeches are ridiculous. You're supposed to stand there and grunt and nod your head like you agree with him or pretend that he's just given you the key to a fabulous mystery.

JUNIOR: Why don't you just run?

ENCO: Because I am a gentleman.

CYLVIO: We don't do that, Junior. You should know that by now.

JUNIOR: I would run.

ENCO: Some of us prefer the fire.

(*The entire house collapses, turning to dust on the ground in front of them. The GUESTS applaud.*)

JUNIOR: Maybe you should hang yourself.
(*Lights cross to the White Palace covered in Red Dust.*)

SCENE TWO

We see the Presidemperor, OCTAVIO, playing with the knobs of a dusty ham radio in a closet of the Palace. Static is coming in loud and clear. Then we hear a weather report from somewhere far away. OCTAVIO wears a raincoat.

MINA THE METEOROLOGIST (*a voice from the radio*): Hello, dear hearts, wherever you may roam. If you step outside, be sure to bring a large umbrella. There are still reports of livestock raining over parts of the Gulf Coast and throughout the Eastern Plains. Reportedly sheep, bison, and even a zorse were seen hurtling across the sky.

(*SHE begins to sing a little jingle.*)
"Don't let the weather bring you down.
There's other reasons to get the fuck out of town."
Thank for listening to WSKP.
This is Mina the Meteorologist saying stay safe or you'll be sorry.

(*The radio returns to static.*)

OCTAVIO (*with a smile*): A zorse...there's nothing "woarse."
It's all coming true.

(*HE turns off the radio and hides beneath a dusty tarp, pushing it against the dark, back of the closet. LUJURIA bangs on the closet door.*)

LUJURIA: Mr. President?! You have to come out now.
The news conference is in ten minutes.

(*Pause*)
How can I keep you safe, if I can't see you?

(*Under her breath*)
Freakin' lunatic.

(*Calling to the housemaids*)
Tullia! Vita! Please help the President out of the closet.

(*TULLIA and VITA come running in. THEY are dressed as classic French maids in impossibly short skirts, with dildos poking through as they move. Cue cards or supertitles appear translating TULLIA and VITA's Pig Latin.*)

TULLIA: Eway ereway onway eakbray.
[We were on break.]

VITA: Oday usway away olidsay, Odayñaway Ujurialay, andway onday'tay
akemay usway ogay inway erethay. Ehay isway alwaysway yingtray otay ucksay onway ymay ittiestay andway eythay areway eryvay ensitivesay.
[Do us a solid, Doña Lujuria, and don't make us go in there. He is always trying to suck on my titties and they are very sensitive.]

LUJURIA: It's the titties that entice him out of there. We need your Titties, Vita.

TULLIA: Enthay ywhay oday Iway avehay otay ogay ootay?
[Then why do I have to go too?]

LUJURIA: You're the one who keeps him in check. We don't want those titties bitten off, do we? No matter how sweet and plump they are. Your job is to protect Vita.

TULLIA and VITA: Ahway, atthay'say osay eetsway. [Ah, that's so sweet.]

(*THEY kiss. THEY enter the closet. LUJURIA locks the door behind him.*)

LUJURIA: Whatever it takes. Sober him up, ladies.
(*The sounds of a struggle. Silence. LUJURIA unlocks the door. OCTAVIO comes out covered in blood.*)

OCTAVIO: Those were very bad maids.

LUJURIA: I wish you would stop doing that.
People don't like doing the domestic thing anymore. I hate those interviews.

OCTAVIO: I wasn't so impressed.
(*LUJURIA begins to wipe off the blood from OCTAVIO's face.*)
You would be a divine domestic.

LUJURIA: Yes. But I prefer security. The last war was good training.

OCTAVIO: I could force you to be my maid.

LUJURIA: But you wouldn't. I'm such a good bodyguard.

(*Finishing wiping him clean*)
All clean.

(*Leads him to the mirror on the wall*)
Look.

(*SHE and HE both see the resemblance between them.*)
Perfect.

OCTAVIO: Yes. Your nose…?

LUJURIA: Don't think about—You have a speech to give—Prayer for the masses.

OCTAVIO: Yes. I have just the thing. I like palavering to the people. I like that word. Palavering. Can you smell the blood on me?

LUJURIA: Yes. I can always smell it.

OCTAVIO: Me too.

(*Lights cross to the Palace Gardens.*)

SCENE THREE

MALPUSO sits in the Palace garden during a storm. HE sits in a wooden swing with an awning of branches protecting him from the elements. HE writes on a flip up PC tablet made out of parchment with an elaborate quill pen. He dips the quill into his veins to write across the "screen."
He is adorned with ornate jewelry.

MALPUSO: Yea, though we walk through the shadow of the valley of —

(*Scratches it out*)
Too depressing.

(*HE begins to write again.*)
I love treason, but hate a traitor…

(*Scratches it out*)
Too Julius. (*meaning Caesar*)

(*HE begins to write again.*)
What's past is prologue…

(*Scratches it out*)
Too historical.

(*HE begins to write again.*)
I have nothing left.

(*HE scratches it out.*)
Too honest.

(*HE begins to write again.*)
I have nothing left.

(*Pause*)
There's only other people's thoughts in my fingers now.

(*HE jangles his jewelry—now WE can clearly see that he is chained to the swing.*)
I want to go inside. He thinks I find my inspiration in nature. And there are some who believe that—but I prefer a blank room, a comfortable chair, a glass of rum. Putting together families of words is hard work made easier with a bit of spirits.

(*Something goes flying past him, over his head.*)
Was that alive? I hate the out of doors. Bugs, weather, rising smoke. Hate it.
Don't make me stay here!

(*Pause*)
Why does he make me stay here?

(*It begins to rain. There is lightning.*)
I'm not afraid of you!

(*The rain and lightning eases. LUJURIA enters and unchains him and leads him to another bench, and chains him to that one and exits.*)
It's her I'm afraid of...I knew who she really was the moment I saw her. That's when I suggested in a Menippean Satire written for his majestic-ness' birthday banquet six Moon-years ago, that he hire her. "Mighty sturdy like the winds of change on the six hills of the Capitol," I said. I know how to entice my Majestic Presidemperor...and she said she'd kill me if I didn't. I believed her. Blood knows blood. But some family ties need to be undone. She believes that I'll leave her all my money, if she

tortures me. But, Ha! She's never read my will—to get the money, she'll have to eat me when I die. A poet's flesh makes good barbeque. Inspiration, where are you?

(FILOMENA enters and MALPUSO watches her walk off.)
Ahhh...there.

(HE writes.
Lights cross to the Chief of Staff/Security Office.)

SCENE FOUR
In the White Palace Chief of Staff Offices. This is
LUJURIA's office that is painted a bright hot pink.
FILOMENA, LUJURIA and OENOTHEA have a meeting.

FILOMENA: Is everything ready?

LUJURIA: Check. Check. And double-D (*bra-size*) check.

OENOTHEA: I plotted a new chart for him.

(SHE bends over to unroll a massive astrological chart, her breasts spilling over it.)
There are major planetary changes coming in...

(FILOMENA moves to view the chart. As she walks, different lights in the room turn on or off.)

LUJURIA: (*to FILOMENA*) Your energy is fierce today, Madame.

OENOTHEA: Aries is in his 4th house—and since Aries governs his Sun—oh, wow!
So the ancestors are dominating his astral sphere. Look!

FILOMENA (*Transfixed by the other women's breasts, then shakes herself loose from their spell*): Is it necessary? Really? All that flesh?

(*LUJURIA and OENOTHEA pull their low-cut tops up to make them slightly less obscene.*)
Better. I wish—

LUJURIA: You can touch them if you'd like.

OENOTHEA: Like grappling with two giant Codfish on one hook. I almost don't fit a whole one in my mouth. But I work it in there. It's always worth the effort—to reel those babies in.

FILOMENA: There'll be none of that. Like my husband always says: Physical beauty is an obstacle to the determination to fight! Why did my husband hire you? You're both so distracting.

LUJURIA: I am supposed to save him and you—and she is supposed to save me.

OENOTHEA: Poor thing! Doesn't she know how much danger she's in? Do you love your husband?

FILOMENA: I—well, why, yes—I love him.

LUJURIA: Show us.

FILOMENA: I show him how much I love him every single—

OENOTHEA: You know what she means...
(*Pulls up FILOMENA'S skirt trying to catch a glimpse between her legs*)
C'mon. Open it up. We're all just women here.

FILOMENA: I am the Presidemperor's wife. You do not get to see what's between my legs.

OENOTHEA: It was different at the circus though. Don't you remember? My tent was right next to yours. You showed everyone for a few ducats and nice bottle of wine.

FILOMENA: Whiskey. I hate wine. It gives me headaches!

LUJURIA: I saw you too...when I escorted our Presidemperor to your show...I never saw anything like you before.
(*Both LUJURIA and OENOTHEA shake their heads "no."*)
They said you could heal people. Just one drop of semen from your shrunken member could cure all kinds of things. So when you came to apply for a maid's job, he had to have you—he's so afraid of dying. He found his woman that day and (*meaning OENOTHEA*) so did I.

OENOTHEA: You were an omen for us—a vision. You have the future between your legs, Madam Filomena.

FILOMENA: Please don't ruin the President's birthday. He may not have many more. His numbers are way down. People have stopped believing.

LUJURIA: Don't worry. He'll have a wonderful birthday, Madam. We have special plans for him.

OENOTHEA: Extraordinary plans. I saw it in his chart. His Leo's in Mars—which governs his Sun—which is in Aries. So there's triple Aries. Plus, two other houses in Leo. And then Taurus, another Taurus, and, oh snap!—that asshole Pisces is in his twelfth house. You should be careful: enemies, solitude, secrets—it's all there. Yep, Pisces men always break your heart. Look at this!

(*Pointing them out on the chart as SHE names them.*)
Fire, Ambition, Time and Comedy—And if he's looking to change professions, he'd make a good precision hair stylist...he's good with his teeth...Oh, shit! Stuff is going to explode.

OENOTHEA and LUJURIA (*in unison*): Bam!

(*OENOTHEA and LUJURIA exit. FILOMENA examines the chart more closely.*)

FILOMENA: I wish I believed in this crap. Looks pretty enough. Planets. Houses. Ascending. Descending. Blah. Blah. Blah. This is madness on paper. But I can pretend. Like I pretended for all those years that allowing myself to be milked for my bodily fluids was a sacred calling.

(*Pause; Lights grow to include LUJURIA and OENOTHEA on the other side of the wall, masturbating each other as THEY watch FILOMENA through a peephole.*)
The first time I saw my sister naked I cried. She didn't have a penis. I cried for myself then. Then I cried for everyone who looked at me and wanted to suck on me—because they wanted to taste my power.

LUJURIA: What's she doing now?

OENOTHEA: Touching herself.

LUJURIA: Oh, baby. That's so freakin' good…

FILOMENA: (*Continues*) I just hung there limp like the holy object they expected me to be. Made a lot of money for my parents I think. Who says no to money? The circus was my home. That was when I knew the only thing to believe in was here on this planet—this Earth where my parts were sore from all the milking.

LUJURIA: (*Pulling her hand out of OENOTHEA as if she's been burned*) Ouch!

OENOTHEA: Sorry. It does get real hot down there sometimes…

FILOMENA: *(Continues)* Some days I even pretended to enjoy it.
(*She takes out a knife and holds it close to her penis.*)
I've got the jump on you, boy. Don't make any sudden movements. Could be your last.

(LUJURIA and OENOTHEA come.)

LUJURIA: Are you a goddess poured down from Mount St. Helens to erupt all over me?

OENOTHEA (*Pulling a lit cigarette out of her crotch*): Puff with me, baby.

LUJURIA: You are a handy little wench.

(*THEY pass the cigarette back and forth between them, alternating puffs.*)

OENOTHEA: Do you think they'll like me?

LUJURIA: My mother won't like you—you're too pretty. But my brother will love you. He loves things that burn.

(*LUJURIA kisses OENOTHEA as the lights cross to PODEROSA's bedroom.*)

SCENE FIVE
JUNIOR plays with a piece of thin rope that he ties into different sailor's knots. HE speaks to a sleeping woman, his mother, PODEROSA.

JUNIOR: I used to be so good at this. Now I can hardly make a simple slipknot.
(*Pause*)
Maybe it's the rope.

(*Pause*)
(*Singing a song*)
"Enemies never, never let you rest,
Until you put them to sleep.
Hijos de puta best fight to the death—
Put maggots in them deep.
Don't let them hear you weep, mother-puta.
Let the maggots in you–seep."

(*HE takes the perfect knot that HE has made and places it over the face of PODEROSA.*)

PODEROSA (*Speaking without opening her eyes*): Good morning.

JUNIOR: Good morning, Mother.

PODEROSA: Beautiful day yet?

JUNIOR: Every day in the greatest Empire in the universe is beautiful.

PODEROSA: What do you know of the Universe?

JUNIOR: Only what you taught me.

PODEROSA: I didn't think you were listening.

JUNIOR (*Handing her the rope*): This one is a little tighter than the last one, don't you think?

PODEROSA (*Feeling the rope*): Very nice. Is there any coffee?

JUNIOR: On the table.

PODEROSA (*SHE pulls an envelope from inside her dress and hands it to JUNIOR.*):
It's time.

JUNIOR: Is this—

PODEROSA: —Yes, but let me get my coffee first?
(*SHE rises to get the coffee.*)
Happy Birthday.

JUNIOR: My birthday's not until next month.

PODEROSA: I lied to you. It's today. Open it.

JUNIOR: Why would you do that?

PODEROSA: Read it.

JUNIOR: Is this some joke?

PODEROSA: No. Can't you—

JUNIOR: You know I can't.

PODEROSA: What is that man doing for you? He calls himself a writer and all he does is bathe. He promised me he'd teach you something.

JUNIOR: He didn't want to. He said it was dangerous.

PODEROSA: It's your birth certificate. Your father kept it hidden all these years, but I finally got a copy from...an old friend who works at the palace. This paper proves you're his.

JUNIOR (*Pulling it out of her hands*): Let me see.

PODEROSA (*Pointing at one part of the birth certificate/letter*): There. You see his name? Octavio Constantino. Just like you. See that "O"?

JUNIOR: I'm the OCTAVIO's son??

PODEROSA: And mine.

JUNIOR: Why are you telling me this now?

PODEROSA: Can't you feel it? How everyone's afraid? Everyone but you. You can take his place, Junior. Destroy him.

JUNIOR: Maybe he wants to get to know me. I could be—

PODEROSA: No. He thinks you're dead. He thinks I killed you. (*Pause*)
Will you rub my back?

JUNIOR: No.

PODEROSA: Will you get one of your friends to come over and rub my back?

JUNIOR: No.

PODEROSA: I should have killed you.

JUNIOR: I know.

(*PODEROSA goes to her tub and gets in.
JUNIOR speaks but SHE cannot hear him.*)

JUNIOR: You know what? That goes both ways.

(*Lights cross to ARROZ con GANDULES.*)

SCENE SIX
ARROZ con GANDULES rehearsing their act on a stage in a nightclub under construction. ARROZ does a dance move while GANDULES watches.

GANDULES: Nuhuhh. That's not right. Try the twirly-twirly first, before the drop.

ARROZ: The twirly-twirly? You mean my sick - pirouette before the grand jeté?

GANDULES: Whatever, dude. Sorry I didn't stick a bag of crawl-up-my-dancing-stuck-up-ass in my mouth before I came.

ARROZ: There's nothing right about you, Gandules. Maybe we should try the song first.

GANDULES: I wrote a new song.

ARROZ: Who asked you to?

GANDULES: Initiative. That's what success is all about.

ARROZ: Right. Let's hear it then.

GANDULES: Can you...?

ARROZ: Oh, ok. Like...
(*ARROZ establishes a beat for him using his own body to pound on/make noises with.*)

GANDULES: I wanna dedicate this song to my dear mother who died of Breast, Ovarian, Liver, Lung and Skin Cancer last Saturnalia, but before she did—she gave me birth and then gave me life. I love you, Ma.

(*A harsh punky song.*)
"KILL ALL THE CRAZY MOTHER-FUCKERS.
DON'T LET THE MAN KEEP HIS DICK UP YOUR ASS.
TELL HIM: PULL OUT, STOP THE LIES. MOTHER-SUCKER—
OR I'LL BE LAUGHING AT YOUR FUNERAL MASS."

(*ARROZ is stunned.*)
That's just the first rough draft.

ARROZ: Uh huh. (*Pause*) I like it. Let's see what Junior thinks.

GANDULES: I know it's not very melodic, but I think with some orchestration...will you sing it with me, Arroz? I think it could be our anthem. All bands have a signature song, right? This could be it.

ARROZ: It could. There are a lot of crazy mother-fuckers.
(*JUNIOR enters.*)

JUNIOR: What are you doing?!

ARROZ con GANDULES: Rehearsing.

JUNIOR: You're supposed to be cleaning. The club has to be ready by Monday, Remember?

GANDULES: Yeah, but—

ARROZ: You said—

JUNIOR: You don't need to rehearse. It's me they'll be looking at.
(*JUNIOR exits.*)

ARROZ: He should be careful how he talks to us.

GANDULES: Yeah. He should. He's not the boss of us.

ARROZ: Yeah, he is. But he should still be careful.

GANDULES: He doesn't know trouble.

ARROZ: Not yet.

(*ARROZ con GANDULES put on bandanas, aprons, and gloves, and start cleaning. PODEROSA enters and watches them for while before SHE speaks.*)

PODEROSA: My son didn't tell me you were so beautiful.

ARROZ: He told us you were a whore.

PODEROSA: That's right.

GANDULES: You look like one—I mean that in a nice way. I mean, you look like who you are. That's good.

PODEROSA: No one likes surprises. It could be disappointing. (*SHE begins to undress.*)
I like to clean in the nude.

(*ARROZ con GANDULES look at each other for a moment and then begin to undress also. Nino Rota music plays. Lights cross to a public space where President OCTAVIO is giving a speech.*)

SCENE SEVEN

JUNIOR, CYLVIO and ENCO, disguised as women, watch OCTAVIO giving a speech. It seems they are in a crowd of shrouded figures. These should be like bunraku puppets—the citizenry. There are many of them and they are all very sad.

OCTAVIO: Them between neutral not is God that know we and war at been always have, cruelty and justice, fear and freedom. Certain is outcome its yet, known not is conflict this of course the people American the for security and freedom for struggle this waging in relent not will I rest not will I, yield not will I. (*an aside*) Words flow like water; but any relevance, they have none! (*Back to the speech*) It inflicted who those and country our to wound the forget not will I. You thank.

CYLVIO (*Whispering to the others*): He's lost it.

ENCO: I used to write his speeches.

CYLVIO: They made more sense then.

JUNIOR: He's not interested in sense. He's interested in dollars.

ENCO: I didn't know you thought such things, Junior.

JUNIOR: You'd be surprised what I think about.

ENCO: No doubt.

CYLVIO: Why do you insist on staying with Enco, when I'm the one who loves you?

JUNIOR: You don't pay me.

ENCO: This is a prudent boy. Don't corrupt him with your trifles, Cylvio. At least wait until I'm gone.

CYLVIO: So he's really going to go through with it?

ENCO: Yes. He's summoned me to the Execution Hut on Friday.

CYLVIO: Maybe if you try writing him another speech. Something coherent. He might remember why he needed you.

ENCO: That's the problem, isn't it? Remembering why? He's not very smart, but there is a cleverness about his choices. Like a roach in a honey-trail, he'll get stuck, but as long as he can eat, he won't care if he's sinking into the muck.

CYLVIO: Is that you or him?

JUNIOR: Roaches in honey will drown.

CYLVIO: Good. Never believe anything we tell you, Junior.
(*Turning to ENCO*)
He's delicious. Please let me have him.

JUNIOR: I choose to stay. There are worse places.

ENCO: That's right. You tell him, my love. Everything could be worse.

OCTAVIO: I weld my flesh and my blood with the people! We will become like the teeth and the mouth! Together we will gnaw through the bones of society—the effete and overly polite

society—of ingrates, morons, writers and thinkers. We do not think.
We act!

(*The PEOPLE applaud half-heartedly. LUJURIA steps forward and intimidates the crowd into cheering.*)

LUJURIA: City- City! Bang-bang! Watch Octavio do his thang! Ooh, oom-gaw-wah, got Octavio powah!

(*The PEOPLE join in.*)
Ooh, oom-gaw-wah, got Octavio powah!

(*Then LUJURIA hustles OCTAVIO into the Palace.*)

CYLVIO: Well that was cheery. I love this continent. Don't you?

ENCO: Maybe I'm going about this all wrong. Maybe I should kill him.

JUNIOR: Not easy. The palace security is tight. Look at her.
(*LUJURIA, dressed in a skintight rubber jumpsuit, has stepped out into the audience and begins to jostle people at random.*)
She doesn't miss a beat.

ENCO: I've got to find her weak spot.
(*OENOTHEA comes out on the veranda to admire LUJURIA.*)
Bingo.

CYLVIO: Can I have your jabot collection? You won't need it when she rips your neck open.

ENCO: I'm getting tired of being afraid.

CYLVIO: Me, too.
(*Pause*)
Let's send the boy.

ENCO: I was thinking the same thing. He can distract her, while we pounce.
Look, he's doing it already.

(*JUNIOR has moved closer to LUJURIA who sees him but pretends not to. LUJURIA speaks to JUNIOR while pretending not to.*)

LUJURIA: Move away from me.

JUNIOR: I can't. You're so beautiful in your full rubber jacket mode.

LUJURIA: You're going to ruin everything.

JUNIOR: Push me.
(*LUJURIA pushes him.*)

Now knock me to the floor.
(*SHE does so.*)

Now kick me.
(*SHE does so.*)

LUJURIA: What's next? I tell you I love you?

ENCO: Don't hurt him!

CYLVIO: You're such a brute. The boy meant no harm.

LUJURIA: (*Rolling him toward ENCO with her foot*) Go home.

CYLVIO: WE are not the people. We have rights. I am the former head of Party Planning and he is the Empire's best scribe. Doesn't legacy mean anything to you?
If we tell the Presidemperor, he'll be mad at you.

LUJURIA: If you tell the Presidemperor, he'll cut off BOTH your heads. I know exactly who you are. Go home before I change my mind.
(*ENCO and CYLVIO help JUNIOR to his feet.*)
Leave him. I have something special planned for him.

ENCO and CYLVIO: But—

LUJURIA: You heard me.
(*ENCO and CYLVIO leave quickly.*)

ENCO: Don't touch his face.

CYLVIO: What a coward!

ENCO: We're the ones running.

CYLVIO: I mean you. How could you let her keep our Junior?

ENCO: Why do you always think the worst of me? I have—I may, uhm, have a plan.

CYLVIO: Oh.
(*When ENCO and CYLVIO are gone, LUJURIA goes to JUNIOR.*)

LUJURIA: Don't come to these rallies. People are watching.

JUNIOR: I thought you were the watcher.

LUJURIA: I am but there are others. Don't look at me like that.
(*SHE knocks him to the ground and puts a foot on his back.*)

JUNIOR: Like what?

LUJURIA: Like we're family.

JUNIOR: We <u>are</u> family.

LUJURIA: So, tonight you perform at his party and you're so good that I convince him to go to your club tomorrow night. Got it? Are you ready for this? Don't look at me.

JUNIOR: Why don't you do it? Why does it have to be me?

LUJURIA: Ask your mother. It's her idea. All of it.

(SHE lets JUNIOR get up. JUNIOR exits. LUJURIA realizes that MALPUSO has overheard everything. After the "people" exited, HE was left still tied to a bench. HE pretends to be asleep.)

LUJURIA: Did you know that you snore? Why is it that today you make no sound?

(*MALPUSO begins to softly snore.*)
Did you write that stupid speech? And what about your will—is it done?

(*MALPUSO snores a bit more loudly.*)
That's what I thought. There's nothing I don't know, grandfather.

MALPUSO: (*pretending to talk in his sleep*) Adopted...Adopted grandfather.

(*LUJURIA kicks him. Lights cross to OCTAVIO's closet.*)

SCENE EIGHT
In OCTAVIO's closet.
HE is trying to tune into his ham radio. HE sits on a stool intensely staring at the radio, but HE just hears static.

OCTAVIO: Come on, come on. We don't have a lot of time.

(*MINA The METEOROLOGIST's voice tunes in clearly.*)

MINA (*voice over the radio*): Hey there, lovers and dream-cats. What do you want most in the world? Clear, sunny skies lighting up your lanai? Flawless days with cool ocean breezes vibrating across your veranda? Not happening today my friends. Today, we'll have snow and red rusty hail the size of a Mini-Cooper. Stay inside. Don't drive. But if you do venture forth, lovelies—don't forget your helmet. Klein's has them on sale today and everyday—'til they stop.

(*Singing the jingle*)
"Klein's has the cap for your cranium.
Made with tough love and titanium.
Wear it if you and yours want to live, live, live!
Buy four and a discount we will give! Give! Give!
That's Klein's...."

(*Speaking*)
Dear listeners, comrades, soldiers, discount shoppers, I just wanted to thank you for listening to Mina. The life of a meteorologist gets so lonely. It's only knowing that you're out there—in the dark—listening—in your little closet—on your little stool.

(*OCTAVIO peers around the closet into the darkness trying to see if MINA is watching him.*)

I see you. Yes, I do. All of you. I even see inside of you. What's that? Your heart is pumping for me. Remember that's the feeling of love—not fear. Remember that's just Mina.

(*OCTAVIO turns the radio off and throws the dusty tarp on top of the radio.*)

OCTAVIO: Shush...no one is supposed to know...

(*Lights cross to FILOMENA and OENOTHEA—who is giving FILOMENA a mani-pedi.*)

FILOMENA: Of course I know. I've always known. Since the first day I met him...
He locks himself in there and talks to people. That's what he thinks he's doing—but that radio doesn't even work. I tried it. Ouch! Can you spend a little more time on my right hand? It seems to never stop aching.

OENOTHEA: (*Massaging FILOMENA's hand*) How's that? Are your knuckles always this swollen? And these cysts on your wrist—can't you see a surgeon or something?

FILOMENA: I could. But I don't trust people who cut things off or out of other people.

OENOTHEA: I guess I can understand that.

FILOMENA: Does she ever stop wanting you?

OENOTHEA: No.

FILOMENA: He wants me too much. I know I should let him. But sometimes I'm so tired and so hungry—for words I mean. I want to read and talk and listen to people reading and talking. Just because I have what I have doesn't mean I'm always up and about. You know?

OENOTHEA: I know.
(*Showing FILOMENA her scarred hands.*)
I know. I am somebody who's up—but when I get about and down to it, I burn. Masturbation is supposed to make you go blind, not combust, but I got used to it. One gets used to having too much or too little. One gets used to the flames.
But then what does it matter? Do you love him?

FILOMENA: He saved me from the circus.

OENOTHEA: Do you love him?

FILOMENA: I get better shoes here.

OENOTHEA: Yes. They look healing—those shoes.

FILOMENA: They are—because my life has always been a road map—a torn one. And I was missing the legend—the key—others had to keep interpreting it for me. But with the right shoes, I find my way—I'm finding my way.
(*OENOTHEA massages her feet in silence.*)
You got so quiet.

OENOTHEA: I said too much already. Lujuria won't be happy.

FILOMENA: She's so jealous and angry all the time. How do you stand it?

OENOTHEA: I like it. I'm grateful. To have her. I like how the inside of her ears smell. I like the taste of her bathwater. It's like drinking the rain of her.

FILOMENA: You learn most of what you need to know from water.

(*Lights cross to PODEROSA's bath.*)

SCENE NINE
In PODEROSA'S bath.
ARROZ and GANDULES are naked with her inside the bath. One scrubs her back and the other scrubs her legs.

PODEROSA: I need to buy you boys some new brushes. These are getting stiff with age. Usually it's the other way—they get softer—but I don't know…you boys make everything deliciously hard…

ARROZ: Why do you say those things to us?

GANDULES: Yes. You're so obvious. Do you think that's what men like?

PODEROSA: You're not men. Not yet. I'm not done with you—yet. I want you to wash each other's hands. I want to watch you washing each other's hands.

(*THEY do so.*)
Beautiful. There is nothing lovelier than the hands of beautiful boys. I like everything about hands. The way they feel on my body, the way they look when they beat against my supple flesh. Hit me. I want you to hit me.

(*ARROZ punches PODEROSA and knocks her out.*)

GANDULES: I don't think she meant for you to do that, dude.

ARROZ: She talks way too much. I like to take them quiet.

(*ARROZ moves to rape PODEROSA, GANDULES stops him.*)

GANDULES: Not in the tub. You got a chapped dick the last time. Water can be harsh on delicate parts.

(*JUNIOR walks in. HE is dressed for the Garden Party performance.*)

JUNIOR: Get off my mother. Get out of our house.

ARROZ: She invited us.

GANDULES: It's her house—not yours.

JUNIOR: She doesn't know what she wants anymore.
(*Pulling out his ropes.*)
You heard me. Go.

(*ARROZ and GANDULES climb out of the tub quickly, pulling towels over themselves.*)

ARROZ: We can bathe you too—if you want.

GANDULES: We like to soak. That's how we got our names.

JUNIOR: I don't give a shit about your names or where they came from. Get out of my house.

*(ARROZ and GANDULES exit.
PODEROSA comes to.)*

PODEROSA: Where'd my bunny-boys go?

(JUNIOR punches her again. SHE falls back into the tub, but HE keeps her from drowning by draping her over the rim of the tub and draining the water.)

JUNIOR: Must've had another whore to visit, Mom.

PODEROSA: That proves it. You love me. You never would've saved me if you didn't.

JUNIOR: It just proves I don't want you dead—not yet anyway...

(JUNIOR exits.)

PODEROSA: I don't buy it, baby-boy. You wouldn't know how to wipe the milk from your "chupa-chupa" without me. Noo...things get so clear once you take in too much water. Once you take that water in—you get your future all laid out for you—like a dream that's like a movie starring Charlton Heston where all the old people have been turned into food called "Beef-Boy-Are-Bits" and little chunks of it get caught in Charlton's throat and he chokes and that's how he figures out what happened. By almost dying...

(Pause)

I can see what you're planning, baby boy, but we won't make any money your way... Now, my way...uh huh...that's the way better plan.

(*Pause; SHE puts her head back under the water and holds it there for almost too long and jumps up sputtering.*)
See? I'm good at almost dying.

(*SHE grabs a towel, jumps out of the tub and exits as the lights cross to the White Palace.*)

SCENE TEN
JUNIOR is standing in front of the White Palace, practicing his knots with his eyes closed. OCTAVIO paces on his balcony over where JUNIOR stands. HE sees JUNIOR and tries to hide, then notices that JUNIOR has his eyes closed anyway. OCTAVIO resumes his pacing, then decides to say hello to JUNIOR.

OCTAVIO: Hey.

JUNIOR: Hello.

OCTAVIO: What you got there?

JUNIOR: Knots. In a rope.

OCTAVIO: Can I see?

(*JUNIOR throws the rope up to OCTAVIO. He tries to duplicate one of the knots but just succeeds in untying it.*)
I'm better at this here governing stuff.

(*He throws the untied rope back to JUNIOR.*)
What's your name?

JUNIOR: Jack.

OCTAVIO: That name gives me the willies. I'll call you, Joe.

JUNIOR: Alright. I'll be Joe. Joe is strong and direct. He's a good husband and a better friend.

OCTAVIO: He loves baseball.

JUNIOR: No, he doesn't. He likes soccer.

OCTAVIO: No. He likes baseball...and hockey.

JUNIOR: Hockey? Okay, hockey. And backgammon.

OCTAVIO: Yeah. Sure. And beer.

JUNIOR: Lots and lots of beer.

OCTAVIO: He sounds like me. Like how I used to be.

JUNIOR: Yeah? Maybe. I can teach you about knots if you want—I mean the tying part.

OCTAVIO: No...would you? That's okay. I don't need to know.

JUNIOR: I guess you got a lot of people in there tying ropes for you.

OCTAVIO: Not right now. But if I decided to tie some ropes—they'd be tied—if you know what I mean.

JUNIOR: Don't your fingers get bored?

OCTAVIO: You mean—nah, you mean—you're kidding right?

JUNIOR: I mean, don't you get lonely?

OCTAVIO: No. I can talk to my wife—if I need to.

JUNIOR: I really love this one.
(*Holding up the rope showing a Clove Hitch knot*)
It's easy but so strong and versatile. Wanna try?

OCTAVIO: You have unusual eyes—I mean, the color.

JUNIOR: Gray.

OCTAVIO: Maybe it means something to have gray eyes. Maybe something means something. Like your eyes. I never met anyone else with those eyes—besides my sister. But she died in a hospital, so long ago. I don't think they took good care of those eyes in there. They were taking care of the rest of her head, but they didn't touch her eyes, and you'd think—well, it wasn't me. I wasn't the Presidemperor then. But I don't see how no one else asked for her eyes to be cared for. I wonder about the love thing. Like Parents and sisters are supposed to have. "Where is it?", I say.

JUNIOR: This one is called the Figure of Eight Stopper. I don't know why it's "Of" eight. Easier to say Figure eight—like in skating, but maybe that's to set the sailors apart from ordinary people who like to skate. I would rather sail though. How about you?

OCTAVIO: Would you like to come to my birthday party?

JUNIOR: Really? But I'm just—you don't know me.

OCTAVIO: But I feel like I know you.

JUNIOR: Oh.
(*Pause*)
What kind of party are you having?

OCTAVIO: Dancing-in-the-Garden Party. It's about to begin. I need to get ready.
You go on ahead!

(*OCTAVIO exits as JUNIOR crosses to the garden. ARROZ and GANDULES are warming up for their dance, with exaggerated stretches and very tight tights with cod-pieces. JUNIOR takes the mic. The GUESTS give him a beat.*)

JUNIOR:
Virate. Virate mi gente, Virate.
Pasalo. Pasalo por mano , pasalo.
Damelo, da'me en mi culo, damelo.
Like the economy, set it free.
Virate, Virate, mi chula, Virate.
Virate, Virate, mi chulo, Virate.
Damelo todo—even a la modo.
Damelo.
El sexo y el poder es pa' la gente.
El pretexto es lo suyo, Señor Presidente.
Virate, Virate mi gente, Virate.

Dance break!
(*ARROZ y GANDULES take the floor and do a wild modern/hip-hop dance.*)
Eso! Así, así!

(*MALPUSO sits in one corner of the garden writing sonnets to himself.*)

MALPUSO: I despise the sonnet—"Octave" rhyming in honor of hizzHonor. The Petrarchan sonnet—abba abba, then cdc dcd or cde cde—fourteen lines, blah, blah, blah. Boring meter, such a predictable rhyme scheme...For the Gods' sake! Anyone who can count can do it—but <u>not</u> everyone's a poet. Only those who've never trusted words alone are the true poets. Poets believe in people. Blood. Love.
I can say that, because tomorrow I'll kill myself.
I'm waiting for my daughter to come visit first. My adopted daughter. It's better when there's someone to mourn you.

(*Pause*)
It's better when you wait.

(*Pause*)
Do you see? Did you feel that tension? Will he shoot himself in the head or throw himself into a pit with hungry lions? Tension. That's what makes a good poet.

(*HE pulls out a gun, holds it flat against his forehead, closes his eyes and smiles.*)
I can see the future now. Oh, damn. I'm not in it...I prefer the Past.

(*MALPUSO enters a memory. HE carries a baby in a basket. HE writes a note to put inside.*)

MALPUSO: We can't wash the tears of his mother out of his hair. Time is out of joint—the secret, you love him.
(*HE places the note into the basket.*)
You can't expect me to hand him such a dark little baby boy.

(*A younger, maybe blonder, PODEROSA enters. MALPUSO hands her the basket and exits. The baby begins to cry.*)

PODEROSA: You told me you'd take care of Junior!
(*to the BABY*)
Some grandfather, you got there, little boy! First he makes me fuck his boss, then he tells me to kill you. Fuck the intellectuals!

(*The baby's cries turn into nightclub music. Jazz and something darker. Young PODEROSA exits. MALPUSO returns. The scene changes back to JUNIOR at the mic singing something. MALPUSO sees JUNIOR.*)

MALPUSO: Oh...that's what happened to the baby.
(*MALPUSO watches JUNIOR with ARROZ con GANDULES.*)

JUNIOR: I'm thinking about adding something to the act. Some magic. Watch.
(*HE takes out his string and starts weaving with his hands.*)
This is called the "Witch's Broom."

ARROZ con GANDULES and MALPUSO: Wooah! Amazing.

JUNIOR: I can do so many of these. People don't get tired of them.

ARROZ: No?

GANDULES: It's not magic. You're just pulling strings.

ARROZ: Yeah. Just strings.

GANDULES: Why don't you ever let us do our own material?

JUNIOR: Because I've heard you.
(*Lights cross to the Oval Office.*)

SCENE ELEVEN
FILOMENA and OCTAVIO knitting in the Oval Office.
THEY listen to a radio softly tuned to the "music" from the previous scene.

FILOMENA: I like when we do things together. We should find more time to do this. I love spending time with you, Octo. You're the best husband ever.

OCTAVIO: And this is the most boring thing ever. When can I go? You can finish this on your own.

FILOMENA: You promised me. One night a week. We do what I want to do.

OCTAVIO: And since when do I keep my promises?
(*HE throws his knitting into the air.*)
Done. See you.

FILOMENA: Don't move, mister. I said this or no more of (*indicating her crotch*) this.

OCTAVIO: I'm getting tired of that too.

(*Confiding*)
I hear voices, Fila. All the time. Telling me to do bad things. I'm afraid to come near you. I don't know what I might do. Last week, I was supposed to burn you. The week before that, cut you—

FILOMENA: You didn't.

OCTAVIO: I did. Just a little. I burnt your fingernail clippings. And the week before that I cut your bangs.

FILOMENA: I'm not afraid of you.

OCTAVIO: Why not? Everyone else is.

FILOMENA: I think if you wanted to do something to me, you'd have done it already.

OCTAVIO: Maybe I'm just waiting for the right time. Maybe it's time that's saving you from me. I don't control that. I tried resetting all the clocks and taking away the minute and second hands, but it left me unsettled...all those one-handed clocks. If you don't mark time, does it pass?

FILOMENA: You don't have to do bad things, Octavio. You could sing.

OCTAVIO: I do have a beautiful voice, don't I?
(*HE sings the first verse to (1973) Steve Miller's "The Joker."*)
"Some people call me the space cowboy.
Yeah! Some call me the gangster of love.
Some people call me Maurice,
'Cause I speak of the pompatus of love."

FILOMENA: You bring me to tears every time, my love.

OCTAVIO: I'm still your love? The people hate me, why don't you? Sometimes I think you're retarded or have some kind of learning disability. You really should not love me.

FILOMENA: Maybe that's why I love you. It picks you. Love. And I am perfectly normal.

OCTAVIO: (*Looking FILOMENA over*) Really?

FILOMENA: Except for that.
(*Checking the knitting*)
Yes. We're done.

(*THEY have constructed a long cape with a train, a royal robe, for OCTAVIO. SHE unfurls it. It is like a spider web of knitted mesh.*)
It's so beautiful. Put it on.

(*HE does so. JUNIOR comes on sneakily and mounts the train. OCTAVIO drags him around the room as HE paces.*)
It suits you. You have such quiet strength sometimes...like you're pulling the weight of the world on your back...like Atlas.

(*JUNIOR begins to sing as the OCTAVIO stops to admire himself in the mirror.*)

JUNIOR: (*Singing; only OCTAVIO hears him*)
"In a spider's web, my father looks so good.
He wears deception well. I love the way his jacked-up wife has stood behind his dead-eyed hell.
If I would slash a knife across his throat,
no one would ever say I'm wrong.
If I could do it while the world made note,
history'd show who's truly strong."

OCTAVIO: Fila, did you hear that?

FILOMENA: I was enjoying the silence.

OCTAVIO: (*whispering into the air*) Go away, voice. I hear your blood rushing through my head now. Get out! I can still remember when you weren't there.

(To FILOMENA)
Remember our honeymoon?

(*Lights cross to OCTAVIO's memory by the Trevi Fountain, in Rome.*)

SCENE TWELVE-A
GOOD LUCK, a memory
OCTAVIO and FILOMENA in Rome on their honeymoon. It is as if, THEY are in an Italian movie. THEY stand in front of the Trevi Fountain. OCTAVIO throws coins in the fountain, one by one as FILOMENA hands them to him.

OCTAVIO: How many...before your wishes can come true, Fila.

FILOMENA: Don't you remember? We saw the movie.

OCTAVIO: Three. That's enough then.

FILOMENA: What did you wish for?

(*Music begins to play. Like Nino Rota's "Dolce Vita" soundtrack. FILOMENA takes OCTAVIO by the hand and leads him in a slow dance.
OCTAVIO dances like a girl.*)

OCTAVIO: Would you do anything for me, my love?

FILOMENA: There's something I haven't done?

OCTAVIO: I'd like you to fuck a giraffe.

FILOMENA: They're so tall.

OCTAVIO: But they're almost extinct. I dream about it.

(*No more talking as THEY continue to dance.*)

FILOMENA: When will I be enough, my love?

OCTAVIO: When I've had everything else...there was a time...

FILOMENA: It's starting to rain.

OCTAVIO: We won't melt.

FILOMENA: Not today.

OCTAVIO: This rain stings. There's something in it. That's why they won't let us drink it. At the hotel. The guards.

FILOMENA: Feel that. You're the only one who can make me hard anymore.

OCTAVIO: (*Slapping her viciously to the ground.*) You fucking freak. Don't make me cut it off.

FILOMENA: Go ahead. I'm tired of it anyway. I'd like a bigger one.

(*OCTAVIO kicks her hard.*)
I'm tired of this dance. Let's go home, Octo.

(*HE kicks her again.*)
Please stop. Not like the last time. I'll be a good girl.

(*HE kicks her again.*)
I'm not going to get up one day.

OCTAVIO: We have a lot more to see.

(*HE turns and walks away.*)

Next stop, the Golden Palace! Domus Aurea. Everything there burned once.

(*HE turns back to FILOMENA.*)
Aren't you coming?

(*FILOMENA, still on the ground, opens her purse and reapplies her make-up.*)

FILOMENA: A lady doesn't go anywhere—without a touch of make-up.

OCTAVIO: I would never get anywhere without you.

(*HE offers her his hand. SHE takes it after reapplying her lipstick. HE pulls her up.*)

FILOMENA: That's for sure. The Domus is that way.

OCTAVIO: See what I mean?
(*HE pulls her in for kiss.*)
Better?

FILOMENA: So far. (*Pause*) Will you keep hit—

OCTAVIO: I never know what I'll do before I do it. I just do.

FILOMENA: Did you know what you were doing yesterday?

OCTAVIO: Yesterday I married the most beautiful girl in the world.

FILOMENA: No, you married me...

(*OCTAVIO kisses her again sweetly.*)

OCTAVIO: Let's go. I have a surprise for you when we get there.

(*Lights cross to a crumbled relic of an ancient palace. It looks a lot like the ruins of La Perla Nightclub.*)

SCENE TWELVE-B
DREAMS UNEARTHED—the memory continues.
OCTAVIO and FILOMENA at the site of Nero's never-completed Golden Palace, the Domus Aerea.

   OCTAVIO: It must have been magnificent in Nero's day.
   (*Pause*)
   You know I was born on the same day as him.

   FILOMENA: You keep telling me. December 15.

   OCTAVIO: Even the same hour of the day, I think.

   FILOMENA: How do you know that? How could anyone? I think every "fact" we've read on every building here is just made up. There are no real records. It was so long ago. How could there be records?

   OCTAVIO: There are records! There are records! Don't you believe in history?!

   FILOMENA: I believe in the stars. Destiny. It scares me.

   OCTAVIO: I scare you?

   FILOMENA: Oh, yes. The sixth president in the 6th election year after the sixth assassination.

   OCTAVIO: (*with a smile*) I am.

   FILOMENA: You are.
   (*OCTAVIO pulls FILOMENA in a tight embrace.*)

OCTAVIO: Feel that? You're the only one who can make me hard anymore. Let's do it in the Coliseum. Or the Circus Maximus...I'll circle your Maximus—
(*HE bites her hard.*)
I love the taste of your blood.

FILOMENA: (*a cry of pain that's almost pleasure.*) Ahh. But leave some of it inside, baby. I need it.

(*Lights cross back to the Garden Party.*)

SCENE THIRTEEN
The Garden Party at the White Palace. Sunset.
We see several people tied to stakes. They have been sexually mutilated. They are bloody and broken. One of them is MALPUSO, the poet. A band plays something like Rota's "Ecclesiastical Fashion Show Theme" from the movie *ROMA*. Rich people dance. OCTAVIO enters wearing the woven robe. FILOMENA stands two steps behind him.
HE gets on the stage and takes over the mic.
LUJURIA is standing guard.

OCTAVIO: Is everyone having a good time?
(*Applause and cheers*)

PARTY GUEST ONE: There's not enough hot passed hors d'oeuvres.

FILOMENA (*stepping to the mic*): Thank you dear guests for being here to celebrate the man who brought night-to-day in this Empire.

PARTY GUEST TWO: I like those chicken satés on a stick.

OCTAVIO: SHUT UP! SHUT UP!

(*LUJURIA throws PARTY GUEST One and Two out. The other guests applaud.*)

MALPUSO: I have a poem for you, your Imperial Majesty.

OCTAVIO: It talks. Haven't I cured you of that yet? There is nothing worse than a bad poet, writing poems in your honor. So awkward. You want to be grateful—flattered even—but you can't help but think if you thank a bad poet, you elevate him to a status he has not earned. And I once thought you were good. Shame on me.

MALPUSO: Please, your imperial majesty. You will like this one.

OCTAVIO: It is certainly your last one. Proceed.

MALPUSO: Birds fell from the sky, with birth's sweet cry—a son was born—

OCTAVIO: Where did the Sun go?
(*OCTAVIO sets him on fire. GUESTS step forward and light the others.*)
Now there's light. Let's dance.

(*Silent screams of agony in time to the music.*
Lights cross to PODEROSA's dressing room at La Perla Nightclub.)

SCENE FOURTEEN
In PODEROSA's dressing room.
Morning after the Garden Party.
PODEROSA, mostly naked, putting on make-up and talking to passed out ARROZ con GANDULES.

PODEROSA: You understand, don't you boys? About love. About how love is the reason for everything? I put this powder on for love. I applied and re-applied my lip stain to mark the opening to my breath, because in my breath you can smell all you need to know about me.

(*Looking at ARROZ con GANDULES*)

You boys are weak. I don't admire a weak man though they're usually easier on the eye.

(*SHE nudges them with her foot. THEY grumble.*)
Just checking. Last year someone died on me. My son never forgave me. A friend of his.
I thought they were lovers but no and no, he doesn't like sharing with his mama. That took me by surprise. I thought I raised him better. Greedy young man takes after his father. I had a thought about that—about what would happen if I just covered myself all in body paint and showed up on the steps of the White Palace. Would I get past the gate? Probably not—but he'd see me—on the surveillance tapes. Maybe photos. Maybe just etched into the side of a wall. I'm like an ancient language he doesn't speak anymore. That's what happens when people get famous. They forget how they once spoke. They only remember things in the present. What kind of fucked-up language is that? One you can never remember because it never happened, it only happens. What the fuck? What do you boys think? I wish you'd sober up.

(*SHE finishes powdering her entire body. Then SHE rolls out a piece of cloth—like a canvas. She rolls herself on the surface of the cloth. Then looks at the image she left. It is blood-red. Red pours from between her legs.*)
Oh. How predictable.

(*ARROZ comes to.*)
That's right. The red between my legs is like caffeine. Or cocaine. Gets you up. Which one are you?

ARROZ: Arroz. What did you do to us, bitch?

PODEROSA: What??

ARROZ: Ma'am...

PODEROSA: That's even worse.

ARROZ: I think we should go. We have to rehearse.
(*HE pulls on GANDULES to wake him up.*)
C'mon, Gando.

PODEROSA: I do like watching you boys dance. I could have been a dancer.

ARROZ: Every-damn-body says that. "I could have—" whatever. Let's see something.

PODEROSA: Oh, you want to see my moves? Hang on.
(*SHE straddles him and gyrates.*)
They go like this and like this and like this.

ARROZ: Why are you made up like a ghost?

PODEROSA: I want to scare somebody today. Maybe you.

ARROZ: I don't scare that easy, lady. Wooh, slow down, Junior's mother. He didn't say you were this much of a freak.

PODEROSA: Do you think I'm sexier with White skin all over?

ARROZ: No, uhunh. More freaky is all.

PODEROSA: I'll show you freaky.
(*SHE gyrates more furiously. A messed-up twerking.*)
Leaves the boys speechless.

ARROZ: Because you're covering my damn mouth. Get off me, lady.

(*Pushes PODEROSA off his face.*)
It's time to go.

(*Pulls a groggy GANDULES up.*)
Gando. Let's go, now.

GANDULES: Ah, man, I was having a juicy dream and shit. There was this lady with big tits and a medium dick chasing me into a room filled with bubbles. And they were red. And it was fucking awesome. Like the bubbles didn't pop or nothing. They were more like balloons and you could roll on them, and they made you light and you could rise up on them and the dick-girl was chasing me and trying to put her tits in my mouth and I was into it. And all like, (*makes a yummy, head-flapping, tongue-slapping sound*) lahyayowuhmmmy! And that little dick was like—

PODEROSA: I thought it was a medium dick.

GANDULES: Yeah, but that was all like a figure of speech, and shit. And lahyayowuhmmmy! I was into that too—in the dream.

ARROZ: Right. The dream. Let's go, Gandules. You need some fresh air.

GANDULES: I thought we were like outside already. With the snow-lady.

PODEROSA: This is powder.

GANDULES: Ohhh...
(*Lights cross to LUJURIA in the Palace Gardens.*)

SCENE FIFTEEN
In the dark, we hear all the women begin to speak Cicero's words in English, perhaps as a round, as the lights come up on LUJURIA. It's the afternoon before the Night everyone goes to the nightclub.
"But inasmuch as things human are frail and fleeting, we must always be searching for someone whom we may love and by whom we may be loved; for if goodwill and affection are taken away, every joy is taken from life."
—Cicero, De Amicitia (On Friendship) paragraph 102—

(*LUJURIA is naked beneath a butcher's apron, sawing up two people. SHE places some of the pieces in a large terrarium—others SHE discards into a pit behind her. The last parts she picks up are the heads and those she places more carefully into the terrarium, so the faces are facing out at the audience and at her. It is a fish tank environment. Fake little trees, a little castle and plastic sunken ships line the tank—along with the heads. When SHE's done, SHE turns the light on, admiring her work.)*

LUJURIA: Hello, my darlings, my starlings. My darkly-fated serving birds.
Birds in fish houses shouldn't throw sharp beaks.

(*TULLIA and VITA, the housemaids, are in the terrarium.*)
You were such pretty things. He couldn't keep his hands off you.

(*Pause*)
Our Presidemperor has such big appetites. And isn't that the way of history? Men in power pounding their peniculum mentulas like anatomical clappers, ringing a warning against the sound rim of a woman's sex. We should know better, Sisters. Gotta watch who you let into your bell tower. But we all like adventure, don't we? Me, I travel. With my wife—my future wife. My vibrational pulls are still my own. I don't owe my ecstasy to anyone. Even my Oenothea. She tastes like burnt meat, but I do like mine well-done. A glaze of charcoal. A chewy bit. They say it gives you cancer, but what doesn't these days? I'll take my chances. I'd rather burn with her than become some man's statuary. Another tune at his garden party.

(Directly to the heads of TULLIA and VITA.)
He played you, ladies. And we know there are some who must always win. Some whose hearts were lost long ago, and the hollow men they've become must be kept filled. Fingers laced tightly around a gentle neck will do just fine. That's why it's important to do those neck rolls. Keep your muscles in shape. And learn how to run away from danger. And why did you think his lady would take care of you? Shim doesn't even know how to care for shimself.

(*FILOMENA walks in quietly behind LUJURIA, surprising her.*)

FILOMENA: What did you just say?

(*LUJURIA covers the tank with a canvas tarp.*)

LUJURIA: Do you always sneak up on people?

FILOMENA: Not always. Is this where you're having them line up for the interviews?

LUJURIA: Interviews?

FILOMENA: For the maid's job?

LUJURIA: Are you applying, First Lady?

FILOMENA: Not again. That's how I found this place, remember? Is that the new uniform?

LUJURIA: Maybe.

FILOMENA: Airy. Doing some butchering?

LUJURIA: Yes. We eat meat around here.

FILOMENA: You know I have no problem with meat.

LUJURIA: Have them go through those doors to the left. Speak to the housekeeper.

FILOMENA: You're not—

LUJURIA: I have enough to do. The housekeeper will help you with those interviews.

FILOMENA: (*Turns towards the door then turns back*) Can I ask you something?

LUJURIA: Maybe.

FILOMENA: Do you have any tips? I've actually never hired a maid before.

LUJURIA: Ahhh... uh huh. Well, be sure to let them know to avoid eye contact and never let the man of the house get closer than this.
(*SHE reaches out as if to strangle FILOMENA but from about two feet away, then letting her arms drop.*)
That would be my advice.

FILOMENA: Ok. Thanks.
(*Pause*)
You're nicer than you think you are.

LUJURIA: How would you know what I think?

FILOMENA: I've seen you. Walking around.
Giving away your lunch to those homeless kids outside the gates...

LUJURIA: Nope. Not me. Through those doors.

FILOMENA: Oh, ok. Thanks again. (*Begins to walk away but then turns back*) Listen—

LUJURIA: I'm busy here.

FILOMENA: I know, but—

LUJURIA: Do you mind? I have work to do.

FILOMENA: I still say you're nice.
(*LUJURIA watches her go through the Palace back doors. SHE pulls the tarp off the bloody terrarium, and addresses the two heads inside.*)

LUJURIA: She fits right in, doesn't she, Tullia? What do you think, Vita? It was problematic hiring sisters. His Imperial, Majestic and Apostolic Douchebag, doesn't like relatives. Poor dark birds.

(*SHE completes the scene with plastic terrarium stuff. Then SHE stuffs a knife in a baggie and places it under the fake coral in the tank. SHE pulls the tarp back over the tank and sits on top of it.*)
I think it's time for a cocktail.

(*Pause*)
That's when your wife is supposed to magically appear with a shaker, some ice, a bottle of vodka and two glasses.

(*LUJURIA gathers all her butchering equipment and puts them in a wheelbarrow. Over the tarp, she throws a rug of Astroturf with fake flowers embedded in it. Then, as SHE crosses off, OCTAVIO enters.*)

OCTAVIO: This is a perfect spot! Hurry up will you.

(*FILOMENA enters pushing a wheelbarrow full of picnic foods, checked blanket, a chilled bottle of vodka, two martini glasses and other picnic things. It is heavy and SHE is struggling.*)

OCTAVIO: (*Striking a pose*) Don't I look perfect in this light? Can you get the camera? We don't want to lose this light...

(*Practicing various poses and looks as HE sings a verse from Joe Tex's "I Gotcha." FILOMENA pulls out a digital camera from the wheelbarrow and takes shots like a pro.*)

"Now, kiss me, hold it a long time, now hold it. Don't turn it a-loose, now hold it. A little bit longer, now hold it, come on. Hold it, hold it, hold it, hold it. Now ease up on me now, hey, Good God Hey, The girl's alright, y'all, ha-ha. Good God."

(*FILOMENA and OCTAVIO set up their picnic. THEY lounge atop the terrarium, which seems like a perfect picnic platform. OCTAVIO puts his head in FILOMENA's lap and SHE reads to him from Cicero's De Amicitia, para.102.)*

FILOMENA: (*In the middle of reading*)...est e vita sublata iucunditas.

OCTAVIO: Yes, that's right. Every joy is taken from life with love. Read that last part again...it sounds like Christmas Bells and condiments. Yes, like someone is pouring salt on top of a giant set of gongs in a stone cathedral, in a dark forest, with dark pudding to eat afterward...

FILOMENA: Ah, pudding. I miss it so. No one made it like Tullia. Except maybe for Vita...Why did you fire them?

OCTAVIO: The only thing They did properly was that pudding. What stupid, clumsy girls. We can't surround ourselves with incompetence, Fila. I'm sure they're somewhere warm. And tropical.
(*A fluorescent light glows from under the picnic platform. A shadow of a palm tree swaying.*)
Read.

(*FILOMENA begins to read in Latin. Translation: "But inasmuch as things human are frail and fleeting, we must always be searching for someone whom we may love and by whom we may be loved; for if goodwill and affection are taken away, every joy is taken from life." Cicero, (On Friendship) para. 102.)*

FILOMENA: Sed quonium res humanae fragiles caducaeque sunt, semper aliqui Anquirendi sunt quos diligamus et a quibus diligamur; caritate enim Benevolentiaque sublata omnis est e vita sublata iucunditas.

OCTAVIO: You make me happy, Fila.

FILOMENA: I'm your dark pudding. More chocolate than blood...yes?

OCTAVIO: Mmmm...yes. Can I tell you a secret?

FILOMENA: You can tell me anything.

OCTAVIO: Do you know what I do in the closet?

FILOMENA: It doesn't matter to me what you do in there. A man's prerogative. Everyone has needs.

OCTAVIO: I contact the dead.

FILOMENA: Oh. Like a séance?

OCTAVIO: Yes, but alone—and with a machine.

FILOMENA: How do you know the people are dead if they're in a machine? It sounds like they could be in an office. Or a ship. Or anywhere.

OCTAVIO: It's the dead alright. They speak to me and they say encouraging things.

(*Pause*)
They know my birthday. Only a dead person would know that because I'm keeping my age a mystery, like all the great men of history. Once you reveal your age, people try to take your power. Don't ever tell anyone my birthday!
(*HE slaps her. SHE scrambles away from him.*)

FILOMENA: I didn't. I never.
(*Pause*)
But why do you have a birthday party then?

OCTAVIO: Never on my real birthday. Never then. Never tell anyone anything about me. I'm taking you out tonight. But it's NOT my birthday!

FILOMENA: No, it's mine. And I prefer to stay home.

OCTAVIO: (*Slaps her.*) You do not! You do not let me go out in public without you, Honeypot! How do you think that would look?

FILOMENA: And what about the dead people? What else are they saying besides "Happy birthday?"

OCTAVIO: Are you making fun of me, honeypot?

FILOMENA: How could I? I'm just your wife.

OCTAVIO: They tell me the future, Fila. Our future. They tell me whom to trust. Where to hide the knives. Where to get good coffee beans—where they don't burn them. I hate burnt coffee. It smells like piles of placentas baking in the sunlight. I don't want to remember that smell.

FILOMENA: So who do you trust?

OCTAVIO: Not you. You dress like one thing and undress like another.

FILOMENA: And what will you do about that?

OCTAVIO: Read to me some more.

FILOMENA: No. You're just going to do to me what you do to everyone.

OCTAVIO: What's that?

FILOMENA: I'm going inside.

OCTAVIO: You're going inside to get changed for tonight.

FILOMENA: Of course. Gold or Platinum?

OCTAVIO: Platinum. Less flashy, but more expensive.

(*SHE goes to leave, HE grabs her hand.*)
Don't make me go alone.

FILOMENA: Why do you always doubt me?

OCTAVIO: You make me. (*Pause*) The dead told me something else.

FILOMENA: What?

OCTAVIO: We're going to die together. Isn't that romantic?

FILOMENA: Picnics are romantic.

(*OCTAVIO pulls FILOMENA down and places a kiss on her throat.*)

OCTAVIO: There. For good luck.

(*OCTAVIO and FILOMENA begin to make love. The lights cross to OCTAVIO's closet where JUNIOR takes out a reading a piece of paper and reads it.*)

JUNIOR: "O gods in heaven, what a night we kept,
How soft the bed! Together warmed, we slept
So twined in love, so crossed upon a kiss,
It seemed her soul was mine and mine was hers.
Goodbye, I thought, to every grief of man.
Farewell, all care!—That night my doom began."
Daddy, you're so romantic—Mother gave me that. To prove to you that I am me. But how do I prove that to myself?
(*HE takes out a knife and slices into his own palm.*)
See how thick it runs in here. That must mean something.
That I have slow flowing blood straight up and pumping.

(*Lights cross to LUJURIA and OENOTHEA in the garden. OENOTHEA is hosing the blood and remains of TULLIA and VITA off LUJURIA.*)

OENOTHEA: I had no idea how messy your job was. Since when does the Chief of Securitatis have to prep the meat for the kitchen?! You should get a job description.
Ever since those maids ran off, they've been taking advantage—

LUJURIA: You have no idea what you're taking about. When is the last time you worked security?

OENOTHEA: Well, I never have, but—

LUJURIA: You are working my nerves today. Just believe me when I say that you don't know anything about my job and you could never do my job. So stop being so bitchy—

OENOTHEA: Bitchy?! I'm defending you. I'm protecting you. I'm acting like a future wife needs to act towards her woman.

LUJURIA: Who said we were getting married?

OENOTHEA: Really!? Now who's the bitch?!
(*Throws the hose at LUJURIA*)
You are my life, Lu. What am I to you? Some fool holding your hose? Cleaning you off? You treat me like I'm your maid.

LUJURIA: You are a maid, Thea. A maid with a burning hot—

OENOTHEA: Not that! Say what I need to hear.
(*Pause*)
I won't wait forever, Lu.
(*SHE starts to exit in a huff.*)

LUJURIA: I have to clear my schedule, Thea. Then we can talk —about it.

OENOTHEA: Whatever.
(*SHE disappears from view.*)

LUJURIA: You are the only thing keeping me from killing myself.

OENOTHEA: (*Peeking her head into the scene*) By the way, I know that's human flesh and blood on you. I know the difference between food and people. I just wanted you to tell me the truth. You act like I'm some girl who can't take it. But I can take it. Where's the trust?

(*SHE throws another hose at LUJURIA.*)

LUJURIA: That's enough with the hoses. Damn, girl! I just— Wanted to keep those heads.

OENOTHEA: Yeah. Those girls were cute. I liked how they talked in secret code. You think they were lovers?

LUJURIA: Hmm...they never fought and worked as a team. I think they were sisters.

OENOTHEA: Oh...But sisters fight sometimes.
(*Comes back into the garden*)
I don't mind the things you do, but I don't like it when you keep them to yourself. I worry about you, going through so much alone. Let me help you next time. I'm good with chain saws.

LUJURIA: Okay, baby. Okay.
(*THEY kiss.*)
Maybe one day—

OENOTHEA: Yes, yes, yes!!!

LUJURIA: I don't know why it means so much to you. We don't need no stinking papers to tell us we're in love and we're real and we're here right now. Together. What else is there?

OENOTHEA: You have better credit than I do.

LUJURIA: That's true.
(Pause, as THEY stare into each other's eyes.)
You want to see? I put them in a nice terrarium.

OENOTHEA: Maybe later...

(THEY kiss again. Longer this time, as they lights cross to La Perla Nightclub.)

SCENE SIXTEEN
In PODEROSA's nightclub *La Perla*. Capitol City.
JUNIOR is finishing up some decorating for his band's performance. HE has covered the entire animatronic genitalia wall with webs of fishnet lace, so now we see penises and mouths poking and puckering through the sheath of black and red lace.

PODEROSA: It's fucking radiant. It's going to be some special club tonight!

JUNIOR: Mother, stop quoting *Charlotte's Web*. You sound retarded.

PODEROSA: I love what you've done. Who's Charlotte?

JUNIOR: Pretty isn't it? Men like to sit in lacy things.

PODEROSA: As long as you build in a few strategic holes. Ripping through lace is not fun. I had a guy once who stripped the skin off the underside of his penis by getting a little too anxious to get to me. There was blood everywhere. *(Pause)*
I was fine of course.

JUNIOR: Of course.

PODEROSA: And by the way, my new investors are coming over soon! Be nice.

JUNIOR: Bend over more. I was the one who sent them to you, Mother.

PODEROSA: That's right. It's all about you. Always has been. Children are terrifying that way. How they arrive and your life's blood gets drained slow and steady until you wake up one day and the shell of your body can't pick itself off the bed to take a shit. That's why I tried so many times to drown you. But you were extraordinary underwater. You could hold your breath for so long. Swam as fast as a bull shark. And just as many teeth. After many test dives, I decided you were part fish and left you alone. Those skills could come in handy.

JUNIOR: You say the sweetest things.

(*ENCO and CYLVIO enter. CYLVIO runs up to JUNIOR and tries to kiss him hard on the mouth. JUNIOR turns his head so CYLVIO ends up kissing his neck passionately instead.*)

CYLVIO: So shy. Not in front of mama?

ENCO: He's clearly disgusted by you, Cyl.

CYLVIO: Is that so?

ENCO: (*Putting an arm protectively around JUNIOR.*) Isn't that right?

JUNIOR: (*Clearly lying*) You know I love you both.

CYLVIO and ENCO: We know.

CYLVIO: This place gets more naughty ever time we come.

ENCO: Fishnets?! What's next?! "High heels and bustiers" only parties?

PODEROSA: What a nice idea!

(*Indicating her clothing*)
I'm all set for that night, gentlemen.
So what did you want to discuss?

ENCO: We were wondering—

CYLVIO: —if it isn't too much trouble—

ENCO: —if we could have a table with our name on it.

PODEROSA: Like a plaque?

CYLVIO: Yes. And special toys—just for us.

ENCO: We don't like sharing.

(*ENCO and CYLVIO both sneak a glance at JUNIOR.*)

PODEROSA: I'll have to think about this. We run a democratic establishment. I'd hate to alienate any customers who might not be able to afford the special treatment.

CYLVIO: But people love exclusivity. They love to watch and envy it if they don't have it. Gives them something to do, poor things.

ENCO: Poor things...

JUNIOR: Poor things.

PODEROSA: Give me a few days. I need to run it by the bank.

ENCO: Of course.

CYLVIO: And we can have anything on the menu for free.

PODEROSA: No. Not anything.

CYLVIO: Can we borrow Junior for a while? I desperately need a shave.

JUNIOR: I quit, remember. Today I start my new career.

ENCO: He quit, Cyl. Stop harassing him. Want to come over later and watch a movie with me?

CYLVIO: I suppose I'm free.

ENCO: I was talking to Junior.

CYLVIO: Oh. Okay.
(*Silence*)
Can I come too?

ENCO: Why? Why can't you let Junior decide whom he likes better?

CYLVIO: Junior's not ready for any big decisions yet. He's just a baby butler.

JUNIOR: I'm a tiny piece of glass in the back of your eye. One day you'll wake up bleeding and you won't know why. Blood will weep out of your eyes, and you'll taste the hard, nickel liquid metal of me flowing down your throat.

ENCO: Scary baby butler.

CYLVIO: The help is always somewhat frightening.
(*Pause*)
But I have a surprise for you...you're going to like it.
(*To PODEROSA*)
So are you.

JUNIOR: I know you reserved a table for tonight. Is that it?

CYLVIO: Maybe. Maybe it's who I'm bringing to the table.

ENCO: He's going to make you guess. He's annoying that way.

PODEROSA: Is it Marvin Gaye?

CYLVIO: He's dead.

PODEROSA: John Lennon?

ENCO: Dead.

PODEROSA: Selena?

JUNIOR: Dead. Moron.

CYLVIO: This person is still alive.

ENCO: Just tell them, Cyl.

CYLVIO: Wellllll....ok. It's the leader of the free-ish world.

PODEROSA: No way! I didn't believe he'd ever come to us—here. What do you think about that, Junior?

CYLVIO: Yes, Junior. Love me the best now?

JUNIOR: How did you do it?

CYLVIO: Well, I...

ENCO: Well, he...

CYLVIO: I heard him say he was coming—and I nodded at him enthusiastically.

(CYLVIO and ENCO both nod their heads enthusiastically.)

JUNIOR: Oh. Well, I...couldn't love you any more than I already do. I better go rehearse.

ENCO: This is going to be a big night.

PODEROSA: Absolutely...

(*Lights cross to JUNIOR's bedroom.*)

SCENE SEVENTEEN-A
The morning of the nightclub opening.
JUNIOR's bedroom. JUNIOR practices being himself.

JUNIOR: (*Traces his lips with a knife as HE speaks to a poster of OCTAVIO*) There's something I need to tell you.

(*Traces the knife along his throat; PODEROSA enters and listens.*)
Hmmm...Not menacing enough...

(*HE tears it off the wall and stomps on it.*)
I mean it. I'm here to make you explode. Bah-boosh! You got that? Like a dick on crack—you'll be up hard until you shatter into tiny shards of black glass.

(*HE struts around the room with a sassy bounce to his step.*)
I know that you know what I'm here to do. You owe me. I should just take it, but I'm going to wait a little to see if you'll do right by me. Some people don't. And those aren't people you see for long. They disappear.

They vanish. Like White girls in wedding dresses. White on white won't do, nah-uh. White on white is not what we aim for. We aim to be seen, in all the colors. You know what I'm saying? All the inter-star-like-galaxy colors where there's nothing but darkness so complete that Earth looks blue... dark blue like my heart—that you—abandoned to this misery.

PODEROSA: Boo-hoo.

JUNIOR: Asshole! Why are you creeping up on me all the time? Damn! Trying to catch me with my pants at my ankles, in one of your boyfriend's mouths—him sucking on me with his dentures out?

PODEROSA: Nope. Just wondered what you wanted for dinner.

JUNIOR: Oh.
(*Pause*)
I'm not hungry. I can't ever eat before a show.

PODEROSA: I was going to scramble up some eggs with Spinach. Or maybe kale. I need my greens. Did I tempt you?

JUNIOR: Get out.

PODEROSA: I only let them do that so I could buy you things.

JUNIOR: Uhhuh. Get out now.

PODEROSA: Mr. Arroz and Mr. Gandules are having something to eat with us.

JUNIOR: Mother, you make me sick.

PODEROSA: Sick is a good thing. Like "you should see his beautiful new car, it's sick." Right?

JUNIOR: You know what I mean.

PODEROSA: I keep you alive. I gave you everything I had.

JUNIOR: The Mayans invented that shit—ZERO! Nothing. You.
(*Pause*)

PODEROSA: This town is making you sassy.

JUNIOR: Get the mother-fuck out of here!
(*PODEROSA exits. HE watches her go.*)
I can't even talk to myself alone. That's why I keep this.

(*HE takes out a tape recorder. Records.*)
It's old school, but I like it. I like how I can see the tape and see how my voice gets turned into plastic ribbons. And when it gets all filled up, I can just tape over it and then it has layers of me all in there. I wind and unwind and rewind. I can point to my own voice and see where I've been. It's proof. I'm going to set myself on fire one day. Tape burns fast. Turns to liquid. And that'll be me—a puddle on the floor, flowing into the ocean. All of me into all of that. All of me water.

(*Stops the tape recorder and rewinds. Plays. WE hear the recording.*)
"ocean. All of me into that. All of me water."

(*Stops. Rewinds. Plays.*)
"burns fast. Turns to liquid. And that'll be—"

(*Stops. Rewinds. Play.*)
"...fire one day."

(*Stops. Rewinds. Listens to the sound of the rewinding until it stops.*)
That's why.

(*PODEROSA pokes her head back in.*)

PODEROSA: I found some tangerine juice.

JUNIOR: Douche with it.

PODEROSA: That's the old way to stop sperm from taking. Sperm hate citrus.

JUNIOR: That's funny. I hate you.

PODEROSA: You didn't used to. This is what happens to mothers and sons in new places. They end up fighting about nothing and stabbing each other in the eye. My friend, Mina, told me about it. She knows everything. That girl could be a dentist or something.

JUNIOR: You know the best people, Mother.

PODEROSA: I know right?! She's so smart and shit. Maybe you should marry her. I think she's got money too. Damn… Maybe I'll marry her myself.

JUNIOR: You should. Right now. Tonight.

PODEROSA: I have to open the club first. You sure you don't want some? Good for your blood sugar.

(*JUNIOR jumps on PODEROSA, choking her.*)
This is what happens when you don't drink your juice.

(*HE lets go of her. SHE falls to the floor.*)
This is what always happens.

(*ARROZ con GANDULES enter and stand between them. THEY help PODEROSA to her feet.*)

ARROZ: I thought you were going to make us some chow-chow boogie.

GANDULES: Don't kill the cook until after the meal, son.

JUNIOR: Back-up dancers should never get between a man and his mother.

ARROZ: Don't threaten us.

GANDULES: Are you threatening us? Or is that more like a saying—like "Bitterness afflicted the anus; but it entered by way of the mouth" —like that?

JUNIOR: Sumerian quips, huh? You think that makes you so smart?! You think this is funny?! That I'm joking here?! I will end her. And you won't stop me.

PODEROSA: They won't, but I will. I always do. I try to kill you. You try to kill me. That's how we show how much we love each other—we'll go to such darkness to keep our love real.

JUNIOR: I know. I know what you really want from me. Once you get it, maybe you can leave me alone. I need a new life—one not floating in shit.

ARROZ: I think the Sumerians knew a lot about shit.

JUNIOR: What's with you two and the Sumerians?

GANDULES: They understood the importance of backup, invention.

ARROZ: They wrote things down. We're keeping a record of all this. So one day we'll be part of history.

PODEROSA: Everything repeats. That's how the wheel gets reinvented. I better go powder my nose.

(*SHE exits as ARROZ con GANDULES take out notebooks and begin to write things down. JUNIOR watches them—then slashes the books.*)

(*Lights cross to ENCO and CYLVIO.*)

SCENE SEVENTEEN-B

In ENCO's bathroom on the afternoon of the
night club opening.
ENCO is looking in his bathroom mirror.
HE was shaving with a straight razor, in his white boxer-briefs that are
now bloody, since HE decided to cut small pieces of flesh from his arms
and neck. HE watches himself bleed. CYLVIO enters, watches for a
moment, and then speaks.

CYLVIO: Enco...What's it to be then?

ENCO: If I just keep doing this, I could make myself into a
patchwork quilt and start all over again. You could sew those
pieces, Cylvio. You would. You're a never-say-die type.

CYLVIO: And you say it so often that it has no meaning.

ENCO: You could make a suit of me and wear me once a year
on my birthday.

CYLVIO: How romantic!

ENCO: It could work this time. Just let me—

(*HE picks up the razor and CYLVIO kicks it out of his hand.*)
I didn't know you could kick like that. Tae Kwon Doh?

CYLVIO: Tae Bo.

ENCO: Is that still a thing?

CYLVIO: I think it was a person—who could kick really high.
(*Rummaging through ENCO's first aid kit and beginning to
bandage ENCO.*)
You have to keep your kit better stocked. You're almost out of
antiseptic.

ENCO: Yes. I didn't think I'd need much more.

CYLVIO: My dearest, I won't be here someday and then you will really bleed.

ENCO: What are you saying? Are you ill?

CYLVIO: Yes. And that's enough about that.

ENCO: A new virus? Must be since we cured the other stuff... hmm. How did you contract said disease?

CYLVIO: Never mind.

ENCO: Could I catch it? Oh, please give it to me!

CYLVIO: It doesn't work that fast. It won't save you from the execution hut. Just take a plane and get lost over the Java Sea or Nikumaroro or Bermuda. No one looks there.

ENCO: You know I hate heights.
(*Pause*)
You're so lucky to be dying. Nothing to lose. No wonder you're such a jolly fellow.

CYLVIO: I'd like to help you, Enco. But your attitude has been bad for a long time. There's no way for you to escape your fate without hope.

ENCO: Thank you, Dr. Cyl. That was gratuitous and sentimental. I have hope. I hope I die without being murdered.

(*Silence.*)
I'm sorry, Cyl.

(*Silence.*)
I didn't mean to yell at you.

(*CYLVIO tightens the bandages around ENCO's neck.*)
Hey!

CYLVIO: Isn't this what you wanted, old friend? I could do it so easily. It's just a matter of degree. How tight is too tight? How long can you go without breathing?
(*HE loosens the bandage.*)
You're right. Too much hope. It keeps me from ending your self-concerned blather. I think surely he'll hear himself one day. Surely he'll see that there are people who love him and then stop hurting them. Surely.

ENCO: Surely.
(*HE holds CYLVIO in a tight embrace.*)

CYLVIO: Enough. My suit is wrinkling.

SCENE SEVENTEEN-C
In OCTAVIO's closet.
The White Palace. The Night OCTAVIO and FILOMENA go to the club. OCTAVIO, in a red tux, is frantically trying to fix his ham radio by wrapping the antenna and the electrical cord in aluminum foil. When he has all the foil in place, he turns the radio on.

(*MINA The METEOROLOGIST's voice finally tunes in clearly.*)

MINA *(voice over the radio)*: Hey there, lovers and dream-cats. I've missed you. Where have you all been? Out making our dear Republic safe for fake-Demosociocrats and wannabe Conservicans? Listen up, Dearhearts. I don't have much time. My station is closing and I won't be able to give you many more pep-talks, warnings or whimsical song stylings.
So I'll be brief: there is a storm coming over the Greater Antilles. It will vortex over the Isthmus of Catanzaro. They say this is where Spartacus defeated the Roman legion just by digging to the water and flooding the land where the Romans tried to cross, at the narrowest point of land in all of Bel Italia, separating the Ionian Sea from the Tyrrhenian Sea. Know where that is?

(*OCTAVIO shakes his head "no."*)

Then you're butt-fucked by a Beaver's furry teeth.
Wooh. That was so many words, gentle folk, that I just be-drooled myself. Now take precautions. Lock your basements. Something is coming up from below. Danger this big, can't be kept behind walls and under concrete floors anymore. It has come to your house, under your bed. What can I do you ask yourself?

(*OCTAVIO nods "yes."*)
You have to be able to use an atlas. If you can't find where the enemy is hiding, you'll never defeat it, you'll never find a place for yourself. Be afraid, my darlings. Keep your third eye open to change and it will take you to the future. You follow that third eye into the seventh chakra of the world and sleep with it inside you. Ssshh, go to sleep now. I won't bother you anymore. Ssshhh...go to sleep. And then go listen to some music. That will relax you. You need to hear this music. Your soul is going to sing tonight. Listen for it. Close your eyes and listen. And the truth will be in a song.

(*Static. MINA's voice is gone.*)

OCTAVIO: I'll do it. I'll close my eyes. I'll listen, Mina. Why don't you ever stay?
I'd make room for you here in my—

(*There's a knock. FILOMENA enters dressed to kill and speaks through the door to OCTAVIO.*)

FILOMENA: Are you in there? Octo?
(*No answer.*)
I know you're in there, my love. Why don't you come out and we can get ready? I'm wearing my Alexander McQueen. The one you love with the cutouts. That matches your sandals. And helmet. You know you want to go out tonight. It's the full Worm Moon.

(*Aside*)

The birds will be back soon to eat all those earthworms and you'll love me again. I can smell it in the cold air.

(*To OCTAVIO*)
Please come out.

(*OCTAVIO opens the door and walks into the room.*)

OCTAVIO: Why do you always know where to find me?

FILOMENA: The scent of your bath water, lavender and thyme. It hurts my eyes sometimes.

OCTAVIO: I'll try to remember that.

FILOMENA: Our chariot awaits.

OCTAVIO: Will you let me hold it in the car?

FILOMENA: If you want. But I bandaged it all up—so it wouldn't show through the dress, so can you just cup it?

OCTAVIO: We'll see.
(*HE takes a small pen-knife out of his pocket.*)
I have this. It cuts through such things.

FILOMENA: You'll be careful.

OCTAVIO: (*Tracing the knife along her lips*) Always.

(*THEY exit to go to La Perla as the lights cross to PODEROSA'S dressing room.*)

SCENE SEVENTEEN-D
PODEROSA's dressing room.

PODEROSA: GANDULES! ARROZ! WHERE IS MY WHITE BUSTIER!

(*ARROZ enters wearing it.*)

ARROZ: Oh. Were you going to wear this old thing? It doesn't suit you. Red is your color. Or brown.

PODEROSA: Take that off now!

ARROZ: Okay.
(*HE does so.*)
But can I have it back after the show? I have a date—

(*PODEROSA slaps ARROZ. After a pause, ARROZ slaps her back. THEY slap each other back and forth until one of them backs down.*)
You're crazy, lady.

PODEROSA: Maybe. But I don't share my bustiers with anybody. Help me get into this.

(*SHE turns her back on him so HE can lace up her bustier.*)
Tighter.

(*HE pulls it tighter. SHE staggers because it's so tight.*)
That's it. I like when I can barely breathe. Perfect.

ARROZ: (*As HE exits.*) It looked better on me....

PODEROSA: Now the show can begin!! Get the carts, boys!

(*ARROZ con GANDULES each push a cart with a silver box on top of it, across the backstage area. THEY are following PODEROSA's every order.
There is the hum of a crowd in the audience behind the curtain. PODEROSA holds hands with each of them and stops to say a final prayer.*)

Holy Mercury, guide these boys to the seat of my power. Restore my soul and make me a woman again.

(SHE places each of their hands on her breasts.)
Let them feel these huge pledges of Heaven's favor.
Allelujah. Allelujah.

ARROZ con GANDULES: Allelujah!

(The curtain opens and the Nightclub show begins.)

SCENE EIGHTEEN
At PODEROSA's nightclub *La Perla*
It has been renovated and made magical. On one wall is a sea of genitalia, animatronic penises, vaginas, and breasts.
Like an adult version of the "It's a Small World," ride, there are patrons strewn about the club in gondolas, equipped with adult pleasuring devices and an intercom to order up pleasure partners or simply snack foods. ENCO and CYLVIO are seated
in a gondola, wiping off their hands and genitalia with a wet wipe. It's the opening night, and not everything works perfectly.

ENCO: I really am getting better at this.

CYLVIO: What's your criteria?

ENCO: Shooting distance for one.

CYLVIO: Volume is only a measure of how long it's been—not how good it is.

(PODEROSA enters in an outrageously revealing costume to open the show. As SHE sings, dancers/performers enact sexual acts of every kind.)

PODEROSA: Bienvenidos, mis compays y mis comays.
Tonight we'll have multiple trips—
kiss many lips—from tops to bottoms—
from head to sucking toes.
Tomorrow, you'll want to forget us—
But after one bite you cannot deny, mis compays
this is the way of this world.

(The music comes up—it is a strange hybrid of jazz, reggaeton and orchestral movie music. The dancers move in a grotesque form of burlesque, forming tableaux vivant of varied sex acts. The AUDIENCE snaps its fingers like it is at a beat poets coffee house event.)

ENCO: I wonder where Junior is?

CYLVIO: I wonder what he's putting on? He's the one who told me about this place.

ENCO: Really. Told you? Not me.
(*A Voluptuous Woman enters and kisses CYLVIO. HE attacks her breasts with his mouth.*)
Now that's something you've never had before.

CYLVIO: It's like swallowing—everything—you're not supposed to anymore.

ENCO: That's sweet. (*HE raises a hookah pipe that's built into the gondola.*) Want some more?
(*THEY both suck on the hookah.*)
I'm going to marry him. I know you're not supposed to marry servants, but I am completely enthralled by him. I imagine a line of dancers, like this one, following us, romping—

CYLVIO: Romping?

ENCO: Yes. Romping. Creating love and pleasure and oneness—

CYLVIO: What if he doesn't want you?

ENCO: Won't matter. A servant does what he's told.

CYLVIO: That doesn't sound like love.

ENCO: Love. Obsession. Possession.

CYLVIO: Good luck with that. He's the one with the upper hand. To be loved is to be strong and to love is weak, Enco. You know that. I know that.

ENCO: I only broke your heart a little.

CYLVIO: Where's that little piece now? My electrical circuits aren't complete.

ENCO: You don't trust me, do you?

CYLVIO: Of course not. You're my best friend.

ENCO: I feel like going again...

CYLVIO: Use this one. *(HE pulls out an enormous purple anal plug from a shelf in the gondola.)* It will take you to the Gods.

ENCO: Will you help me?

CYLVIO: Of course. I'm your best friend.

ENCO: Sshhhh! The show's about to begin.

CYLVIO and ENCO (*in unison*): I'm so excited!

(Lights come up fully on the Nightclub.)

SCENE EIGHTEEN-A
La PERLA nightclub.
The club is decorated like a giant spider web made of nautical knots and rope. There are puppet patrons and mostly human performers swinging from hammocks. It looks fun and dangerous. The show is about to begin. The music is neo-funk/punk. PODEROSA enters with ARROZ con GANDULES close behind her pushing two tables each holding a box covered in silk cloth. The music gets softer.
In the audience are ENCO and CYLVIO.

PODEROSA: Welcome devastated darlings! Sorry I was late but I had to—

(*SHE unties the cloth covering her animatronic bodice, revealing lips on her breasts. ARROZ con GANDULES pulls strings on her bodice that make a tongue stick out between the lips and THEY react like she's licking them.*)
—eat...didn't I?

(*To ARROZ con GANDULES*) That's enough. Go sit over there, boys.

(*THEY go.*)
Now, we can really talk...

(*SHE lifts the cloths off the boxes to reveal TULLIA and VITA's heads.*)
Go for it, ladies.

TULLIA: We have nothing to say.

VITA: Yeah. Eway avehay othingnay otay aysay, Itchbay!

PODEROSA: (*Pinching their faces hard*) Sooo...headstrong, you know. Maybe you could sing us something? (*Goading the audience for applause*)
What do you think people? Give them some love!

(*ENCO and CYLVIO applaud. ENCO's arms and neck are wrapped in bandages.*
CYLVIO pats his bandages with a white hanky where blood is seeping through.)

PODEROSA: I give you—Tullia and Vita—the singing cerebellums—Caput et faciem!

TULLIA and VITA (*Singing in unison*):
We once were whole and now we're heads,
That's how our story goes.
We had warm blood and now we're dead.
That's all our story shows.
If we were better at self-preservation—
We'd have escaped his perverse mutilation.
But we weren't, we didn't, we couldn't run—
His skill with his hands can't be outdone.

TULLIA (*Indicating VITA*): He ripped her.

VITA (*Indicating TULLIA*): He raped her.

TULLIA and VITA (*Pointing at each other with their lips*):
And then he had the nerve to asphyxiate her.
It wasn't a very good date. (*Spoken*) Non erat tempus ipsum.

(*ARROZ con GANDULES make the heads bow, as the next act enters. It is MALPUSO on his cross, still smoldering.*)

PODEROSA: That was lovely, girls. Don't you love those sister acts?! But now we have a big surprise for you, my sweet-meated voyeurs. The mostly extinct and somewhat ferocious of all Earthly species: CinderPoet.
(*MALPUSO tries to speak but ashes fly out of his mouth when he opens it.*)
Hmmm, there seems to be some technical diff—

MALPUSO: I'll speak! Let me speak! I have a song of love for you. (*HE sings beautifully.*)
Te quiero con esperanza, me muero de amor por ti.
Soy siempre tu macho, mi hembra, muchacha.
Animales mansos entre nosotros, bestias asquerosos con otros.
Pero tu y yo, juntos, somos como unas estrellas en los cielos—
Bellos—sin igual. Un llanto—sin respirar.
Quiero partirte hasta las nalgas, mi negra, hasta que la luna pasa delante del sol.

(ARROZ con GANDULES come and roll him off.)

PODEROSA: That was quite sweet, but a bit overwrought. Sheesh! Poets?! Am I right?! This next gal reminds me of myself when I was touring in Berlin with the Cirkus Fearkus of Victoria Espinoza de Santurce. She's sweet, she's hot and she's not for the faint of heart. Just wait till you feel the scorching flames of her desire. The incredible, the edible, and the highly flammable, Oenothea.

(OENOTHEA enters in a chariot of fire pulled by ARROZ con GANDULES in a chaos of sound including the sound of elephants trumpeting.)

OENOTHEA: Gentlefolk! Kind people of the last district of the last mountain in the last millennium. I need a volunteer from the audience. Don't be shy. This isn't a lame speculum up my coochie kind of act. Oh, no! This is the real chookie-chookie. Put it in and see what happens. Feel the warmth of my inner love! Who is man or woman enough to take the heat of my innards?!

(LUJURIA comes forward and begins to fist OENOTHEA. Sparks come flying from between her legs.)

PODEROSA: More fingers! More fingers! Just put the whole fist in there. And pull it out slowly...Yes! You see ladies and gentleman. Not a burn on her.

(ENCO and CYLVIO gasp. Lights dim on PODEROSA and brighten on them.)

ENCO: It's just simply miraculous—as in I want one.

CYLVIO: Really??

ENCO: I mean, as in I would like it in a different package—but the same. You know. Don't be obfuscational when I'm just trying to have a good time for a change. This week has been shit.

CYLVIO: I know, dear. Who tries to cut his own throat? That's unheard of, Enco. And with a pair of tweezers. That was just cray—

ENCO: I'm not crazy, Cyl. I just want to go before he gets me.

CYLVIO: No one is going to get you, dear. Well, you are due to be executed, but that's a whole village kind of thing…There's no "he."

ENCO: Who is it that comes into my study and rips all my paper vertically in half? What kind of madman cuts paper like that?

CYLVIO: Maybe somebody who likes lists? That long—

ENCO: And who is it that keeps knocking on my bedroom window? Leaving unctuous yellow fluids dripping down the pane?

CYLVIO: What if I said that was me?

ENCO: Why would you do that?

CYLVIO: I didn't say it was me, I just said what if…

ENCO: I'd never speak to you again, that's what. Was it you?

CYLVIO: …no…

ENCO: Seriously? You know how terrified I've been?!

(*Lights brighten on PODEROSA and the PATRONS; dim on ENCO and CYLVIO.*)

PODEROSA: (*Picks out a volunteer from the crowd with an enormous phallus*) You! Put it right in there!
(*PATRON places himself inside OENOTHEA and burns up like a firecracker.*)

ENCO and CYLVIO: Oh, yes! Bravo!

PODEROSA: Now remember, folks! You all signed an "I won't sue you" paper at the door. This club is dangerous. And that's how we like it, don't we?
(*The PATRONS scream approval.*)
All righty then.

(*Lights rise on CYLVIO and ENCO as the club action lights dim.*)

CYLVIO: I was just trying to get your mind off your troubles. Give you a little mystery to chew on. And I like watching you. But the torn paper is not me...<u>that</u> is spooky.

ENCO: It doesn't matter. This kitten's on his ninth life. Something will take soon. I saw it in my chart. Life-altering events are about to happen. Life-ending...

CYLVIO: Why do you believe that sputum?

ENCO: You do too. You are always saying what a perfect Scorpio you are—jealous, voraciously sexual and unkindly honest and handsome.

CYLVIO: That's true. But why do <u>you</u> believe it? You're a piss-poor Aquarian. There's nothing happy-go-lucky about you.

ENCO: There's so much more to us, Cyl. I hope Junior's on next.

CYLVIO: Me too.

ENCO: Will you stop wanting everything I have?

CYLVIO: I don't think so. Isn't that what friends do?

(*ARROZ con GANDULES do a sexy dance with twine and packing tape onstage as the lights cross to JUNIOR and LUJURIA backstage.*)

SCENE EIGHTEEN-B
JUNIOR's dressing room.
JUNIOR is putting on make-up to go on stage.
LUJURIA is looking for trouble.

JUNIOR: You're not supposed to be back here.

LUJURIA: Is that so?
(*SHE starts to comb his hair.*)

JUNIOR: You're the hairdresser?

LUJURIA: Maybe.

JUNIOR: Poderosa said you'd be early. It's late.

LUJURIA: I'm surprised our fucked up mother said anything at all about me.

(*Pause*)

JUNIOR: Ma said you'd help.

LUJURIA: Yes. That's what I'm doing. Do you ever use hairspray? I think it would help. Some hair can't be kept down with just conditioner.

JUNIOR: Why are you helping us now?

LUJURIA: Time had to be right. Without the right time there's a lot of broken watches shaped like hearts.

JUNIOR: Huh? You <u>are</u> crazy like she said.

LUJURIA: What else did she say?

JUNIOR: That you were just like me.

LUJURIA: I have better hair.

JUNIOR: I have the music though.
(*Singing/rapping*)
Flagellate, incorporate, syncopate, fate.
Dead down dog facing the Sun.
But it's behind you cause you hate.
Dead down dog facing the Sun—
It's just begun, Son. Don't be so hung, Son.
Gotta get it good on the karma tip.
Don't show your panties everywhere you slip.
Somebody always got something to say.
If not for tomorrow, then why not today.

(*HE kisses her. SHE wipes off the kiss. HE speaks.*)
Did you just throw up in my mouth a little? I like it.

LUJURIA: You taste like family.

JUNIOR: I know.

LUJURIA: He'll be here in two minutes. I put a tracer on his car. It's not as easy as—

JUNIOR: I know. Why didn't you do it already? Why did you wait for us?

LUJURIA: I needed to be sure. I needed time and I fell in love. That takes time too.

JUNIOR: Love always gets in the way...especially a father's love.

LUJURIA: Octavio's nice to me sometimes—but he doesn't know yet, who I really am. Maybe it's because I can kick his ass, but it makes me remember…there was a time when I wanted a father.

JUNIOR: Me too.

(*HE pulls string between his fingers.*)
Pick one.

(*SHE does. It makes a penis-like shape.*)
That means your firstborn will be a boy.

LUJURIA: I'm not having any children. They suck. They suck the life right out of you. Take all your body juices and turn them into a salty powder you can blow away over your left shoulder—right into Satan's eyes.

JUNIOR: You're scared to shrivel. I'm scared to melt.

LUJURIA: Together, we're almost human.

(*LUJURIA has pouf-ed JUNIOR's hair into a giant curl.*)
Now you look like something.

(*HE hands her a small knife. SHE tucks it into his hairdo.*)
That'll fit just fine.

JUNIOR: You're good at that.

LUJURIA: (*Pulling out a knife from her own hairdo*) I know. Right?!

(*Lights cross to OCTAVIO and FILOMENA in the car on the way to the club. FILOMENA is dozing. Her skirt is up around her waist and her pocketbook discreetly covers her privates. OCTAVIO is playing with the radio. After zipping through some static-ky orchestral Nino Rota-type music, MINA the METEOROLOGIST begins to speak to him through the radio.*)

MINA: It's Zulu time here at the WMO and Mina is back with your latest Convective Storm-cast from the SPC in Norman, Oklahoma. The Moon is gibbous in the hindquarters of that jackal Jupiter. So, we're expecting some Microbursts tonight over the Eastern side of the Mid-Atlantic. Advection fog predominates the homosapienic back door Cold Front approaching the region, accompanied by blowing dust, blowing sand, blowing snow and blowing spray increasing the probability of a bomb cyclone in the next 24 hours. The Coriolis Force of the Earth may prove too much for the Cyclonic rotation and may cause some massive decouple-ing this evening with the onset of Derechoes, Diamond Dust, and Dust Devils

OCTAVIO: What does it mean?

MINA: It means you're fucked, Octavio. The Combined Seas of 25 meters will sink the coast of any place you're near and the dust will make it hard to see when you fall into water that wasn't supposed to be there.
(*OCTAVIO begins to masturbate.*)
This Fujiwhara effect of storm collision will create tornadoes of F5 on the Fujita scale with multiple violent suction vortices. My advice is...What are you doing?

OCTAVIO: (*putting his penis away quickly*) I was...you know. It sounds bad so I thought—

MINA: So you thought you'd diddle yourself while the world explodes?

OCTAVIO: Yes.

MINA: That-a-boy! Remember it was me who tried to warn you. Keep listening in. You might not survive without me—at least you'll know what's coming—so to speak.

(*Lights cross to JUNIOR's dressing room.*)

SCENE EIGHTEEN-C
Backstage at the Club, in his dressing room, JUNIOR holds his head in his hands. TULLIA and VITA try to cheer him up.

TULLIA: Your sister's very strong-jawed.

VITA: Almost square. Like a melon—in a box. Like a square melon box.

JUNIOR: The hairdresser?

TULLIA: Vita, "Ixnay" on the "etaphormay"! The boy's up to no-good tonight—just how we like it.

VITA: Yeah. If we could hold him down for you, we would. But her I'd "arrymay." Did you know I had a beard once? I called her "father."

JUNIOR: Why are you talking to me?

VITA: We like you.

TULLIA: That's right. We like you.

JUNIOR: It sounds like it's that woman you like.

TULLIA: Humans aren't meant to hold their heads in their hands.

VITA: That's something you come to realize when you're just a head.

JUNIOR: My head's pounding.

VITA: That's the blood.

TULLIA: Rushing. Taking action. Aren't you sure?

JUNIOR: Something has to stop that sound. My mind's a record on skip. And each skip scratches it's long yellow fingernails on my brain.

VITA: I like acetabuproxen. For those kind of aches.

TULLIA: Fingernail pain is so hard to remove.

VITA: I have a theory. It's about singing. Opening your mouth wide and letting sound come out. Clearly. It helps.

TULLIA: Moves all those bugs around from the corners of your brain like the pieces of your eye that break off and become a part of your consciousness, always floating in front of them like a ghost of a reminder of a memory that you see for the rest of your life.

JUNIOR: It's telling me I'm almost done.

VITA and TULLIA (*in unison*): Ever-clay, oy-bay.

TULLIA: The secret is to never reach for your weapon until you're about to use it.

VITA: The secret is that once you reach for it, use it.

TULLIA: And once you use it you go as far as you can go.

VITA: There's no other option.

JUNIOR: (*Pause; HE sings.*)
"I have a purpose—I was told—
— when I was a little boy— I had a purpose.
A witch looked at me and erupted.
—a real witch who saw my darkness.
She took me in and spit me up—
like a bad piece of roast pork skin—
with a bristle of pig's hair

brushing your insides with its wrongness.
Not supposed to be in your mouth—that feeling. It's an omen.
(*Pause; HE continues singing.*)
I saw a black bird this morning, flying Southwest.
It passed an owl. On the right. It's an omen."

TULLIA and VITA (singing):
"That's so bad—like the blood after a shave.
That's so wrong—like the blood of a slave.
It's an omen. It's an omen.
It's an omen, men have watched for many centuries.
Where are the Sacred Chickens, Junior?
Where does he keep his fowl?
Feed them cake and if they eat all is well..."

JUNIOR:
"It's an omen. It's an omen.
My life is fucked—it's like Hell."

VITA and TULLIA:
"So far it sucked. It's an omen.
Wake up and smell your mother's hole.
Papa put his junk in and rusted out your soul.
That's the (s)cent that's five to the dollar—
A stank you've turned into a hollar."

JUNIOR:
"That war cry steals my breath from my mouth.
I can't live this North of South.
It's an omen."
(*Spoken*)
You have to keep an eye out before they come and make a home inside here.

(*THEY cover their eyes as birds' nest hats float in and settle on all three of their heads.*)

(*Lights cross to the back of OCTAVIO's limo.*)

SCENE EIGHTEEN-D
In the back of the limo,
OCTAVIO sleeps while FILOMENA speaks.

> FILOMENA: When I was a little girl, I had a doll covered in black feathers. Her name was Augurie. And she told me the future if I listened closely. She told me the earth would start to melt. That the Sun would get too close. She told me I should learn how to swim and fly, because it would be too hard to walk on earth anymore. There'd be no soil left.
> Nothing would grow anymore except under water. Babies would keep their gills and swim like fish—And eat each other the way fish do. She told me to prepare—To watch for the warnings. Mad men would run the government. Well, that's been going on for a while...then, I'd lose my most precious thing. That happened eleven days before I met you. When I lost Augurie, I didn't know which way to walk—forward or backward—and then...(*Strokes OCTAVIO's brow*)—she would never have approved of you. She was sweet like an angel. And she knew how to make people listen. She knew without ever saying a word. Except with her mind. She told me things were about to start sinking, hard things. She said someone would want to cut me, so I would be just a woman and so dismiss me, but I made it this far. With all my parts—oh, there's been a nick or two—but I stopped the bleeding—Augurie told me where to find the bandages—before she disappeared. I think I threw her into a fire while I was sleeping. I think I felt her feathers in the dark and thought she must be a tasty Capon—but she wasn't. In the morning, I found feathers sticking out of my mouth. Bad dreams can taste good sometimes. That's why you write them down—to read later—once you wash the white dust out of your eyes, the darkness is clear.
>
> (*SHE takes a small dagger out of OCTAVIO's inner breast pocket and puts it in a hidden pocket of her dress.*)
> We're almost there. I'll have to wake you soon and pretend to love you. Take your hand and smile demurely. Walk beside you, but one step behind, taking note of all the exits.

(*Pause*)
I think I have to take some more swimming lessons now. Put in some time at the pool. Before it all goes away. You don't know how to swim do you?

(*Kisses him.*)
Awaken, my love.
(*HE wakes with a start. And swings at her and she falls to the floor.*)

OCTAVIO: Why are you always sneaking up on me? Well?! Get up! We're here.

(*HE pulls her to her feet.*)
You're a disgrace...but...

(*HE kisses her.*)
You never pull away. I like that in a woman.

(*OCTAVIO puts on his crown as HE and FILOMENA make their way out of the car and into the club, the lights cross with them. PODEROSA is doing a mime act. It is terrible. SHE is pretending to be a dictator like Mussolini or Franco or Hitler or Trujillo or Castro or Bush—perhaps all six. ARROZ con GANDULES holds up flags of those countries to help the audience identify the dictators. The People are guessing and shouting out names.*)

THE PEOPLE: (*Dolphin-skinned puppets*) Mussolini! Franco! Hitler! Roosevelt! Buchanan! Castro! Thatcher! Bush! (*etc.*)

(*OCTAVIO and FILOMENA are seated center stage. The tables move slowly toward them, blocking their escape. Only FILOMENA notices. OCTAVIO is fascinated with the mime. And the décor. ENCO and CYLVIO try to be invisible in their seats sinking low and pulling their collars up.*)

FILOMENA: I think we should leave, Octo. Something's not right.

OCTAVIO: You are so boring, Fila. WE are the country. We have to represent. Fun! Attention! Intellect! Sex! The people want it all from us!

FILOMENA: I know...

(*ARROZ con GANDULES shoo off PODEROSA with a giant dildo filled with foam. THEY chase her off and JUNIOR come on dressed like his father. OENOTHEA and LUJURIA enter and stand behind OCTAVIO and FILOMENA seeming to be guarding them.*)

OCTAVIO: You see! We're safe.
(*Pause*)
Oh, this is going to be delightful. He's a handsome young man. He will be someone important one day. Watch. He came by the house the other day. With string or rope or something. These show people are so resourceful. Amerika would be nothing without them. They do so much with so little.

JUNIOR: (*Sings*)
"I never had a father, but I had a man inside me.
He spoke to me with silent screams—
I knew he had to look to see.
The son he brought into this world, the dark boy with the dark curls."

(*TULLIA and VITA are pushed on by ARROZ con GANDULES.*)
Unwanted but undercover of night
Crept back to him to shed some light."

TULLIA and VITA: (*Singing*)
"He has no wife. He has a knife.
He has a knife. But where's his life."

OCTAVIO: I like this song.

FILOMENA: Of course you do...

OENOTHEA: *(Whispering)* I'd like to have a wife.

LUJURIA: Jesus. Will you relax?!

JUNIOR: (*Sings*)
"I used to think he'd come for me.
In the night, I'd dream of him.
That the day would begin again
And I would wait and see—"

(*PODEROSA comes out to listen to JUNIOR's song.*)

PODEROSA: (*An aside*) Ese mojon de mi coño siempre tiene que joder conmigo como un ojo de culo. Shucks! He never had it that bad—he had me.

TULLIA and VITA and ARROZ con GANDULES: (*Sing*)
"But he never came to Junior's bed—
He never stroked poor Junior's head.
But now he can sing about it
And no one can ever doubt it."

JUNIOR: (*Sings*)
"A father was all I ever wanted in a man.
A man was all I thought he'd be,
But he'd look a lot like me…"

PODEROSA: Thank you, Junior. What a depressing song! Wasn't it folks?

OCTAVIO: I liked it. Come here, boy.

(*JUNIOR goes to him.*)
I'd like you to sit right here. On my knee and whisper something in my ear. Something about the weather. It's been so strange.

(*JUNIOR sits in his lap. OCTAVIO pulls JUNIOR's head to his own, as HE does so, HE finds the knife hidden in JUNIOR's hair*

and pulls it slowly out. As HE pulls out the knife, the OTHERS pull out their knives.)
Oh. That's the plan.

(*FILOMENA stabs OCTAVIO as HE is about to stab JUNIOR.*)

FILOMENA: Stop it!

OCTAVIO: Mina warned me. She said someone I loved would free me.

(*OCTAVIO collapses. The OTHERs rush to see. THEY prod him to see if HE's truly dead and then THEY stare at FILOMENA.*)

(*Since THEY were all ready to stab OCTAVIO, THEY all have knives out. JUNIOR turns to FILOMENA.*)

JUNIOR: Thank you...I think.

ENCO: Is she the Presidemperor now?

CYLVIO: I think so.

PODEROSA: Blah, blah. You were supposed to get him, Junior. All those plans and you let his woman do your deed for you?! It was never going to be easy, but this is just an embarrassment don't you think?
(*JUNIOR takes the knife from OCTAVIO's body and stabs his mother.*)
Okay...I see where you went with this...all these years and I didn't see it coming.
Holy Mercury, where are you now?

(*PODEROSA dies.*)

LUJURIA: Thea, will you marry me?

OENOTHEA: Is this the—?

(*Pause*)
Yes.

FILOMENA: I'm a certified Justice of the Peace. Please join hands.
(*LUJURIA and OENOTHEA join hands.*)

(*ENCO begins to sob.*)

ENCO: Can you believe it, Cyl? I'm not dying anymore.

CYLVIO: The brides are so beautiful.

(*ENCO and CYLVIO hold hands. JUNIOR, ARROZ and GANDULES hold hands. TULLIA and VITA have no hands. THEY bite a strand of each other's hair instead. FILOMENA says a silent prayer over the brides. JUNIOR hands the brides a piece of red string to hold between them.*)

ENCO: The woman behind the man always carries the sharpest knife.

CYLVIO: Indeed.

(*FILOMENA cuts the string between LUJURIA and OENOTHEA. THEY are married. Applause. The animatronic walls vibrate. JUNIOR speaks.*)

JUNIOR: It wasn't how I imagined it—but it seems right.
(*JUNIOR hands FILOMENA the crown that OCTAVIO was wearing.*)
A Puerto Rican Woman President.

FILOMENA: Your parents should have been so proud…

JUNIOR: I came from a black pearl of an island.
That is the only jewel I ever needed.

MALPUSO: This can't happen.

(EVERYONE except JUNIOR suddenly lunges forward reaching for the crown as FILOMENA backs away from the crowd. Then, the lights come up brightly on the audience. Blackout.)

The End for now...

Satyricoño

TWO ROBERTS:
A PIRATE-BLUES PROJECT

TWO ROBERTS

This play was commissioned by the Lark Play Development Center, John C. Eisner, producing director and Megan Monaghan, artistic program director, 2009.

Special thanks to Sra. Marta DeValle Quintana, Elisa Bocanegra, Suzy Fay, Candido Tirado, and the actors from the first reading at the Lark: Felix Solis, Joshua Torres, Stacy Osei-Kuffour, Jeffrey Joseph, Bobby Plasencia, Anna Lamadrid, Liza Fernandez, Christopher Shyam Kerson, and Emma Ramos.

Dedicated to my mother, Gregoria Miranda Cruz and her nose.

"When I leave this town
I'm 'on' bid you fare... farewell
And when I return again
You'll have a great long story to tell"
FROM "FOUR UNTIL LATE" BY ROBERT JOHNSON
This memorial marker is placed at the base of this
old pecan tree as was Robert Johnson himself, prior
to his burial nearby...in accordance with the account
of eye-witness Mrs. Rose Eskridge, as told to historian Stephen C. LaVere

—Engraving on a monument marking Robert Johnson's final resting place (one of three supposed resting places around Greenwood, MS, each with its own marker) in Little Zion Missionary Baptist Church on Money Road, on the edge of Greenwood, MS—

CAST OF CHARACTERS:

ROBERTO—34, a 19th Century pirate from Cabo Rojo, the SW coast of Puerto Rico, Ambitious, generous, brutal, an adventurer and seducer of women.

ROBERT—27, a 20th Century Blues singer from Hazlehurst, the Delta region of Mississippi, Ambitious, talented, innovative, an adventurer and seducer of women.

SOPHRONIA—25, Roberto's lover, a fisherman's daughter from Joyuda, P.R., mixed blood—European, African, Taino. Practical. Skilled at fishing. Likes dirty jokes. A jibara, salt-of the-earth type. Fond of sayings (dichos).

SOFIE—35, Robert's lover, an African-American dwarf, born in Itta Bena, MS near Greenwood but now runs a motel in West Helena, Arkansas. Sassy, sarcastic. A fighter. Knows what and who she wants. A free spirit who loves making love and likes to be watched.

WILLIE—27, African-American, Robert's best friend and traveling companion. Plays guitar, harmonica, and sings. Likes playing back-up, not lead. Loves Count Basie and likes to sing Bing Cosby songs. Born in Clarksdale, MS. Smooth, handsome, a little dangerous. A ladies' man. Risk-taker. Jokester.

WILFRED—33, Puerto Rican, Roberto's pirate crew member, his ship's doctor, from Mayagüez, P.R. Aristocratic, gay on the down-low. In love with Roberto. Likes to shock and terrify. Has an African Gray Parrot that goes everywhere with him.

EPIFANI THE DEVIL-GAL—30s, Interested in architecture, infrastructure, a builder, a shape-shifter. A lover of books. Plays various other humans, like Lil, Robert's lover just before his death, and Maria Germana, Roberto's mother.

CORNELIUS THE DEVIL-GUY—30s, Interested in 1970s fashion, games of chance, a destroyer, a shape-shifter. A lover of music. Plays various other humans, like Lil's husband, and Virginia, Robert's wife.

NOTES:

Roberto Cofresí—(June 17, 1791-March 29, 1825) A 19th Century pirate from Cabo Rojo, the Southwest coast of Puerto Rico, born of an Austrian-Italian father and a Puerto Rican mother, died at 34. He and his band of men outsmarted the United States, Spanish and English Navies for seven years or so, until the Spaniards decided to help the Americans stop him. Considered the "Robin Hood" of Puerto Rico, because he shared his booty with the poor people of Cabo Rojo who helped shield him. Supposedly sold his soul to the Devil so he could outmaneuver any ship and score with the ladies. A statue of him in Boqueron Bay simply states his name. His nose is strikingly similar to my mother's nose, also a native of Cabo Rojo, Puerto Rico.

Robert Johnson— (May 8, 1911-August 16, 1938) A 20th Century Blues singer/composer from Hazlehurst in the Delta region of Mississippi, born illegitimate from an African-American farmhand father and a migrant farm worker mother with ten children from a previous marriage to a prosperous wicker furniture maker, died at 27. His acoustic blues on slide guitar—an essential contribution to the Blues— is the direct precursor to rock 'n' roll. Robert Johnson is known as the "Grandfather of Rock." He played professionally for seven years or so, until a jealous husband of one of his lovers poisoned his whiskey. He supposedly sold his soul to the Devil so he could out play any musician and score with the ladies.

- Roberto Cofresí's schooner was called the "Ana." This is the one he was finally captured from by the combined US/Spanish forces, leading to his execution.
- His first small boat was called "El Mosquito."
- Robert Johnson's guitar did not have a name anyone remembers, but he supposedly sold his soul at a "Crossroads." A crossroads in the South could be the place where two railroad tracks meet.
- In England, criminals were buried at crossroads, because many roads confuse the dead. In Santeria, it is a place where offerings are left for the Gods.

- Many famous musicians from all over the world and from many different eras are said to have sold their souls at a crossroads for their musical abilities.
- A jook (juke) joint is a roadhouse with mainly liquor, some food, where workers go to unwind on the weekends after a long hard week's work. Jook joints were popular in the Mississippi Delta of the 1930s.

This play is about two men very much like Robert and Roberto.

LANGUAGE NOTE:

The African-Americans speak with the Hazlehurst/Greenwood, Mississippi area dialect from the 1930s. I have tried to reproduce some of that dialect, but I welcome the actors' interventions in sound and cadence.
And the Puerto Ricans speak with an early 19th Century flourish and an island speed that the actor can make their own.
Actors: please adjust to your natural accents and cadence.

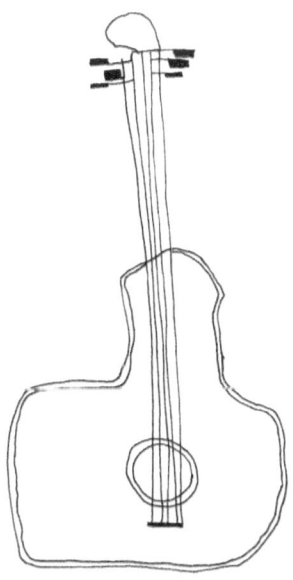

TIME:

The near future in an afterlife.

PLACE:

A deserted island, filled with abandoned jook joints. A crossroads. Two railroad tracks. Betwixt and Between.

PROLOGUE:
On a beach.
In the dark, we hear the sound of a raging storm that segues into the sound of a blade being sharpened against a whetstone. A light comes up on a fight-scarred ROBERTO, sharpening the blade of a cutlass or machete. He speaks to the lifeless body of the man HE has recently hacked (CORNELIUS). HE is stained with blood—his and the other man's.

ROBERTO: Hear that?
(Sound of the wind kicking up)
That's the sound of dull steel turning to gold. Ready to pierce the entrails of a man richer than me, whom I will prick, rip, enter and gore—and then I'll rob him.

(Pause; as HE enjoys that sharpening sound.)
I've heard it said that robbing a man after death is bad luck. His hair falls out. His penis shrivels. He loses all his money. And his women betray him. But I have never felt any of those ill effects.

(HE drinks from a jar filled with red liquid. HE studies the jar, turning it over in his hands. HE holds the jar out to the dead man.)
I found this in your cabin. Fair size. Well-proportioned. Good for keeping things. Holds a fine libation. Thank you, dear corpse. You were lucky I used my long blade on you.

(HE returns to his sharpening.)
I have my shorter blades forged into triangular points so that no

surgeon can ever sew that gushing wound closed. Slowly, and in great agony, after perhaps, three weeks of suffering, finally, a very rich man will die—but that's never mattered to me. All that concerns me is that his seaward possessions become mine—half for me. A quarter for my men. And the last quarter for my country—well an eighth anyway. Add this last extra bit to my collection. I am a patriot—a man who stands for something. That hidden eighth will one day make my daughters rich. I will only have daughters.

(Pause)
I always sharpen my own blade—always take charge of my own destiny.

(Pause, as HE cuts out the tongue of his enemy and places it in the red-liquid jar.)
There. Sharper blade. Faster work.

(HE swirls the stuff in the jar and stares at the floating mess.)
When you live by water, all liquids seem like home.

(ROBERTO freezes in place as a light comes up on ROBERT. HE is in the midst of replacing a string on his guitar. HE has just removed all the strings and is polishing the neck and fret board. HE speaks to the passed-out WOMAN [LIL played by EPIFANI], he has gotten dead-drunk.)

ROBERT: You too crazy, Lil. I'm puttin' your name in one of momma's Good-Bye Bottles. You got to keep away from me, gal. Look at you there—gone to a place what smells like your own spit. I can't be wit that. Yeah, that's how it's gonna be. You ain't gonna see me no more. You don'gotta go sniffin'round me for trouble no more. Uh, uhhnn.

(Pause, as HE takes a jar from inside his guitar case that appears to be the same jar ROBERTO had. He shakes it, swirling the stuff inside.)
My momma told me that to make people run crazy and keep

them away from her door, her granma would put some chopped-up dark red onion, into a bottle, add some Four Thieves Vinegar, and then put that person's name in the bottle. I found two of those bottles floating in the river by our house once—an'I opened them up—jus' to see whose name was inside.

(HE opens the jar and takes a long drink. CORNELIUS enters as LIL's husband. HE waves goodbye as ROBERT drinks.)
Mmmm. Your husbeen got good taste in whiskey anyways.

(Takes another long drink.)
And don'you know?! Inside those old jars was my name on a piece of lace. In both jars mind you. I thought about what to do. I figured if I drank it then it might lose its power. Never could tolerate onions much but this tasted more like flowers. That's when it started though. My good luck—from that day on...and I also come to find that vinegar-onion stuff is good for cleaning the neck of my guitar. Musta had some kind of oil in it too 'cause it polishes up nice. Works well. Hoodoo. Momma kept a big jar of that vinegar in her cupboard and she'd drink it when she felt sick and it would clear everything up. Tole me that besides the red onion, it had lavender, sage, hummingbird mint, some other spices, plus a handful of garlic cloves all blended with apple cider vinegar. You let it sit at room temperature in a cool place for six weeks and then—I feel sick.

(Lights come back on ROBERTO now dressed in Pirate finery. We hear the sound of a firing squad as both ROBERT and ROBERTO fall to the ground dead. EPIFANI and CORNELIUS rise as THEY fall. THEY watch ROBERT and ROBERTO in silence for a moment. THEY strip away their 1930's clothes and have modern looking Alexander McQueen-esque clothes underneath.)

EPIFANI: The truth overtakes them.

CORNELIUS: Bet a little. Lose a little. *(Pause)*
Funny how some things seem random but they're not.

EPIFANI: Like names—of chance...names floating in the water. I do like the old magic.

CORNELIUS: People took it more seriously, didn't they, Piff.

EPIFANI: Yes, Neely, they did. Fear and longing used to mingle. And now that we have them both, I think the magic may begin again...this was such a good idea...

CORNELIUS: You think they know.

EPIFANI: Not yet.

(EPIFANI and CORNELIUS kneel on the ground. Sand appears at their feet. THEY pat it into their hands as if THEY are making snow/sandballs, then they rub their faces with the sand, like it is soap they are using to wash their face. As THEY do this, a ship appears on the horizon, and the sound of a raging storm resumes. Lights cross to ROBERT and ROBERTO lying face down in the sand. Their lower halves are in the water. ROBERT is wearing a 1930s style pin-striped double-breasted dress suit with wide lapels; his guitar is strapped on his back with twine. ROBERTO is dressed like an 1820s pirate. ROBERTO comes to first and pulls ROBERT all the way out of the water. ROBERT wakes up as ROBERTO pulls him out.)

ROBERT: I can't breathe.

ROBERTO: Spit out the sand.

ROBERT: How—?

ROBERTO: A shipwreck.

ROBERT: What the hell was I doing on a ship?! One minute I'm in my bed with the worse stomach cramps ...and then...there ain't no water there.

ROBERTO: Were you dying?

ROBERT: Felt like it...What are you supposed to be? A movie actor?

ROBERTO: A Privateer.

ROBERT: A private what?

ROBERTO: A pirate.

ROBERT: That's the goddamnedest thing I ever heard. I died and went to a pirate ship. Sheeet!

ROBERTO: None of this makes sense...I thought you'd be different.

ROBERT: Who do you think I am?

ROBERTO: An angel—or a ghost.

ROBERT: Oh...An angel would know how to swim. The water just carried me here by itself. And a ghost wouldn't haint hisself, would he?

ROBERTO: This is a test.

ROBERT: This is a joke.

ROBERTO: No, this isn't funny.

ROBERT: There's plenty jokes not funny...What's perfect pitch? Throwing a banjo on top of a guitar attached to a negro.

ROBERTO: I don't understand.

ROBERT: *(Holding up his guitar)*
Me neither.

ROBERTO: Where are we? Where are my men? Are they all...

ROBERT: I only have one real friend. And I never take a trip without him.

ROBERTO: He missed this one.

ROBERT: Some things you have to do alone...

ROBERTO: In my country, you would attach the guitar to a pirate.

ROBERT: I don't care to know anything else about you. I'm leaving soon.

ROBERTO: Good.
(THEY sit in silence for a moment.)
Me too.

(Pause; to himself out loud)
What is this place? They should have just shot me like they said they would. Marooning a sailor is worse than death. But I know these seas. I will find a way to sail out of here...the storm's moving.

(The sound of the storm begins to retreat into the distance.)

ROBERT: It's stopping.

ROBERTO: Storms don't stop. They change location.

ROBERT: How long do you think it will take them to find us?

ROBERTO: You think someone is looking?

ROBERT: I'll be missed for sure. I had a gig in Greenwood on Saturday.
Got one bottle of pre-payment.

ROBERTO: I was supposed to be shot on Saturday. My body hung in El Morro for 24 hours and then they were going to bury me somewhere outside the cemetery gates.

ROBERT: And today is...?

ROBERTO: Lost track of time.

ROBERT: Just like us...lost.

(Searches through his pockets and finally finds a bottle of whiskey. HE uncorks the unopened bottle, takes a swig. ROBERTO takes it.)

ROBERTO: Is that what we are?
(Takes a swig and puts the bottle in his own pocket.)

ROBERT: *(Extending his hand)*
Excuse me?

ROBERTO: *(Ignoring ROBERT's request for the bottle.)*
What if we're not lost?

ROBERT: *(Putting on a mock church voice)*
"Oh, laws, we's found! Thank the Lord Almighty, we is found!"
Gimme back my bottle.

ROBERTO: *(Tossing ROBERT down into the sand and standing over him)*
Will you squeak, bilge-sucking American rat!

ROBERT: Get offa me. What the hell..!?

ROBERTO: Demon. Defiler. Thief.

ROBERT: Me? No.
(Indicating his guitar)
This is me.

TWO ROBERTS

ROBERTO: Americans are clever. They take many shapes. But I'm never fooled. Why should I let you live? Do you know to whom you speak? I am he. The most feared man in the Caribbean. Tell me why you're following me and I'll spare you the mouth pear.

ROBERT: I'm not foll'ing—I don't even—

ROBERTO: I could drown you in your own blood puddle, you chuckle-headed fool.

ROBERT: I don't know what you're saying. I just play music.

ROBERTO: That's your answer. Music? You must be insane. *(Pause as HE relaxes his hold on ROBERT a little)*
I do, usually, spare the insane…Alright then, today I'll spare your life in the name of my people. I'm nothing if not generous and good-hearted. Some call me their Robin Hood. Man of the People. Irresistible to women. Ruthless murderer.

ROBERT: Me too. Irresistible, I mean.

ROBERTO: Maybe that's the reason we're here together.

ROBERT: The beach of all fine male specimens. So where are all the ladies?

ROBERTO: Must have taken a different boat. My name is Roberto.

ROBERT: I uh? Really? Me too. Robert.
(ROBERTO pulls ROBERT to his feet by one arm.)

ROBERTO/ROBERT: We *(Simultaneously, still grasping each other)* Robert/Roberto.

(THEY release their hold on each other as the lights follow the storm to another side of the island.)

ACT I: SCENE ONE

An island beach at the tail end of a hurricane.

Two women wander the wreckage of a 19th Century Schooner called the "Ana." Hanging from the starboard side of the ship, we see a small boat, labeled "El Mosquito." Hanging from the port side, we see a small guitar-shaped boat labeled "Crossroads." One woman is dressed in 1820s style and the other 1930s. We hear a tinny recording of "Come On In My Kitchen" by Robert Johnson, that is orchestrated/manipulated in a way to evoke the feeling of a hurricane.

> *[Sung]*
> *"Mmm... you better come on in my kitchen babe,*
> *it's goin' to be rainin' outdoors*
> *The woman I love, took from my best friend*
> *Some joker got lucky, stole her back again*
> *You better come on in my kitchen babe,*
> *it's goin' to be rainin' outdoors*
> *Oh, she's gone, I know she won't come back*
> *I've taken the last nickel out of her nation sack*
> *You better come on in my kitchen, baby,*
> *it's goin' to be rainin' outdoors*
> *[Spoken] Oh, can't you hear that wind howl?"*

SOPHRONIA and SOFIE: *(Shouting into the wind)*
Roberto/Robert!

> *(Recording continues)*
> *"Can't you hear that wind howl?*
> *You better come on in my kitchen, baby,*
> *it's goin' to be rainin' outdoors*
> *When a woman gets in trouble, everybody throws her down*
> *Lookin' for her good friend, none can't be found*
> *You better come on in my kitchen, baby,*
> *it's goin' to be rainin' outdoors*
> *Winter time's comin', it's goin' to be slow*
> *You can make the Winter, babe, that's dry long so*
> *You better come on in my kitchen,*
> *'cause it's goin' to be rainin' outdoors."*

TWO ROBERTS

(The women, SOPHRONIA, in 1820s attire, and SOFIE, in 1930s attire, search frantically in the storm, under the broken masts, and fallen sails— a dance of mass hysteria, mourning, desperation. Then suddenly, the wind begins to die down and THEY speak but cannot hear one another.)

SOPHRONIA and SOFIE: ROBERT/O...
(Overlapping, SOPHRONIA in Spanish/SOFIE in English)
He's not coming back./¿Adondé puede estar?

(Simultaneously)
My love./Mi corazón.

(Overlapping)
I can smell the sweat on his soft neck. / El viento me lo trae.
(*THEY can now see and hear each other. THEY try to make sense of it all.)*

SOFIE: I knew he'd be taken one day. S'what happens when you love too many women.

SOPHRONIA: He could have just been with me. I would have made him happy.

SOFIE: He made <u>me</u> happy. That's all I know.

SOPHRONIA: You? ¿Cómo se dice "señora" en japonés? Ta usao (Esta usado).

SOFIE: You better not be talkin' about me—like you're so somethin' or uther, with that squeaky little bird voice.

SOPHRONIA: Había un hombre que vendía un loro que estaba alegre y jodiendo la vida. Y un día se acerca una vieja y le dice " ¿Que hace de especial este loro?" "Pues si le jala la pata derecha habla español y si le jala la izquierda habla inglés." La vieja pregunta "¿Y si le jalo las dos a la misma vez?" El loro contesta: "¡ Me caigo, imbecil!"

SOFIE: What you sayin'? Pata? That's leg right? And somefin' about a parrot?
(SOPHRONIA looks surprised that SOFIE understood.)
An innkeeper needs to know things.

(From the port side of the deck appears EPIFANI the Devil-Gal. SHE is dressed to make an impression in a combination of 19th Century and 21st Century clothing.)

EPIFANI: It's not just about a parrot.

SOFIE: It's about us, isn't it—with our legs all pulled out from unter us. And that's not funny. I never laugh at anything about legs. Well, maybe, chicken legs. Chicken legs are funny. Human legs—no—they are not.
(pause)
I need a stepladder. Cain't look over the railin' even. How'll I ever find my true love?

SOFIE and SOPHRONIA: *(In unison; a prayer)*
Let him find me.

(THEY sit on the deck of the ship as it begins to storm again. THEY pull a ripped sail over their heads.)

SOPHRONIA: His breath in the wind—

SOFIE: —his taste in my tears.

SOPHRONIA: His touch released from the small of my back as I awaken.
And his heartbeat—

SOFIE: —throbbing at my temples.

SOPHRONIA: Y ahora lo sé—que estoy metida con él.

SOFIE: I drowned that first day I saw him.

EPIFANI: When you live by water, you learn not to fear it. But that's always a mistake.

(A strong gust of wind blows the sail away. The WOMEN are left sitting unprotected in the storm. Lights cross to the MEN: WILLIE, dressed in 1930s attire, WILFREDO, dressed in 1820s attire, and CORNELIUS, dressed in the clothing of 1970s soul icon Don Cornelius—probably a patchwork suede suit in different shades of brown. THEY are trying to hold onto the sail.)

WILFREDO: Don't let go! We'll never be able to move out of this storm without it.

WILLIE: Sheet! What the Sheet! I don'—what. I don't know about sail ships. What the hell is this? C'mon. There ain't no sail ships in Mississippi. A paddle boat or something maybe—an old row boat. But what is this?! I thought I was taking a bus to Naw'lins. Where'd you book us this time, Robert? Goddammit.

CORNELIUS: It's a schooner. Super-bad, huh? A two or more masted fore and aft rigged vessel with a foremast and a main mast stepped nearly midships with the main mast generally taller than the foremast. Can you dig it?

WILLIE: Oh. Why din't you say so? A Schooner. What the hell am I doing on a schooner??

WILFREDO: What else is there? It's the only way to get there. Where he is. I never should have left his side. They could have taken him anywhere. Dropped him on any island. The Caribbean is full of them. Just a pitiful spit of sand with three days' worth of water. He'll die if we don't find him soon.

WILLIE: I think we got different goals here—

CORNELIUS: We're here.

(The wind stops blowing. The rain dies down. THEY now see that they are on a beach. THEY look around in the sudden silence and then jump down onto the sand from the deck of the ship.)

WILLIE: This do not look like Naw'lins.

WILFREDO: *(Calling)*
Roberto! Roberto!

WILLIE: Robert, where you hidin'?! C'mon now. Let's close our eyes and get back on that bus. We've come out of wurst nightmares than this. Remember Iowa?

CORNELIUS: Maybe you'll both find what you're looking for...maybe not.
(HE picks up a piece of rope from the sand, ties it into a nautical knot like a Rolling Hitch around his own waist.)
We're here. Thirsty?

(CORNELIUS holds the end of the rope out to WILLIE and WILFREDO who do not take it. CORNELIUS shrugs and begins to do a "Soul Train" walk toward a dilapidated jook joint trailing the rope behind him like a snake. After a time, WILLIE and WILFREDO follow. SOFIE, SOPHRONIA and EPIFANI approach the jook joint from the opposite direction.)

EPIFANI: Almost there, ladies.

SOPHRONIA: Why are we following you?

SOFIE: Yes. Why?

EPIFANI: Only one place to go and two men to look for...

SOFIE and SOPHRONIA: Oh...

(SOFIE and SOPHRONIA exchange a look as lights cross to ROBERT and ROBERTO.)

246

I: SCENE TWO-A

Sunset on the beach.
ROBERTO puts the finishing touches on the enormous ship HE has built out of sand and driftwood. ROBERT strums his guitar. ROBERTO shakes his bangle-laden arm like it is a percussion instrument.

> ROBERT: I never told no one this before. Before today, I had no reason to. Didn't wanna lose track of the women I left behind, so I made a notch on my thigh for each one. My legs are looking like the bark of an old oak tree. So many rings. The ladies ask me about it, but I just say that's where my momma used to hit me with a switch. They like those kind of stories.

> ROBERTO: Hmmm...my women like giving me these.
> *(Shaking his arm to make his bangles jingle.)*
> I have a bangle on my arm from each one of my ladies. Each fine piece of slim silver or gold reminds me that I am longed for. Missed. Someone is waiting for me on the other side. They are. I know it.

> *(HE shakes his arm again.)*
> A gypsy siren call...

> ROBERT: This here is how I get the women.
> *(Plays an open "G" on the guitar)*
> Spanish tuning. I got it from the Sears and Roebuck instruction manual that came wit the guitar: 'How to Play the Spanish Fandango." We all learned that way. Wit that song, I mean. I found a copy in the shed behind my stepfather's house. Lula Mae McNair went back there with me once and I showed her my Spanish tuning up close.

> ROBERTO: Women do appreciate a man with certain talents.
> *(Pause; as HE hacks off pieces of driftwood from the "ship" with his machete.)*
> The music is entertaining, but it would be a very good idea for you to help me with this.

ROBERT: Really?
(ROBERTO looks at ROBERT while continuing to hack at pieces of wood.)
So...what do you want me to do?

ROBERTO: I'm done for now. But next time, I'd like some help. A man needs his brotherhood. A man alone becomes envenomed by his own work if he doesn't share it.

(HE flips his machete into the sand by ROBERT and throws himself at ROBERT to admire his "ship.")
Ships are like sweet young maidens who let you make all sail and luff into the wind.

ROBERT: I like the old ones—make a good living and don't mind sharing it with the right man.

ROBERTO: I like short ones. Less demanding on the neck and shoulders.

ROBERT: I really like the ones with big behinds and small breasts. Not sure why. Behinds are necessary.

ROBERTO: I like both. I like to bite them. I was called a savage more than once. In a good way.

ROBERT: I was always a gentleman. That's why the married ones really liked me. Men don't have time to be nice to their wives. Girlfriends are so demanding.

ROBERTO: But I was closest with my men. I killed for them and them for me. Tying men on the deck was Wilfredo's idea, but it was effective. I always let my men decide on the torture. It gave them something to look forward to. And we only tortured the ones who had killed one of us. I let the innocent live. Always. That part of the story, no one tells.

ROBERT: *(ROBERT looks at ROBERTO and plays a chord in open "G.")*
Hear that? Don't gotta do no killin' if you got them thrillin'...

ROBERTO: Who are you supposed to be?

ROBERT: Just a songster. A musicianer.

ROBERTO: Still not an angel?

ROBERT: Nuh-uhah. They play harps. I used to play Jew's harp, but that ain't the same thing. Just passing through, I think.

ROBERTO: I've been waiting a long time to pass through. I've been close to death so many times that I've made friends with it. We play cards—in my head, death and me. And I keep winning. I'm waiting to lose. I close my eyes and slowly squeeze them open to narrow slits to see if I can peek at her. She's gorgeous.

ROBERT: Death's a woman?

ROBERTO: Of course. Luscious. Round. A waist made for my hands to fit securely in that place between her hips and her back. Another place above her sex and below her stomach where I can rest my head. Perfectly. But if I open my eyes, she disappears. Have you ever played cards in the dark like that? Letting death hold you?

ROBERT: I do like a good game of stud poker.

(ROBERT plays a Spanish Fandango as ROBERTO listens. This music brings ROBERTO into a scene from his past.)

I: SCENE TWO-B

On the deck of the ship in a storm. A bloody WILFREDO is holding and rocking ROBERTO's bloody and bruised body.

> WILFREDO: (*HE sings a song into ROBERTO's ear. Though not in the memory, ROBERT's guitar seems to accompany WILFREDO's song. Should be a love ballad, Jíbaro-style.*)
> Leró, leró, leró
> De mi leró
> Pa poder "tiburiar"
> Que vengan las parejas
> Toditas a bailar
> Con Roberto Cofresí
> Que vengan a bailar
> Con Roberto Cofresí.
>
> ROBERTO: Que me van a matar.
>
> WILFREDO (*Gently with relief*)
> So...decided to stay with us a while longer, Captain? I was afraid—
>
> ROBERTO: You were afraid, Wilfredo?
>
> WILFREDO: I mean—
>
> ROBERTO: Me too. Those Spaniards know how to kick ass.
>
> WILFREDO: I wasn't afraid of that.
> (*Pause; WILFREDO helps ROBERTO drink water.*)
> You don't always need to be the first on deck.
>
> ROBERTO: I like knowing that you're all at my back. That's how I float. Suspended in your trust.
>
> WILFREDO: Pretty speech. What a loyal crew you must have. Six jumped overboard. Three are in worse shape than you. And you are truly fucked my captain. Do you think you can walk?

ROBERTO: So that leaves ten of you. A good number. Can still crew a ship. You're the captain now—and the surgeon.

WILFREDO: No. You'll always be the Captain—but this surgeon is sending you to bed. And then I'll see if I can save that foot. You stepped on one of those French tossers—with the spikes.
That's when the giant Moor with the axe caught up to you.

ROBERTO: Did you kill him?

WILFREDO: What do you think?

ROBERTO: Good.
(Pause)
By yourself?

WILFREDO: No.

ROBERTO: Less impressive.

WILFREDO: Daniel took a blow for you. And Mauricio. And Timoteo.

ROBERTO: Are they dead?

WILFREDO: Not yet.
(Pause; ROBERTO closes his eyes.)
Don't do that.

ROBERTO: Did we get their gold?

WILFREDO: Oh, yes. All of it. And five barrels full of smoked fish. Very tasty. Like bacalao, but even saltier.

ROBERTO: I hate fish.

WILFREDO: Really? A sailor—who lives on an island—hates fish?
Stop closing your eyes!

ROBERTO: Give me my sword.

WILFREDO: No.

ROBERTO: Are you disobeying me for once, Wilfredo?

WILFREDO: People always ask for foolish things when they think they're dying. No.

ROBERTO: If you can't save my foot, then kill me—or give me my sword.

WILFREDO: It's just a foot, Captain.

(ROBERTO punches WILFREDO in the face with his fist and pulls his now bloody face close to his so HE can speak right into it.)

ROBERTO: You better save it or I'll kill one of us.

WILFREDO: Yes, Captain.

*(WILFREDO carries ROBERTO below decks.
Lights cross to ROBERT caught in a memory.)*

I: SCENE TWO-C
ROBERT is softly playing a love/gambling song
like *Little Queen Of Spades*.

ROBERT: "Now she is a little Queen of Spades and the men will not let her be. Ev'rytime she makes a spread, hoo, fair brown cold chill just runs all over me."

(SOFIE enters. SHE carries a big pot full of something good.)

SOFIE: You stop singin' that gamblin' song and pretendin' you wrote it for me. I ain't no thing like a little Queen of Spades. Sheet. When a woman is turned into a playing card that cain't mean no good.

ROBERT: Oh, my darlin', my dea'est. Just set that beautiful smellin' pot'o'love right o'er here by me.

(SOFIE takes a big spoon out of the pocket of her apron and hands it to ROBERT.)

SOFIE: You been drinkin'?

ROBERT: No, ma'am.

SOFIE: Why you gotta drink so much? It kills the taste of the food.

ROBERT: That's just bad information right there. It opens up your tongue. Readies it for new sensations.
(HE grabs SOFIE and kisses her.)
See?

SOFIE: You taste like gasoline.

ROBERT: That's 'cause you start my motor runnin'!

SOFIE: Uh, huh. Maybe I can light a match and blow you up. Damn fool.

ROBERT: Mmhmm.
(Tasting the food)
You made this with Turkey fat. Just like I likes it.

SOFIE: Think you're so smart.

(Pause; ROBERT continues to eat as SOFIE watches.)
How long you stayin' this time?

ROBERT: Gotta push off tomorrow. Willie and I got a gig in Iowa.

SOFIE: Iowa? You tryin' to get yourselfs kilt? They ain't no Black folk in Iowa. What they want wit you two?

ROBERT: You worry too much.
(He puts the spoon down and grabs SOFIE.)
Wanna come along?

SOFIE: You know I ain't leaving my hotel wit nobody to watch over it.

ROBERT: You got your mine in the bizness all the time, woman. C'mon with me and Willie. We'll have a time.

SOFIE: You'll have a time alright. Finish up those collards.

ROBERT: I wanna make love with you.

SOFIE: Wit that much liquor in you, you be makin' love AT me. Better find my raincoat. There's a flash storm a'comin.

ROBERT: How many times you saved my life, Sofie?

SOFIE: How many times you been to see me, Robert?

ROBERT: I come through as often as I can.

SOFIE: Uh huhm.

ROBERT: You know I can only see what's right in front of me. And right now I am only seeing you.

SOFIE: Oh…I'll just put that pot back on the stove to keep warm.

ROBERT: Don't be gone too long, darlin'.

SOFIE: Humph! Damn fool.

(ROBERT backs out of his memory into ROBERTO.)

I: SCENE TWO-D

ROBERT: She warned me that time and she din't eben know it.

ROBERTO: Seeing ghosts now too?

ROBERT: Jesus of Nazareth, King of Jerusalem:
I know that my Redeemer liveth and that He will call me from the Grave.

ROBERTO: Deus gubernat navem [God steers the ship].

ROBERT: But it's the Devil brings the hard-blowing wind.

ROBERTO: Always takes two. Ready to play now? Made a pack out of palm leaves.

ROBERT: Deal then, Mr. Desperate.

(ROBERTO begins to deal out his homemade cards. As the ROBERTS pick up their cards, EPIFANI enters dressed like a late 18th Century woman, dragging a small, child-size wooden shovel—like an old-fashioned sand toy. ROBERT pretends not to see her. ROBERTO cannot pretend. She finds a spot and digs in the sand and finds a buried guitar, SHE holds it up to the SUN, and then hands it to ROBERTO, who doesn't take it. HE just stares at EPIFANI. SHE turns it around in her hands and holds it out to him again.)

EPIFANI as ROBERTO's mother, MARIA GERMANA: Play the waves, Betito. In the sea, you can find your way home. Your father came across the sea from Trieste to plant you in my womb, my baby boy. Without the sea, I wouldn't have children. Your brothers and sister were easy, but never you. Screaming, crying, demanding, debating. I was so tired of hearing you

scream that I took you to the sea and thought I'd throw us both in—but I didn't. I walked you to the edge and then...all the way —into the water, till the waves could cover your tiny feet and finally you stopped.
(EPIFANI leaves the guitar at ROBERTO's feet and exits into the water. ROBERTO takes the guitar, tears off the strings, one by one, and carves a bigger circle around the sound hole, then HE places it in the water, steps one foot inside it and seems to float in it over the waves.)

ROBERTO: When she died, I made my first boat. I floated closer every day to where she must be. Seems that mothers are always at sea. And sons get in deep—trying to find them.

(ROBERTO gathers the cards and shuffles them pretending not to see CORNELIUS as CORNELIUS enters dressed in a bloody hospital gown. His legs are bloodstained. HE sits at ROBERT's feet, resting his head on ROBERT's leg.)

CORNELIUS as ROBERT's wife, VIRGINIA: Remember how you just put yah forehead on mine and kept it there till the coronah come and took me away. The doctors and nurses just give up on tryin' to pull you offa me. But when he came you stepped on back. Why was that? He musta had a "she's seriously dead" face on for you to step off like that. One little old White man—but that was dark you seen in his eyes, ain't cha? And they didn't even let you hold our baby. They just threw him on top of me into the freezer, till the preacher could come. Blue— like the sea. I saw that flash before I was gone too. My eyes filled with the blue of him. I drowned there in cold, wet baby flesh. My baby was gone. So was I. I had to be.

ROBERT: My sweet Virginia. Our baby. After that...
(Pause)
I drank and smoked and whored...jus'din't care.

CORNELIUS as VIRGINIA: Music got real good though. Better'n'better each time you played. That's somethin'this...

(Touching the blood, touching ROBERT's face and leaving blood there)
...could give you.

(CORNELIUS exits. The ROBERTS both want to pretend what just happened didn't.)

ROBERTO: *(Deals out the cards for poker)*
I like this game.

ROBERT: Good. It's only been around about a hundred years.

ROBERTO: An Italian sailor taught me. He learned it from a German who spent time in New Orleans.

ROBERT: Right. Jus'don'give me no damn aces or eights.

ROBERTO: What's wrong with aces and eights?

ROBERT: Dead Man's hand. I thought you knew how to play poker.

ROBERTO: No such thing. The dealer isn't always in control.

ROBERT: You're right about that alright.
(ROBERT throws down four cards.)
Don'say nuthin'. Jus'hand dem on out.

ROBERTO: Four? That's a whole new hand, my friend.

ROBERT: Don't I know it.

(Holding out his hand)
Jus' give 'em here.

(Lights cross to SOPHRONIA, SOFIE, WILLIE and WILFREDO seated on broken planks of wood, staring out to sea. THEY have their hands buried in the sand.)

I: SCENE TWO- E

WILLIE: I was jus' holding his hand. Say'n' it was all gonna be awh-ight. Prayin' for it.

SOPHRONIA: God makes you a liar. It's never alright. It never gets better.

SOFIE: The lie is this. That I can eber forget—even if I do get back home. There's no 'mount a'sand that can keep away the thought of him.

WILFREDO: If it wasn't for Chirichin, I'd be dead now too. He warned me—about the Spanish ship. I told Roberto, but he says it's bad luck to listen to birds.

SOFIE: Where do you think we are?

SOPHRONIA: I was on my way to see him—but by the time I got there...
I won't believe it. Ever. I didn't see him fall. There was no sign.

WILFREDO: There are always signs. Earth trampled, bullets fired, sails ripped by the wind that was supposed to take us home.

WILLIE: That's a whole lot of diddly-do.

(SOPHRONIA, SOFIE, WILLE and WILFREDO look out over the sand sea, searching for ROBERT/ROBERTO. The lights go down slowly, and then come up quickly on ROBERT and ROBERTO.)

I: SCENE TWO-F

ROBERT: This here's the longest damn game of cards I ever played.

ROBERTO: When I younger I used to think that games were to be played fast and hard because that's the only way you could be sure of winning. Keep people guessing the whole time, keep them moving, never let them take too many long breaths. You can only breathe so many times, then—

ROBERT: Then...

ROBERTO/ROBERT: You end up here.

ROBERT: No place I needed to get to this soon.

ROBERTO: No. No place.

(Lights go down slowly on ROBERT and ROBERTO, then they come up quickly on CORNELIUS sunbathing and EPIFANI flipping through books on the beach.)

I: SCENE TWO-G

CORNELIUS: What are you so nervous about?

EPIFANI: Something's beginning to go wrong.

CORNELIUS: There are rules. Just lay them out clearly. Look! *(HE points out into the sand sea.)*
A pink dolphin.

EPIFANI: I thought they only lived in rivers.

CORNELIUS: A pink dolphin will be lonely out here in the sea.

EPIFANI: A pink dolphin will never find its way back, once it swims away.

CORNELIUS: That's a strange way to say that, I mean, don't they have to swim away always? Can't swim in place.

EPIFANI: I'm worried about them.

CORNELIUS: It'll be dead soon, so—

EPIFANI: I mean the Roberts.

CORNELIUS: Already dead. Nothing to worry about there. Oh. Wait. Is this a metaphor? Like the rare pink dolphin—

EPIFANI: No metaphors today.

CORNELIUS: Pass me the tanning oil. I want to burn.

EPIFANI: I thought I did too.

(Lights cross to WILLIE, WILFREDO, SOPHRONIA and SOFIE still searching for the ROBERT/ROBERTO. It is evening and they have made torches from Palm leaves. THEY are looking dirty and tired. They have been searching for a long time. THEY pace up and down the beach. Suddenly WILLIE looks down at his feet and bursts into tears.)

I: SCENE TWO- H

SOPHRONIA: I was wondering who would start the crying again. I didn't expect it to be you. Let's not waste time doing that again.

WILFREDO: He has a heart, god damn you, you plain simple witch!

(SOPHRONIA points her torch at him.)

SOPHRONIA: To be a witch would be wonderful —sometimes.

WILLIE: Don't. It is not about that. I was thinking about some'uhm Robert tole me 'bout myself, that I jus' I don'know. I jus' heard it, like he was right here with me. I don't think I eber thought I'd be memberin' that. Som'uhm so stupid. About my shoes.

SOFIE: What did he say?

WILLIE: He said he wanted dem 'cause they so soft. He said "I need me them shoes." And I told him to go fuck hisself. Shit, I wasn't gonna give him my shoes. Jus'cause you love someone don'mean you gotta give them all your stuff.

WILFREDO: They were just shoes.

WILLIE: *(with a sob)* I know.

SOPHRONIA: No. They were his. He needs his shoes himself. Don't make him feel guilty. Nobody would get my shoes. I had to share this pair with five brothers and two sisters. When I had them on, I wore them for the whole family. Not even Roberto could take my shoes away.

SOFIE: I think y'all are missin' the point.
(Taking WILLIE into her arms in a big hug.)
C'mon, big baby. I woulda kept my shoes too.

SOPHRONIA: Sssh! Listen. *(Silence)* Did you hear that? I think they are close.

WILFREDO: I don't hear anything.

SOPHRONIA: Sounds like glass breaking.

SOFIE: I hear it now. Like burning glass.

WILLIE: I had a harmonica sounded like that once. He used to say, "Willie, you got the dust of angels' wings in there…but they like to drink and fight so that sound they little heads going crack."

SOPHRONIA: You're not going to cry again, are you?

(The tinkling, breaking glass sound gets louder and seems to come from the middle of the sand sea. THEY all look out into its vastness.)

SOPHRONIA, SOFIE, WILLIE and WILFREDO:
Something's breaking.

(THEY all hold hands for a quick moment as if THEY can't resist and then let go of each other's hands just as quickly, each walking their own separate ways.
The lights cross to the outside of the jook joint—"Lucky Legba's Lounge." Legba is from the Yoruba legend about the Devil who appears at crossroads. He is called "Legba," and in the Robert Johnson myth, it was he who appeared at the crossroads of Highway 61 and Highway 49 in Clarksdale, MS.)

I: SCENE THREE
Time has passed. The storm is long gone.
WILLIE and WILFREDO sit outside a dilapidated shack that looks like a Mississippi jook joint. The faded sign above it reads "Lucky Legba's Lounge." THEY play dominoes with a set they carved from coconut shells. On the bottom of the steps leading up to the lounge, SOFIE and SOPHRONIA sit burying their feet in the sand.

WILLIE: I got me a happy parrot who jus'loves to say fornicate, copulate, masturbate—all the nasty "ate" words—all the time. One time a lady friend come over for some coffee with my cream —if you know what I mean—but she's real shy. And that darn bird would not stop. I shook him, and yelled up in his face and nothing. He just kept right on. Finally, I got so mad I threw him into the freezer, kickin' and clawin', just to teach him a lesson. But pretty soon he got all quiet in there, so I got scared he was dead and opened up the door. And what do you know if he don't climb right gentle up onto my arm an' says, "Sorry for all the fuss I made. I will try to improve my vocabulary." I was amazed. Could this be the same bird?! But then he turns to me and says, "By the way, what did the chicken do?"

TWO ROBERTS

(Pause; CORNELIUS enters carrying drinks on a tray.)

CORNELIUS: What did the chicken do?

WILLIE: It's a blessing you've got drinks in your hand or I'd have to slap you for the fool you are.

(They each begin to think of the next joke they each can tell. WILFREDO comes up with one first.)

WILFREDO: *(An African Gray parrot is seated on his shoulder)* Había un loro que estaba alegre y jodiendo la vida, que decía muchas palabras malas—

WILLIE: —he swore like a sailor. One day his owner got tired of him—

WILFREDO: —y lo dejo afrente de una iglesia. Entonces—

WILLIE: The priest opened the door and brought the parrot inside.

WILFREDO: El proximo día la cura lo trajo a la misa para rezar por el.

WILLIE: Oh, heavenly father, please take from my parrot all these blasphemous words—

WILFREDO: —For he does not know the difference between good and bad.

WILLIE: And the parrot pushed his beak through the bars of his cage and said:

WILFREDO: Yo, no, Cabron. Dicelo a las monjas que chichate anoche. Haceme daño, Cura-Cabron!

CORNELIUS: Oh, yes, it hurts good. That's it. Hit me again, with your big—

WILLIE: Hey quit that! There's ladies here.

(Simultaneously, all the MEN either tip their hats or incline their heads toward the WOMEN, who ignore them.)

CORNELIUS: How come it's okay for you, but not for me?

WILLIE: I don't engage in the overtly scatological, fool. I'm about smooth and subtle. Like a baby's behind. You're boocoo nasty.

WILFREDO: Are we playing dominos or trying to seduce someone, gentlemen?

(As the WILLIE begins his song, SOPHRONIA takes off her dress and picks up a makeshift fishing pole. SHE trudges into the sand up to her thighs as if she is wading into water. Then, SHE casts the fishing pole into the sand.)

WILLIE: *(Begins to sing "A Fine Romance," by Jerome Kern and Dorothy Field, a la Bing Crosby and the other MEN join in with hums and whistles)*
"A fine romance with no kisses
A fine romance, my friend, this is
We should be like a couple of hot tomatoes (to-mah-toes, dear)
But you're as cold as yesterday's mashed po-tah-toes (potatoes)"
"A fine romance, you won't nestle
A fine romance, you won't even wrestle
You've never mussed the crease in my blue serge pants
You never take a chance, this is a fine romance"

(SOFIE joins in the song, duet style.)

SOFIE: "A fine romance, my good fellow
You take romance, I'll take Jello

TWO ROBERTS

You're calmer than the seals in the Arctic Ocean
At least they flap their fins to express emotion"

SOPHRONIA: Stop singing, you're scaring the fish away.

WILLIE/SOFIE: "A fine romance, my good woman/young man
My strong, aged-in-the-wood woman/good man
You never give those orchids/love notes I send a glance
They're just like cactus plants (oh boy)"

SOPHRONIA: Callensen!

WILLIE and SOFIE: This is a fine romance!

SOFIE: You sing jus' like Bing Crosby.

WILLIE: Yup. I'm known as the "Colored Der Bingle."

SOPHRONIA: How can you sing when Roberto's still missing?

SOFIE: Robert's here somewhere. Like to dis'peer he do. He think he d'onliest man on de planet sometime. Men are like chirrun most ofen' times.

SOPHRONIA: Los hombres son como los músicos: Vienen, tocan, y se van.

SOFIE: He tole me I'm his insp'ration. "Ain't no one ever made love to me like you do, Annie," he tole me. Annie's my middle name. I din't even know he knew it.

EPIFANI: Is that why he writes those sad songs?

SOFIE: His songs ain't sad, they pra'vocative.

(A silence. The sound of the sea fills the quiet. WILFREDO moves quietly up to SOPHRONIA's dress that lays tossed in a pile behind her. HE

smoothes out the dress and looks for the sash at the bodice. Into the sash, HE tucks his parrot, Chirichin, after prying it off his shoulder.)

WILFREDO: Mira, Chirichin. A soft, sweet place for you to nap.

SOPHRONIA: That fucking parrot's dead, Wilfredo.

WILFREDO: *(A whisper; covering the parrot's ears)*
Don't listen to her, Chiri.

SOPHRONIA: They let any crazy man become a pirate...but not me.
(Pause)
I wanted to be a pirate so that I could take from people who have too much and give to people who have too little. Just like my Roberto. The Captain said I would have made the perfect pirate, except that I was too young. And a woman. Though there were some lady pirates—but they were either Chinese or English. Puerto Rican women are never allowed to hold weapons. I guess the men knew exactly what we'd do with one the first chance we had. I could face death if I had to. He's never scared me.

(Pause)
I saw him take my mother away with his small gray gossamer wings. Her last breath drew fast—like a hummingbird's—when she left me.

(Makes a sound with her breath imitating her mother's last breath while WILFREDO makes a similar sound to Chirichin, like a mother soothing her child to sleep.)

SOPHRONIA and WILFREDO: Ssh-sssh-sssh-ssh. Ssh-sssh-sssh-ssh...

SOPHRONIA: I hoped to kill a Spaniard and an American or two. Roberto was going to let me carry my own knife—the one

he made from the pieces of the dock the Spanish ripped up for their big boats. We hate those boats. They tangle our nets and then we can't fish and if we don't fish we don't eat.
(Pause)
I heard that people in the mountains eat dogs sometimes. I'll stay on the sea, thank you. No dog food for me. A pirate has choices. That's what freedom is. I dream of a free Puerto Rico. No dog food for us.

(WILLIE, WILFREDO and CORNELIUS move to the shoreline.)

CORNELIUS: I ate dog once.

WILLIE: You lyin' pug-ugly pickle-head.

CORNELIUS: Barbeque's up, nice.

WILFREDO: A man does what he needs to do. I've eaten alligator, turtle, snake, manatee—but I won't eat dog.

WILLIE: You drunk too much giggle-water, Fellas. Well, Gator is tasty. And Possum. But snake and dog?

WILFREDO: *(Pointing out to sea)*
You see that?

CORNELIUS: *(Without turning to look)*
Looks like a boat.

WILLIE: Looks like salvation...but I'm not leaving without Robert.

WILFREDO: I heard about these pirates in the Dominican Republic—they were French. Of course.

CORNELIUS: Yes. They lived—together, in pairs. In a house. Together. And they shared everything. Killed together. Stole together. And when one died the other inherited his belongings.

WILFREDO: Yes. Matching swords and boots, too. Sweet. You know a lot about these men.

CORNELIUS: I listen. Men like to talk when they're at sea—they like to talk into the wind.

WILFREDO: Yes. We like to talk.

(Silence. THEY continue to stare into the horizon. SOFIE and EPIFANI join them.)

CORNELIUS: You want to marry him, don't you?

WILFREDO: I don't think marriage—

WILLIE: Can I hold your parrot?

WILFREDO: No.

SOFIE: Can I hold your parrot?

WILFREDO: Maybe.

(WILREDO whistles at SOFIE, pretending it is coming from Chirichin.)

SOFIE: He has good taste.

WILLIE: I like birds. I can hold my arm real still—like—
(HE holds his arm in a stiff right angle.)
You see? Your bird would be real comfy on my arm. I won't shake or nuthin'.

EPIFANI: It's getting dark again. You better come in Fisherwoman.

SOPHRONIA: My name's Sophronia. And I'm not afraid of a little darkness. Sometimes the fish bite more in the dark. They're more trusting then. But it can be dangerous. I have scrapes on my legs from the scaly fish that whip against my skin. I like how those scars feel at night. I touch them and they tell me I've caught something. I held something alive in my hands and then sliced its belly open and scaled it and cooked it. That's the best way to eat.

SOFIE: I dun lost my appetite now.

SOPHRONIA: I'm not ever going to stop looking.

ALL the OTHERS: Never.

(Lights cross to ROBERT and ROBERTO.)

I: SCENE FOUR
ROBERTO is building enormous chairs of sand for himself and ROBERT. ROBERT helps.

ROBERTO: I didn't expect to be captured. I'd been at it for seven years. It was supposed to be my lucky year. That's what everyone said. Seven years at sea and never caught. Many wounds. but I still had all my limbs—thanks to Wilfredo. Never questioned my luck. It was like the inside of a fertile egg—I was just waiting for it to hatch when suddenly it fell and broke open and the bad bloody spirits escaped—all dressed in their military best. Three ships it took to bring me in.
(THEY sit in their chairs facing out to sea.)
And they shot me. I think.

(Sitting up and looking more closely at the horizon.)
You see that? I think it's a ship.

ROBERT: We could get rescued.

ROBERTO: Perhaps. Or they could sail on by.
(Pause)
Unless…We can pretend to be helpless women and when they get close, we'll take their ship.

(Offers ROBERT a drink from his own bottle.)
Have some.

(ROBERT grabs the bottle and tucks it into his inside jacket pocket.)

ROBERT: How do we do that? There's no dresses out here.

(ROBERTO puts out his hand for ROBERT to return the bottle. ROBERT does so.)

ROBERTO: We need panties. On a stick. For a flag. We wave—they come in—then we..swoop.

ROBERT: Panties on a stick do sound tempting. But I think that ship's already moving away. No swooping will be done today, Doc.

ROBERTO: I'm a Captain, not a doctor.

ROBERT: You talk like a doctor.

ROBERTO: Chess.

ROBERT: Huh?

ROBERTO: People who're good at chess all sound like doctors because they are decisive—and ruthless. Check. Checkmate. I have you. No, you don't, because I have you. Strategy. Logic. Final outcome. Your advantage. Chase it. Take it. Win.

ROBERT: Uh huh.
(Pause)
You don't make no kind of sense. But White people never do.

ROBERTO: I'll regret not killing you, won't I?

ROBERT: No doubt. I have a lot of regrets. Most of them married.
All of them minxy little bearcats.

ROBERTO: They must fight really hard—those bearcats. I'd like a bearcat to sleep naked on me.

ROBERT: Do pirates know about poison?
(Pause)
I think I was poisoned.

ROBERTO: We don't usually solve crimes. But I can tell you this—
(HE reaches into his own pocket, takes out ROBERT's bottle, takes a deep swig from it.)
Not a bit poisonous.

(HE places the bottle gently into ROBERT's pocket.)
But I prefer rum. Sweeter. Mixes with the body's blood better. Keeps things from getting messy.

ROBERT: I messed myself up. I should have changed a few things.
But it's done, right?

(Pause)

ROBERTO: I wanted to be buried at sea. My last hope...to return. But fool that I am, I'm here—With you.

ROBERT: *(Singing)*
"F' I had a last wish, I'd wish to be with Miz T.
She got a big house and a big car for me.
F' I had a last wish, I'd wish to be with Miz.T.
And I'd take her so deep, she'd be swimmin' in my sea."

(Lights cross to SOFIE, SOPHRONIA, WILLIE and WILFREDO.)

I: SCENE FIVE
SOFIE, SOPHRONIA, WILLIE and WILFREDO,
are each caught in an individual light as each one speaks.

SOPHRONIA: I wish I could keep my eyes closed forever.

WILFREDO: Seeing him always swimming there.

WILLIE: I want to turn it all back. No forward. Only what used to be.

SOFIE: But then they could start again different, and they could be worse.

WILLIE: Truth told, I wish I never met him sometimes. Sometimes that pain is too close. I can hear it like blood rushing through my head. Too much. It might pop one day and I'll be so lost. There won't even be an island.

WILFREDO: The sea is so convincing. The waves sing a song I despise. But I sing along anyway—

SOFIE, SOPHRONIA and WILLIE: What else can you do?

SOFIE: I can't keep going back. I might meet myself and run screaming from that mess.

SOPHRONIA: How long can I keep him there before I scream too?

SOFIE: The river's so convincing. I would wade into it until something with teeth'd come after me.

WILFREDO: There's a story about how the sea came to be. A giant was crying...or maybe it was God? I can't believe I'm beginning to forget that story.

WILLIE: There's another story about the river and how it washed over the riverbanks one day and stole all the light, that's how you knew the Earth was dying. Somebody was dying.

SOPHRONIA, SOFIE, WILFREDO: Always.

(Lights cross to CORNELIUS and EPIFANI.)

I: SCENE SIX

CORNELIUS and EPIFANI sweep the sand with pitchforks/backhoes. They are making perfect and continuous spirals. THEY do this in silence until they reach the edge where land meets sea.

EPIFANI: Fibonacci Spiral.

CORNELIUS: Yes. Your favorite.

EPIFANI: Do you know how special this is?

CORNELIUS: Yes—A self-similar curve which keeps its shape at all scales —if you imagine it spiraling out forever. Very special.

EPIFANI: And its <u>equiangular</u> because a radial line from the center always makes the same angle to the curve.

CORNELIUS: Yes. This curve was known to Archimedes of ancient Greece, the greatest geometer of all time.

EPIFANI: It spirals inward forever—

CORNELIUS: —as well as outward.

EPIFANI: Like water swirling around a tiny drain-hole, being drawn in closer and closer as it spirals—

EPIFANI and CORNELIUS: *(In unison)*
—but never falling in.

(ROBERT and ROBERTO enter and step onto the newly raked sand, as EPIFANI and CORNELIUS watch. ROBERTO measures the circumference of the island by putting one foot in front of the other as ROBERT writes down the measurements on a piece of driftwood. THEY do this in silence for a while. CORNELIUS and EPIFANI observe ROBERT's and ROBERTO's actions.)

CORNELIUS: What's the point of that? Whatever the size, he's not leaving here, is he?

EPIFANI: Setting his parameters. There's always a reason. When you build a house, you have to take measurements of the space where the house will be. Imagine an emptiness—filled. And then you design it, taper it, colonnade it. Place some delicate cinquefoil in the window and the door panels...

CORNELIUS: If we fail to send them to him, he'll take our feet. I can't fit into my new platform shoes with claws and hooves. We'll be crawlers again.

EPIFANI: Maybe not. There are some old ways we haven't tried. Ways you never learned. Ways I had forgotten—
(Pause as EPIFANI stares at ROBERT and ROBERTO or a moment.)
—until I remembered.

CORNELIUS: Don't.

EPIFANI: What are you afraid of?

CORNELIUS: Eternity.

EPIFANI: Me too.

(Then ROBERTO speaks.)

ROBERTO: What do you have so far?

ROBERT: Two thousand, six hundred and seventeen feet.

ROBERTO: Good. That's about two thirds of the way around.

ROBERT: And how does—

ROBERTO: It will. It will help. Information always does. This way, if a storm comes through, we can tell if the island is rising or sinking. Then we have a way to mark time. Storm to storm. That will be our unit of measure.

ROBERT: Uh huh. I want to stop. My feet hurt.

ROBERTO: Take off those ridiculous shoes. They look like tight little caves your toes hide in.

ROBERT: Does this kind of "persuasive" talk really work on anybody?

(ROBERTO yanks the driftwood tablet out of ROBERT's hands and continues on alone, walking, measuring, notating. ROBERT waits until ROBERTO is out of sight, then takes out his guitar and plays something soft and mournful. HE continues to play into the following scene. On another part of the island, SOPHRONIA is still sand-fishing in her petticoat and undergarments, as SOFIE plays dominoes with WILLIE and WILFREDO.)

WILLIE: *(To the others playing dominoes)*
You see White people think the Blues is about being sad and poor and low-down. But that's just what you is. Fact. Now singin' the Blues is about being with people. Nothing sad 'bout that. Washin' off the sweat of work with the sweat of dancin' and lovemaking. That's it right there. Nothing sweeter than a little hoopty-doo.

SOFIE: Some men always got to try to be intellick'shall. Like we'd ever believe anything comin' out of those mugs.

WILLIE: Yeah. But singing like "Der bingle" worked on you, alright.

WILFREDO: Mmhmm. Tienes todas las hermanas enanas coming after you.

WILLIE: Petite but so sweet. And grateful. I like a grateful woman.

(HE puts his hand on SOFIE's thigh, SHE disdainfully removes it.)

SOFIE: This bank is closed, lover.

WILLIE: Too bad, 'cause I got a big deposit to make.

SOPHRONIA: *(Still fishing)*
You have to put it into the sea. Big fish are attracted to the fluids of men.
(WILFREDO retrieves SOPHRONIA's dress from the sand and puts it on, securing the parrot, Chirchin with the sash to the belt. HE speaks to Chirichin.)

WILFREDO: Mira, [mu]Chacho, This is what makes dresses so much more practical than pants.
(Petting the dead parrot and trying to feed him some chewed up fruit from his own mouth.)
What do you think, Chirichin?

SOFIE: Pretty dress.
(SOPHRONIA sees WILREDO in her dress.)

SOPHRONIA: ¡Quitaté eso, pendejo!

(SOPHRONIA jumps WILREDO, who easily pins her down into the sand.)

WILFREDO: ¡Pendeja eres tu!

(SOPHRONIA takes out a knife and puts it to WILFREDO's throat, WILLIE tries to pull SOPHRONIA off WILFREDO, but SHE pulls WILLIE down into the fray. SOPHIE watches and tries not to be amused. CORNELIUS and EPIFANI enter, their arms full to overflowing—one with fish and one with wine.)

EPIFANI: Sometimes you need a little miracle.

CORNELIUS: We could let her kill him.

EPIFANI: No. We need them happy, Neely.
(To herself) I need them.

CORNELIUS: But it would be a good lesson.

EPIFANI: I SAID NO!

(EPIFANI's outburst conjures lightning flashes and a clap of thunder. Everyone stops trying to kill everyone.)

SOFIE: Is anybody else hungry?

(THEY run for cover into the jook joint as the rain begins to fall. WILFREDO, WILLIE, and SOFIE grab the food and enter the jook joint. SOPHRONIA grabs her dress and WILFREDO grabs his bird.)

I: SCENE SEVEN
Jook Joint in the sand. The Devils, EPIFANI and CORNELIUS sing to themselves a medieval chanson as THEY set up the bar for the evening. This song is sung over ROBERT's music from the previous scene.

EPIFANI and CORNELIUS

*"Je me complains piteusement,
a moi tout seul plus qu'a nullui*

> *I lament piteously,
> to myself alone more than to any other,*

de la griesté, paine e tourment

> *the grief, pain,
> and torment that I suffer*

que je souffre plus que ne di.

> *more than I tell.*

Dangier me tient en tel soussi

> *Danger keeps me in such
> anguish that I can't*

*qu'eschever ne puis sa rudesse,
et Fortune le veult aussi*

> *escape his harshness,
> and fortune wishes it so,
> too—but by my faith,
> that's Youth.*

mais, par may foy, ce fait Jonesse."

EPIFANI: I'd like to be a painter.

CORNELIUS: Portraits or landscapes?

EPIFANI: Houses.

CORNELIUS: Like Hitler.

EPIFANI: Not like Hitler. He was a very unsuccessful painter. That's when the troubles began.

CORNELIUS: What kind of houses?

EPIFANI: Houses of worship, I think. A bit of a challenge. All those colonnades and finials and festoons and architraves.

CORNELIUS: My favorite part is the voussoir—a delicate, wedge-shaped part of the arch and it sounds nice. Say it!

EPIFANI: Voussoir...yes. Delightful on the tongue.

CORNELIUS: I wish I could write with my tongue. The things I could...Tongues are more honest than fingers. A slip of the tongue reveals the truth and a slip of the fingers is just a mistake.

EPIFANI: A voussoir could become foutoir (*a whorehouse*). And though the Church has been known to run one or two of those over the centuries, I'd say it would be hard to find one inside an actual church structure—nowadays.

CORNELIUS: Men in skirts and red shoes. Highly suspicious.

EPIFANI: Dressed for temptation.

CORNELIUS: And what do they call us? Defilers. Tempters. I like a nice suit and a strong cup of coffee. What's wrong with that?

EPIFANI: Nothing, nothing at all. Sometimes I think we can't be defined by who we are but by what we do. Painter, builder, architect of my own destiny...

CORNELIUS: Fashion, conversation and mild stimulants.

EPIFANI: Why must everything good be ours to rule?

CORNELIUS: French music was the music of the world once. Why did that change? First Spanish, then, English. The only thing uglier is German. Russian is good. Dutch a bit scary. Greek, well, original. But French...

EPIFANI: You are leaving out many continents.

CORNELIUS: Don't like those. Although a little Urdu, is nice and Igbo, okay. But I have no use for any of those other languages.

EPIFANI: Oh, but Sanscrit is lovely...

CORNELIUS: As is Taa Clicking language, but difficult to sing in.

EPIFANI: We loved Aramaic.

CORNELIUS: Not anymore. Hardly anyone remembers it. And not very descriptive. Not enough adjectives.

EPIFANI: Ah, but such a favorite...for some among us.

CORNELIUS: I think I'll serve Manhattans tonight. With the good bourbon.

EPIFANI: Most ladies won't drink such a harsh drink. Maybe gimlets? Or Cuba Libres? They go so well with sorrow.

CORNELIUS: If you could take two books with you to a desert island, two books for all eternity, what would they be?

EPIFANI: *Lives of the Saints* and the *Oxford English Dictionary*.

CORNELIUS: Volume. But a bit dry. I would go with the History of Art and Pedro Paramo—I like a good ghost story. There are so many ways to interpret the stories of the dead.

EPIFANI: Hmmm...that should kill some time...If you could take one work of art, what would it be?

CORNELIUS: You my love.

EPIFANI: Awh...I wish you were more complicated. Knob Creek or Bookers?
(EPIFANI takes out all the bourbons and places them on top of the bar.)

CORNELIUS: I guess...the Knob. Bookers is so harsh going down. Reminds me of a sweet young woman
(HE signs that SHE is dead and gone to Hell.)
My first job.

EPIFANI: The first is always hard. The last is hard too.
(Pause)
And the ones in between...hard, hard, not easy...hard.

(Pause)
Anyway, never mind...Cornelius, the Knob does make the perfect Manhattan—though I know many a gal who's thrown up after too much Knob.

CORNELIUS: Moderation, Epifani. It's always about moderation.

EPIFANI: Apropos of that—why'd you change your name? A little extreme. So many letters.

CORNELIUS: I have dreams sometimes about being smoothe, well-dressed and black as night. That's none other then Mr. Don Cornelius. I did not want the 1970s to end. "Soul Train" was the perfect representation of all the joy humankind could offer. Everyone looked fly, danced well. No one looked hungry or oppressed. Everybody was smiling. Everybody looked free. You?

EPIFANI: I wanted something Greek, but not so far from Roman and kind of modern like a Soap Opera name—like someone didn't know what they were doing when they named me, but by chance it turned out to be a fabulous name because it is an epiphany—when you realize that you've lived your whole life only to die—it's the ultimate epiphany. But with the "f" and the "i" instead of the "ph" and the "y"—then it's even cute. It's just a winning name I think. And I am really tired of the old ones.

CORNELIUS: I hear you, sister.

(They high-five each other and bump bellies like jocks do. THEY see ROBERT and ROBERTO looking out at the ocean in silence.)

EPIFANI: Those two are going to be difficult.

CORNELIUS: That's why he gave them to us.

EPIFANI: She never makes mistakes.

CORNELIUS: Never, Piff.

EPIFANI: Never, Neely?

CORNELIUS: We get the sad ones. The lost ones. The ones named Robert.

EPIFANI: That's not why. *(Pause)*
I asked for them.

CORNELIUS: I didn't know you could do that.

EPIFANI: You can't—but I can. I'm the oldest.

CORNELIUS: The favorite. Why?

EPIFANI: They're sad in the same way. In the same way I am.

CORNELIUS: They won't let us back in. You know that. These two won't open any doors for us. Just dark business—as usual.

EPIFANI: You're so young, Cornelius. Wait long enough and hope comes back to you.

CORNELIUS: I love your...epiphanies.

(EPIFANI kisses the arches of CORNELIUS' feet. Lights cross to the beach.)

I: SCENE EIGHT

It is the violet time of dusk. ROBERTO is returning from catching dinner. HE carries fish impaled on his cutlass. ROBERT kneels in the sand, stuffing a letter into a glass bottle. ROBERTO is topless. ROBERT is still in his suit and hat. THEY now have all kinds of sand furniture.

ROBERTO: Guess what we have for dinner.

ROBERT: Not hungry.

ROBERTO: Have to eat.

ROBERT: No. I don't.

(Silence)

ROBERTO: Why are you sending that letter? We don't even know what sea this is. What language it needs to be in. Who will read it?

ROBERT: Not a sea. A river.

ROBERTO: Quite a wide river. Look at those stars.

ROBERT: Stars don't come out this early.

ROBERTO: They do here. Must be in the Southern Hemisphere. South Atlantic.

ROBERT: You can tell all that from three stars?

ROBERTO: I can tell a lot of things. I can tell that this circular island is three thousand five hundred and twenty fathoms in circumference. I can tell you don't know how to follow orders. And I can tell you're hungry. How about some fried Codfish?

ROBERT: Catfish. This is a river.

ROBERTO: I know ocean cod.

ROBERT: I know river cat.

ROBERTO: Whatever it is, I will gut it and cook it.

ROBERT: You don'scare me.

ROBERTO: I'm not trying to scare you. I'm trying to eat. All that measuring made me hungry.

ROBERT: You don' scare me 'cause I got expectations. I'm waiting for an answer.
(HE throws the bottle into the water and watches it float away.)
People remember me. They want to talk to me. Won't be long now.

(ROBERTO comes to kneel beside ROBERT and THEY both watch the bottle disappear.)
I want to be found.

ROBERTO: Is this how it ends?
(Pause)

ROBERTO and ROBERT: I saw a woman in my dream last night with no hands.

ROBERT: She was holding a purple flower between her forearms.

ROBERTO: And she came to this place and tried to plant that flower in the grayish green grains of sand.

ROBERT: But when she covered the bottom of its stem, the flower melted—

ROBERTO: —as if she had poured a glass of hot water there.

ROBERT: All that water just disappearing into the sand.

ROBERTO: No sign that that flower had ever lived was left behind. Just the memory of the girl who felt it on her arms—but not her hands.

ROBERT: Then the girl tried to jump into the water—tried to get away, but I held onto her and said if I couldn't leave neither could she.

ROBERTO: And I ripped her clothes off and took her from behind till I felt her blood dripping down my legs—warming the soles of my feet.

ROBERT: Took that girl as fiercely as I have taken anyone.

ROBERT and ROBERTO: And I woke up wondering if the water has memories, too.

ROBERT: And the flower.

ROBERTO: Does the water remember all the blood? All the pain? Is that why I'm still surrounded by it? Blood's as salty as the sea.

ROBERT: And then that girl, she crawled a little ways down the beach and began to dig.

ROBERTO: She dug a hole with her arms and feet, big enough to stand in, and she got in and waited for the tide to come in and finish her. She was happy to let the water take her.

ROBERT: The water makes everyone whole.

ROBERTO: As I watched that hole filling up with water, I thought…

ROBERT and ROBERTO: …love can drown you too.

ROBERTO: Leaves you gasping with nothing but air all around you.
That how it feels to be left all alone.

ROBERT: I wouldn't be smiling if I was her, I thought.

ROBERTO: If I was her, I'd dig myself back out of that hole.

ROBERT: Then she turned my way—

ROBERTO: —steady—like the barrel of a gun pointed right at me.

ROBERT: And she smiled.

ROBERTO: And smiled.

ROBERT: And, finally, melted into the sand.

ROBERTO and ROBERT: —just like that flower.

ROBERTO: Same dream.

ROBERT: We aren't ever going back.

ROBERTO: That's not certain. We have to plan. I've made escapes from stone prison cells. Sand won't hold me for long.

ROBERT: Will you take me with you when you escape into this sea? What's this sea called?

ROBERTO: Open.
(THEY sit and watch the sand sea and the setting Sun. ROBERTO reaches for ROBERT's hand.)

ROBERT: Quit that.

ROBERTO: I like holding hands.

ROBERT: I don't. Not wif men. Not even wif women dat much. I hate how other people's sweat feels on my palm. And how their smell just stays there on you.

ROBERTO: That's the part I like.
(HE takes a deep whiff of his hands.)
I smell everyone I ever touched in the palm of my hands. People I loved and people I killed. I need to remember all that. That's what can keep me alive I think. I think as long as I can smell my enemies resting in the creases of my palms—right there, beside the tears of my mother, then she can wash all that blood away. That's what I think.

(ROBERTO rests his hand casually palm up beside ROBERT. ROBERT slowly takes it.
Lights cross to WILLIE, WILFREDO, SOFIE and SOPHRONIA.)

I: SCENE NINE
Playing a game.
WILLIE, WILFREDO, SOFIE and SOPHRONIA sit in a circle. WILLIE plays the harmonica for this game where THEY are passing around a large green plantain, and whoever holds the plantain when the music stops has to tell the truth. SOPHRONIA wears banana leaves around her head like a turban. The OTHERS all wear variations on the banana wear theme—scarves, arm bracelets, ankle bracelets, etc. Even Chirichin has little banana pants on and maybe a little turban.

WILLIE plays a song like "Stormy Weather" on the harmonica. When he stops, it lands on WILFREDO.

> SOPHRONIA: The plantain of truth has chosen you.
> To honor this plantain, tell us the story of your first day as a pirate.
>
> SOFIE: *(Looking coquettishly at WILFREDO)*
> Oh, yes. I need to hear this.
>
> WILFREDO: I was fourteen. I had walked to the dock to fish and I saw some men there carrying a trunk. They demanded help carrying the trunk to the Captain's house. I said I'd do it if they would take me with them. They did. That night.
> *(Pause)*
> It was a Danish ship. The Danes are fierce fighters. There was one who just wouldn't die. It took three men to hold him down. And then the Captain said it was time to baptize me. If I wanted to be a pirate...he handed me an axe. He told me to cut the man's hands off, so he could never fight again. Such a brave man. Such a good fighter. I couldn't do it. I turned with the axe and got the Captain. With one stroke I got through his neck and left the axe imbedded in his spine. Like he was made of clay. I never knew how strong I was until that day.
> Luckily, his crew hated him, so they were happy to have him dead. They shared their gold with me—not equally, but enough to give me a taste for it. When I got home, I told my mother I had stayed on the dock fishing and sold my fish at the market. She was so happy that day. I thought, if this will make my mother happy, there can't be anything wrong with it. By the end of that month, I'd killed six men, and brought enough money home to begin my education as a doctor. Much later, I met Roberto. I still wonder if he's a devil or a saint. I only know that now I am a healer who kills only for him.
>
> SOFIE: I want to be next.

WILLIE: This is a game of chance, darlin'. You never can know if you're gonna be next.

*(WILLIE begins to play his harmonica again.
The plantain gets passed around again. SOFIE holds onto it for too long.)*

SOPHRONIA: If you do that you'll be sick every time you eat a banana.

WILLIE: Ain't we beyond such nonsense-superstition-bunk-a-do? Just tuck it between your legs, honey, and you'll feel a whole lot better.

WILFREDO: She's right you know. It happened to me. I held on to my mother's platano for too long once and I had—explosions. For two days. Almost died.

SOFIE: *(The platano is finally handed back to her.)*
Ha. Ask me anything!

SOPHRONIA: The plantain of truth has chosen you. To honor this plantain, tell us the story of your first time with Robert.

SOFIE: I guess I can tell you that, because there was plenty of witnesses. We did it in front of the big bay window in the lobby of my hotel.

WILLIE: Yep. I saw it.

SOFIE: Really? How did I look?

WILLIE: You had a real crazed look in your eye, like you just got squirted with a lemon.

SOFIE: It was amazin'. That man, well, he had me stand up on a step stool and then I was just the right height for everything... and sometimes I was upside-down on there and wooh, lord, that

was…that was the night I fell for him. Nobody ever made love to me like that. No jokes.
(Pause)
No turning off the lights so they couldn't see my face. Or my twisted legs. No. He was all there for me. For everyone to see. No one else ever made me feel like a whole person before. No shame.

(WILLIE begins to play the harmonica again and the platano gets passed around again. This time it lands with WILLIE.)

WILLIE: No. I will not tell my secrets to a tuber—or a fruit—or whatever that is.

SOPHRONIA: I'll take your turn.

WILFREDO: The plantain of truth has chosen you. To honor this plantain, tell us the story of the first time you saw the Devil.

SOPHRONIA: How do you know I've ever seen that darkness?

WILFREDO: We all have. It travels with you always. But one day we see our shadow and it is not ours and we can't change it, no matter how much light or distance we move away from it. A steady follower, the devil.

SOPHRONIA: The day my father died. I saw it lift out of him. There were two souls. I had always known there were two, but I didn't know that his evil lived inside him, just waiting, just below the surface. It tried to get inside me, but I said NO! And it left.

WILLIE: It never leaves. It hides.

SOFIE: And it waits. Maybe on a beach.

SOPHRONIA: Snakes, goats and birds hide him sometimes.

WILFREDO: *(Petting his bird)*
Nonsense. My Chirichin is all goodness. I think it hides in women's shoes. They look so painful.

WILLIE: Him? It's a her. Definitely. You ever seen those shapely legs? Those legs that tempt you and turn your stomach around and your tongue hang out like you like to swim in your own spit. And other things move. It's un-natch-ral.

SOFIE: Nahuhn. It's the most natch'ral thing. It is nature. It's like that hurricane, brought us here. Nature is the most pah'ful thing in the whorled. It can open up the ground and drown you in dust as soon as kiss you with a slender ray of sun.

SOPHRONIA: *(Casting a spell)*
Platano maduro, guineo ven a mi,
Traeme mi alma, El Pirata Cofresí.

(She throws the platano into the sea.)
Come back when you find him.

(They all watch the platano float out to sea. Lights cross to the jook joint where the sound of 1930's music is blasting from an old juke box.)

I: SCENE TEN
In Lucky Legba's Lounge. All the tables are tables for two. WILLIE and SOPHRONIA sit together. SOFIE and WILFREDO sit together. CORNELIUS and EPIFANI are behind the bar in matching outfits decorated with seashells. No one sees ROBERT and ROBERTO except CORNELIUS and EPIFANI and ROBERT and ROBERTO can see no one but them until later in the scene.

CORNELIUS: Welcome to Lucky Legba's, you're lucky to be here and you'll be luckier to leave.

EPIFANI: What can I do you for, Robert?

ROBERT: Are you...? I mean, what do you mean "do?"

EPIFANI: You don't recognize me?

ROBERT: Nuhuhh.

ROBERTO: *(Stepping in front of ROBERT)*
My name's—

EPIFANI: Roberto. El famoso Pirata. Who doesn't know you? Do you know who I am?

ROBERT: Looks familiar. Did I ever play here?

CORNELIUS: You play here now.

EPIFANI: Like it...or not.

WILLIE: One day a man who traveled all over the world, found a parrot that spoke 30 languages. He decided to buy it for his mama, had it shipped express. He called his mama the day after it was due to arrive to be sure it got there. "Oh, yes," she said. "It was delicious." "What?! That parrot spoke 30 languages." She thought for a moment and said, "Well, why didn't it say something then?!"

WILFREDO: *(Petting the dead Chirichin who is looking the worse for wear)*
What people don't know is that a parrot has the mind of a 2- or 3-year-old child. Imagine losing that child. Imagine the child knowing that he's going and nothing can stop the death of him. His feathers fluff up around his back as he is cold and his eyes cloud over. Then he stops talking and whistling. Chirichin loves whistling.

(Pause)
All they know is to make fun of a grown man and his parrot and the tears that form behind his eyes as he thinks he may have lost—

(HE begins to sob.)

SOFIE: This is why I have no pets. Ain't there enough already in the world to say good-bye to?!

SOPHRONIA: *(Under her breath to WILLIE)*
He needs to bury that thing already.

(Raises her glass in a toast)
To Chirichachin. Que duerme en paz...pa'lante y pa'tras!

WILFREDO: *(overlapping)*
CHIRICHIN! His name is Chirichin.

(ROBERT and ROBERTO can see all of them now.)

ROBERTO: *(moving to them)*
Wilfredo! Sophronia!

ROBERT: *(moving to them)*
Sofie? And my man, Willie!! I can't believe it!

WILLIE: That toast was real nice, Miss So-fonia.

(WILLIE, SOPHRONIA, SOFIE and WILFREDO continue their conversations in silence, as if a sound switch has been turned off.)

ROBERT: Willie? Willie, it's me. Don't you recognize me? And Sofie, give your papa a kiss now!

EPIFANI: They can't see you. Or hear you.

CORNELIUS: *(To ROBERTO)*
That goes for you too.

EPIFANI: It took us a long time to come up with something that would really hurt.

CORNELIUS: Torturing the soul has very little to do with equipment anymore.

EPIFANI: No fiery treadmills to walk or gigantic burning noxious cogs to turn.

CORNELIUS: Eternal damnation is what happens when all you love is within arms reach—but it no longer recognizes you.

EPIFANI: They're here for you, but they will never find you. You'll see them searching and searching.

CORNELIUS: You'll feel their hearts breaking.

EPIFANI: And they will never get to leave.

CORNELIUS: And you'll watch them get tortured—for eternity. All because of love.

ROBERTO: That's not possible.

ROBERT: I lied about all that. It sold records. Man sells his soul. I was just a good liar.

ROBERTO: No one takes from me what I haven't given.

EPIFANI: What can I get you to drink?

ROBERT: You can't keep us here.

ROBERTO: I'm leaving.

EPIFANI: And miss all this excitement?

CORNELIUS: All this pain?

ROBERT: There never were any crossroads. I made all that up.

CORNELIUS: Gotta be careful—the things you make up.

EPIFANI: Didn't you ever think: "Gee, I wish I had a drink?" And then, "Pracatan!" it lands right in front of you.

ROBERTO: That has happened once or twice. I'm popular. I get what I want.

ROBERT: Are you hurting them?

CORNELIUS: You're hurting them. You went away and they followed and now you won't come back for them.

(Silence)

EPIFANI: Do you want to save them?

ROBERT: Yes.

ROBERTO: Why can't they save themselves?

EPIFANI: There are ways...

ROBERTO: Hah! I knew it!

CORNELIUS: Why are you telling them, Epifani?

EPIFANI: It's time for a new game, Cornelius.

CORNELIUS: I just got these shoes, Piff.

EPIFANI: Oui. Et ils sont trés jolies, mon petit.

(CORNELIUS and EPIFANI turn on the jukebox in the Jook Joint. SOFIE and WILLIE applaud. SOPHRONIA and WILFREDO stare at it in wonder.
WILLIE picks out a song and puts a nickel in the jukebox. When he does

so, ROBERT starts to sing, Robert Johnson's "Last Fair Deal Gone Down".)

> *"It's the last fair deal goin' down, last fair deal goin' down*
> *It's the last fair deal goin' down, good Lord,*
> *on that <u>Gulfport Island Road.</u>*
> *Eh, Ida Belle, don't cry this time*
> *Ida Belle, don't cry this time.*
> *If you cry about a nickel, you'll die 'bout a dime*
> *She wouldn't cry, but the money won't mind.*
> *I love the way you do, I love the way you do.*
> *I love the way you do, good Lord,*
> *on this Gulfport Island road.*
> *My captain's so mean on me, my captain's so mean on me.*
> *My captain's so mean on me, mmm good Lord,*
> *on this Gulfport Island Road."*

(EPIFANI tries to dance with ROBERTO who pulls away. CORNELIUS sits at ROBERT's feet to watch him play. SOPHRONIA, WILFREDO, SOFIE and WILLIE begin to dance. SOFIE and WILLIE pull themselves out of the dance when the amplified sound of blood rushing from one chamber of the heart to another is heard over the sound of ROBERT's singing. THEY begin to rock in silent anguish. WILLIE holds SOFIE. SOPHRONIA and WILFREDO join them. THEY seem locked in silent mourning. ROBERT looks at ROBERTO while HE sings. When ROBERT stops singing, HE speaks.)

ROBERT: Make it stop.

(EPIFANI and CORNELIUS shake their heads "No.")

ROBERTO: So...there are worse things to be haunted by.

(Blackout.)

END OF ACT ONE

ACT II: SCENE ONE

In the back room of the bar.

EPIFANI is reading "The History of Art" as CORNELIUS rubs oil on her legs. To one side, ROBERT and ROBERTO rest on each other's shoulders with their eyes closed.

EPIFANI: Why do you think Pan is always shown playing a flute?

CORNELIUS: He invented it. When he was chasing after that nymph. She turned herself into reeds, so he picked some up, strung them together and blew.

EPIFANI: Birth of the pan flute. I know. But does he always have to play it in every painting? I play the harpsichord, but you don't see me strapping one to my back and playing it all willy-nilly wherever-whenever. There's a time and place for everything.

CORNELIUS: It would be uncomfortable. A harpsichord is pretty big. And no one paints you.

EPIFANI: That's not the point.

CORNELIUS: Maybe you should stop reading that book.

EPIFANI: Why?

CORNELIUS: Puts ideas in your head. And it's so heavy. Must be a burden all that art.

EPIFANI: What are you reading these days?

CORNELIUS: I do Jumbles. Keeps my mind limber. It's very soothing.

EPIFANI: But can you relax your wrists after doing all those—
(disdainfully)
—Jumbles? That's the only way to tell if you're truly relaxed.

CORNELIUS: Oh, yeah.
(HE twirls them around to show how relaxed they are.)

EPIFANI: Mine feel like iron rods are piercing them.

CORNELIUS: Like being nailed to a cross?

EPIFANI: I guess.

CORNELIUS: That's because you're older than me. Old people need to complain. Keeps them lively. In the race. Wanting for something.

EPIFANI: I'm not that much older.

CORNELIUS: If I asked you to say something interesting about yourself with no facts, what would you say?

EPIFANI: Epifani wants to go home.

CORNELIUS: Oh…I'd say, Epifani needs Cornelius.

EPIFANI: Good one.

(CORNELIUS pulls away and settles in next to her to do a Jumble word scramble puzzle from a torn piece of newspaper.)

CORNELIUS: When a man meets his maker in a watery place, he becomes a—
(Spelling it out)
—"t-o-l-r-f-a-e" —hmmm…

(ROBERT and ROBERTO speak from their dreams.)

ROBERT: I saw my father's face staring back up at me from the river. That's when I knew I was dying. I felt the poison rising up my arms into my throat over my face, into my eyes. His eyes. No life left.

ROBERTO: I felt my heart break into moist pieces of drifting wood—that's what the heart of a dying man becomes I thought.

EPIFANI: A "Floater."

CORNELIUS: *(Writing in the newspaper the answer to his Jumble puzzle.)*
Of course.

(ROBERTO and ROBERT suddenly awaken fully as the lights come up on WILLIE, SOPHRONIA, WILFREDO and SOFIE asleep on the floor of the jook joint. WILLIE is the first to wake up. ROBERT and ROBERTO watch. ROBERT sits. ROBERTO stands.)

WILLIE: That was—was it? What day is it—do anybody know when—
(Feels for something in his pocket)
Hey, y'all wake up now. Sheet. Somebody stole Ozella. Sheet! A man can't even sleep no more without some dime becoming a nickel.

(HE searches all around the jook joint frantically, until finally HE spots his harmonica in SOPHRONIA's hand. HE gently removes it, then retreats to his own space. HE whispers to his harmonica.)
Okay, Baby-girl. You're safe...There's really nothing nastier than smellin' someone elses' spit on your lips—I mean unless they kissing you.

(WILLIE sniffs the harmonica as SOPHRONIA wakes up.)

SOPHRONIA: What are you doing?

WILLIE: Jus' you know...it was—she needed to—cleaning. Needed a cleaning.

SOPHRONIA: You play nice. I like how your eyes get big and moist when you play. Almost like you're crying.

WILLIE: Naahahh...really? I don'ever cry.

SOPHRONIA: I guess we have that in common.

WILLIE: Most girls seem to like it—my harmonica playing I mean.

SOPHRONIA: What do you call it? I heard you call it something?

WILLIE: Jus'somethin'...Jus'Ozella.

SOPHRONIA: Who was she?

WILLIE: My mother.

SOPHRONIA: My mother was called Caoniba—but her real name was Valentina Mariana Luciano.

WILLIE: Uh, huh. That's a nice name. Next time I get a new—
(Shakes his harmonica in the air)
—harpoon, I'm gonna name it after your mama.

(SOPHRONIA gets choked up by this.)

SOPHRONIA: That would be—that's so—really?
(SHE starts to cry a little, but looks away to try to hide it.)
She would like that.

(Pause)
She was a bitch though. But maybe because she was so tired all the time. Nine children.

WILLIE: That's a whole mess. Nine. I'd be a bitch too.

(WILLIE takes SOPHRONIA's hand shyly.)

ROBERTO: And this is supposed to destroy me?

ROBERT: I'm happy for him. He been looking a long time for the right woman. Women never paid him the mind he deserved. They was too busy looking at me.

SOPHRONIA: I've never met a man like you, Willie. With such a big heart.

(SOFIE awakens and looks at WILFREDO, asleep still with Chirichin tucked under his chin.)

SOFIE: I'd like to sleep tucked under somebody's chin one day... That's something alright.

WILLIE: That's devotion.

SOPHRONIA: That's crazy.

EPIFANI: That's human.

ROBERTO: This is ridiculous.
(HE stomps out of the Jook Joint.)
A long, relentless nightmare.

(Pause)
And nightmares are warnings. So I must keep guard.

(ROBERTO exits the jook joint as lights cross to the beach.)

II: SCENE TWO

Sunrise on the beach. SOFIE is painting something on a palm frond with lipstick. WILFREDO watches. HE has Chirichin in a sling across his chest. ROBERTO and ROBERT sit in their sand chairs and also watch.

WILFREDO: Is that a note?

SOFIE: Maybe. Don't look.

WILFREDO: I write notes too. But I don't send them.

SOFIE: Why not?

WILFREDO: If you don't send them, you can't expect to get answered.

SOFIE: I'm not surprised you're a doctor, the way you look at me. Do you stare at everybody like that?

WILFREDO: I've never met a dwarf before. It's interesting. I keep wondering why you can't just have some legs made. Out of wood.

SOFIE: That would be something—like a crazy peg leg polly the pirate?! Uhuhnnn. I get enough looks as is.

WILFREDO: You were born like that?

SOFIE: Yup. My mother was afraid of me when I come out. She thought the Devil herself was being born. She was only a scared chile of thirteen herself when she had me—so she left me at Miz Montgomery's house. Miz Montgomery took in strays—like me. Sweetest woman in West Helena. It was her inn that's mine now. Miz Mongomery's . I kept the name she give it. Seemed right.

WILFREDO: *(Approaching her)*
May I—?
(He places a hand on her skirt and waits for her to nod consent before HE lifts it up to look at her legs more closely.)
You have so many scars.

SOFIE: *(SHE pulls her skirt down quickly)*
Girls who caint run get beat with switches a lot.

WILFREDO: I didn't mean to embarrass you.

(Lights come up on WILLIE and SOPHRONIA on the beach. SOPHRONIA is teaching WILLIE how to tie nautical knots with a piece of frayed rope. ROBERTO mirrors her actions.)

SOPHRONIA: This is called the Figure eight knot. At the bitter end, that's the end being used to secure a line, you make a loop by twisting a bight of the rope, pass the bitter end round the standing end, taking the longest journey—not the shortest—pull it through the loop again and there you have the figure eight.

ROBERTO: *(To ROBERT)*
Perfectly done. It's the best knot to prevent lines sliding out of sight or up inside the mast. And its true beauty is how easy it can be undone.

ROBERT: Uh huh. Willie's never gonna get that.

(WILLIE gets it. HE makes a perfect Figure Eight knot.)

WILLIE: Teach me another one.

SOPHRONIA: You learn fast.

WILLIE: I'm beginning to. You're a good teacher.

(Pause; Lights come back up on WILFREDO and SOFIE. WILFREDO speaks to SOFIE and WILLIE speaks to SOPHRONIA.)

WILLIE and WILFREDO: You wanna go on a date?

SOPHRONIA and SOFIE: Yes.

(Everyone exits except ROBERT and ROBERTO.)

ROBERT: Did you hear that?

ROBERTO: Strange. They have no place to go.

(ROBERT and ROBERTO stare at the new couples as THEY exit.)

ROBERT: Maybe it's not where you go, but how.

ROBERTO: I'm going to go kill something.

(Lights cross to SOFIE and SOPHRONIA sitting at the edge of the sand sea.)

II: SCENE THREE
SOFIE and SOPHRONIA sit on the edge of the sea, their feet in the water. THEY are giving each other pedicures with stones and sand. In their hair are rollers made from seaweed. ROBERT and ROBERTO watch them.

SOPHRONIA: You're good at this.

SOFIE: Yup. Uh huh. I used to work in a boarding house for old folks and they needed a lot of feet attention. Mmhmm. Nothing as nasty yellow as all that stuff under they toenails. I don't miss them old feet. But the poor things couldn't barely bend over to reach they feet so I din't mind. Never had my own feet rubbed before though.

SOPHRONIA: Men always seemed to like licking my feet. I think because they're small, compared to the rest of me. Like baby feet. So I always keep them smooth. But even just a walk on the beach can take the old dead skin away.

SOFIE: I never thought about sand like this—like it could scrape away your rough edges and such. I'm used to swampy lands, and riverside sand—sand that sucks you in and cuts you. There ain't no soft white sand like this. We got pieces of wood and weird animals walkin'around. Like gators. They gotta be the weirdest animals. So you walk fast through there. Too fast to smooth any feet anyway.

SOPHRONIA: Gay-tor? Gato-r? What is that? A big cat?

SOFIE: Nooo. It's got long claws and leathery, wrinkly skin. And it's real long—longer than you're tall—with big teeth, like 2,000 teeth or something. And they all crooked and it lives in the water.

SOPHRONIA: Like a fish?

SOFIE: More like a lizard—
(making a chomping face)
but with big chompers.

SOPHRONIA: Oooey! Like a caiman. We have them on my island too. But not so big.

SOFIE: You're lucky then, I guess.
(Pause, as THEY pour sand over each other's feet)
What do you think our Roberts are doing right now?

SOPHRONIA: Walking in this sand. Pulling themselves through the wet heavy sand—just to get to us.

SOFIE: How long you think it'll take?

SOPHRONIA: *(with a shrug)*
Will they remember us? That's what I worry about. So many days have gone by.

SOFIE: And here we planted ourselves like some crazy sea witches.
(Notices that one of SOPHRONIA's seaweed rollers has come undone and begins to re-roll SOPHRONIA's hair.)
I guess that gives us some time to get all pretty anyways…

(The sound of a wave. The women disappear into black as lights come up brightly on ROBERT and ROBERTO.)

ROBERTO: Maybe all of the rest of our lives will just be filled with things we shouldn't see.

ROBERT: Why though? You know they aren't letting us see just anything.
(Speaking into the air as if the DEVILS can hear him.)
Are you?

ROBERTO: You have to cut a lock of your hair on a Friday and throw it into the sea. That's the only way to make the Devil appear.

(EPIFANI and CORNELIUS enter on a tandem mountain bike.)

EPIFANI: Actually, you're supposed to "fling ist thy'n shard of torneth hair into the stormy ayre so ist thou mightist appeaseth the mighty wind so ist will bloweth thou safely hometh." Or something like that. That's what it says in the *Horropedia of Horrobelia*—about summoning Lucifer the "Morning Light that comes as Venus in Lightning from the Sky" anyway.

CORNELIUS: Whoosh! Here we are.

ROBERT: Why are there two of you?

CORNELIUS: There's many more of us.

EPIFANI: Yes, that's what they say…a legion. Do you know what a legion is?

ROBERTO: An army of between 3000- and 6000-foot soldiers and 100 to 200 on horseback.
(Others look at him surprised)
I think I was a Roman in my past life. I dream about it all the time. I see a stone house in my dream and it is filled with stone jars filled with liquids. I am looking for something in the jars. Finally, I find what I'm looking for and I begin to drink it and as I drink it, it becomes a snake with black stripes. I take the snake down into my throat and feel it alive there in my stomach. I can see my stomach moving and stretching as that snake continues to grow there. And the pain of the snake grows with it and I wonder if that snake will tear through me.

ROBERT: I had that dream too, 'cept that snake never makes it down my throat—wraps itself around me and just squeezes—'til I turn to liquid. 'til it's me, running across the floor. The liquid of me, runnin' across the floor and fillin' up one of them jars… y'all are—

EPIFANI: Not my favorite form. Although, stripes are nice…

CORNELIUS: Snakes dream too. They dream about skunks. I have this one dream at least once a century where people are walking all around me, trying to avoid me. But every time one of them passed me, a skunk came up in its place like a skunk garden. All those white striped tails waving in the wind like the flag of a new country—and that country is me.

(Lights come back up on SOFIE and SOPHRONIA. ROBERT and ROBERTO watch.)

SOPHRONIA: *(Pricking her finger on a sharp seashell shard)* Look at me.

(SOFIE looks. SOPHRONIA places a drop of her blood across SOFIE's lips like a lip gloss.)
There.

SOFIE: Is that even sanitary?

SOPHRONIA: Looks good. You have beautiful lips, like ripe quenepas. Have you ever tasted one?

SOFIE: No, uhuhun.

SOPHRONIA: A small, delicious fruit. The outside is hard and green, like an avocado, but inside—she's like a juicy little mango.

SOFIE: *(With a laugh)*
That's me alright.

(Lights cross to WILLIE and WILFREDO on another part of the beach. WILLIE is putting a paste made of sand and water on WILFREDO's face.
Chirichin is resting on WILLIE's rolled up shirt. ROBERT and ROBERTO watch them.)

WILFREDO: You have—

WILLIE: Don't talk. You'll crack.

WILFREDO: *(Speaking slowly to keep the "Mask" from cracking.)*
—such...soothing...hands.

WILLIE: Don't even start, boy. One favor is all you get from me. I figure I owe a man that, but that's all. Why you home-sexuals all like that? Always trying to take more than offered.

WILFREDO: I...can't...without...cracking.

WILLIE: That's 'nuff.
(Moves away from WILFREDO; sits watching the sunset.)
Let it set up. And shut up.

WILFREDO: Going...down...

WILLIE: *(Taking WILFREDO's words as a sexual innuendo)*
WHAT NOW?!

WILFREDO: Sun...

WILLIE: Oh. Yeah. Goin' down.
(Silence)
I know what they said...'cause I was always following him around but he and I...never had a friend like that. When we was in Iowa together—that's when I knew he was my brother for always. Things like that, when men do dem together, it seals you up like a "big-ass-heavy-still-in-Hebrew" bible.

WILFREDO: I-Oh-Wah?

WILLIE: Devil lives in Iowa. Vacations in Naw'lins, though.

WILFREDO: What-happened-in-I-Oh-Wah?

WILLIE: Had a gig. Paid real well. Crazy White people kept coming. Fillin' up the dance hall for three nights straight. But then come to find they were't coming for the music, no sir. Came to see some colored men in person. Made sense once we figured it out. They eyes were so twinkly when they was watching us. So amused. Like dey was watching a monkey unpeel a banana. Look at dose tricks. Watching Robert's hands fly across his guitar, and my lips on the harmonica. They kept offering us more and more money to stay. We was a hit.

WILFREDO: Twinkly...eyes...That's...why...I...carry...an...axe.

WILLIE: Men don'let men laugh at dem. I think dat's the best thing my momma give me—dignity. Don' ever need to complain about what I din't have when I've got that. Protecting that can get you kilt, but people get kilt for a lot of stupid things in dis world.

WILFREDO: I...know...Would-you-put-a-little-on-my—
(Indicating Chirichin, who still rests on WILFREDO's rolled up shirt.)

WILLIE: No. I am not touching that.
(Lights cross to the ROBERTS and the DEVILS.)

ROBERT: What about that time in Iowa?

EPIFANI: What about it? You got paid, didn't you? You took the money? Paid well. You just didn't know what they were really paying for...there you were thinking your musical genius was bringing them in and all they wanted to see was a trained circus animal. You wanted some money. To feel what that's like to have some.

ROBERTO: I gave most of my money away. I shared it with everyone who needed it.

CORNELIUS: Not everyone.

ROBERTO: Not everyone would take. Some people despised us. Said they could smell the blood on us. But everyone has that blood. Our land was taken. Our ports. Our women. Ships full of gold going away from us, not toward us. Taken from under our feet. What did they do for us, but steal from the earth beneath us?

CORNELIUS: The earth is beneath all of us.

EPIFANI: That could be interpreted a couple of different ways...I would prefer not to defend the earth. I miss other places. On earth the work never stops. A girl gets tired.

(Lights up on all the couples and they speak simultaneously.)

ALL, but EPIFANI: Amen.

EPIFANI: I want to see you alone, Robert.

CORNELIUS: And I you, Roberto.

ROBERTO: *(Under his breath to ROBERT)*
This could be our chance. Divide and conquer.

ROBERT: Huh? Uhh...yeah. Maybe. What if she do something outrageous to me?

ROBERTO: Use it. Do it. Courses can be set in a different direction. Take notes. Learn.

(Lights cross to the porch of the Jook Joint.)

II: SCENE FOUR
On the Jook Joint's porch.
ROBERT teaches EPIFANI how to play a song on the guitar.

ROBERT: You picked an easy one.

EPIFANI: I thought nothing you wrote was easy.

ROBERT: This one is.

EPIFANI: People say your songs haunt people. That they can feel the songs vibrate from their fingertips, up their arms to their ribs, and from there straight on into the heart and other places. Me, I feel them in my stomach sometimes. Sometimes in the back of my throat. Like tears I'm choking on.

ROBERT: Hmmmnnn...And you wan'learn to play one? Cash money say you crazy...
(Handing the guitar to EPIFANI and placing his hand over hers to show her how to hold it properly.)
Firs' off, you want to hold her loosely. Hold her too tight and she'll run right from under you. You want to show her conf'dence. Se'kuhtee. Skill. Skill will keep her in your arms. And you'll touch her just right. Finger coming from 'bove, from the top, tips firmly placed and wrists loose 'nuff to walk all the way to the 12th fret.

EPIFANI: This isn't my first time.

ROBERT: I can tell.
(HE lets go of her hand slowly.)
But it your firs' time with the Blues.

EPIFANI: Yes. What's the first chord?

ROBERT: Check the tuning. What you got?

EPIFANI: *(Strumming the guitar to check the tuning)*
Quarter step sharp. Drop D tuning. Capo first fret. Key of A.

ROBERT: Or you can try, Open A, half step down, Capo 2. Now play A7. A diminished 7. D. A. A7G. D to F sharp progression. Watch the rhythm. Swings 4/4 tah 5/4.

(SHE does so.)
I'm 'pressed. Now A to E, E7 and restore to A7.

(SHE does so.)
Good. A7. A diminished 7. A7. A diminished7, A7, D7/F sharp.

(HE sings.)
"Early this mornin' when you knocked up on my door.
Early this mornin', ooh, when you knocked up on my door,

And I said 'Hello, Satan. I believe it's time to go.'"

(Speaks)
Repeat dat last progression. And then D7. And you haf to hammer on and pull off.

(Sings)
"Me and the Devil, was walkin' side by side.
Me and the Devil, ooh, was walkin' side by side.

(EPIFANI stops playing.)
And I'm goin' to beat my woman until I get satisfied."

(Speaks)
Did I lose you?

(EPIFANI faints. ROBERT saves the guitar from falling.)
Hmmm...happens sometimes.

(ROBERT plays "Me and the Devil Blues" to himself, humming.)
She right. It not dat easy.

(Pause)
A lot of notes.

(Lights cross to ROBERTO and CORNELIUS inside the Jook Joint.)

II: SCENE FIVE
In the Jook Joint.
ROBERTO teaches CORNELIUS how to sword fight. ROBERTO throws CORNELIUS a sword.

ROBERTO: Catch.

CORNELIUS: *(HE catches the sword by the blade with bare hands.)*
This is thrilling. I've only had duels before. Too formal. So many rules. But to fight with these things you have to mean business. Close enough to smell the fear.

ROBERTO: If I win, will you let me leave?

CORNELIUS: This is a lesson. Not a fight, is it? It wouldn't be fair to fight without—

ROBERTO: *(Attacks him swiftly, mercilessly)*
Fair?

(CORNELIUS gets up, with his wounds healing almost instantly)
Now that's not fair.

CORNELIUS: Not much I can do about that.

ROBERTO: Do you know that my country has no flag?

CORNELIUS: Yes. I know. It will have. It does have.

ROBERTO: How long have I been here exactly?

CORNELIUS: Can't say.
(HE knocks ROBERTO to the floor.)
Time is different here. You've heard of Island time right?

(Holds the sword on him but doesn't cut him)
Right?

ROBERTO: Do it. I've had enough of this life too.

CORNELIUS: No. Too easy.
(HE backs off ROBERTO who jumps up and attacks him viciously. CORNELIUS begins to giggle.)
You call this a fight!?

ROBERTO: I'll pull out your kidneys and fry them with my fish tonight.

CORNELIUS: Really? C'mon, really? That's what you got?

ROBERTO: *(Pulls out a small bayonet and tries to stab CORNELIUS with it.)*
This is my favorite. Her name is Gloria. She leaves wounds so fierce in my enemies that I only use her on people I really hate. Makes wounds shaped like triangles inside the body that begin a bleeding that can't be stopped.

CORNELIUS: So that's it? That's everything. The secret. You have no true skills, just rage.

ROBERTO: I have nothing. You have all the power here. You take my friends and lovers and parade them in front of me and call me cruel. I didn't devise this little plan. I will rip your lying tongue from inside your putrid head.

(ROBERTO is about to rip out CORNELIUS' tongue when a small guitar-shaped boat floats in.)

CORNELIUS: I know.

(ROBERTO is transfixed by the guitar-boat. It twists in the air and water spills from it.)

ROBERTO: Do you want to know my real secret?
(Shaking CORNELIUS, who does begin to look shaken.)
Do you?! The day my mother died, it was my soul she took with her. I have been nothing for a very long time.

CORNELIUS: That's why you're here.

ROBERTO: Then why is he here? The other Robert? He's just a musician.

CORNELIUS: No, he isn't. Haven't you heard him play? He attacks his chords. He sings all about us. He makes people fall in love with him. He makes men jealous. He is a soul-stealer. Just like you—but different. But alike. But different. But—alike.

ROBERTO: Why us together?

CORNELIUS: Can't say really. Not at liberty at this time... actually, you have to figure that one out yourself...

ROBERTO: If you're really the Devil, why isn't your name Lucifer or Beelzebub?

CORNELIUS: That's what you call us. What we call ourselves is something else again. Why are you called Roberto?

ROBERTO: My father told me that my name means "shining with fame."

CORNELIUS: He had great expectations.

ROBERTO: Yes. He was from Trieste. And his father was from Vienna. Europeans are full of expectations—yet empty of resources. That's why they steal from our world—to maintain their delusions of grandeur. But it was my mother who chose the name. My beautiful mother. She smelled of wildflowers and rainwater.

CORNELIUS: The good ones usually do.

(Lights cross to SOFIE, SOPHRONIA, WILLIE and WILFREDO.)

II: SCENE SIX
SOFIE, SOPHRONIA, WILLIE and WILFREDO are having a date night. SOFIE and SOPHRONIA are seated at the bar in island finery THEY made themselves from found objects—like a Gauguin in the rough. WILLIE and WILFREDO enter with corsages made of palm fronds and various wild island flowers. ROBERT and ROBERTO enter

and watch. CORNELIUS and EPIFANI enter from behind the bar, dressed in their finest Alexander McQueen-esque party clothes.

    WILLIE: *(Handing his corsage to SOPHRONIA)*
    Beautific for the terrific.

    SOPHRONIA: Aren't you the sweetest man? Pin it on me.

    WILLIE: It goes around your wrist.

    SOPHRONIA: *(Letting him place it for her)*
    Oh...I've never seen anything like that before.

    WILLIE: I know. It's just as gorgeous as you, baby.

(SOPHRONIA kisses WILLIE's cheek as WILFREDO steps forward with his corsage for SOFIE.)

    SOFIE: Well, I thought you'd never get around to giving it to me, mister.

    WILFREDO: You're a nice lady, Sofie. But you know...

    SOFIE: I know. I 'preciate your bringing this for me even though.
    (SHE struggles to figure out how to pin it. WILFREDO steps forward and pins it for her.)
    Thanks, Wilfredo. Y'are a gentleman, alright.

(A slow dance tune plays in the background.)

    WILLIE (to SOPHRONIA): Let's polish that floor, milady.

    WILFREDO (to SOFIE): Shall we?

    SOFIE: *(Pulls out a palm frond tie she made with pictures of "Chirichin" drawn on it.)*
    Wait. Try this on.

WILFREDO: Oh, my goodness. That's incredible. How did you draw this? It looks just like my "Chirichin."

SOFIE: *(Pulling his head down to her shoulder)*
I know, darlin'. Just dance.

(ROBERTO and ROBERT go to the bar and get drinks.)

ROBERT: They look real happy.

ROBERTO: I know.

EPIFANI: What'll it be gentlemen? Rum punch? Rum and coke? Coconut rum?

ROBERT/ROBERTO: *(In unison)*
Whiskey.

CORNELIUS: A sad man's drink.

EPIFANI: A real man's drink. Let's make it a double.

(ROBERT and ROBERTO clink glasses and throw back their big shots of whiskey.)

EPIFANI: *(Refilling their glasses)*
Again.

(Pouring Cornelius and herself one)
And one for good luck!

(They all clink and throw their drinks back.)

CORNELIUS: Yowza!

EPIFANI: I forget the warmth of a nice scotch.

ROBERTO: Goes down like—
(Makes a smooth hand gesture accompanied by a whistle)
Don't you agree, Robert.

ROBERT: I agree, Roberto.

(On the other side of the room.)

WILLIE: You a great dancer, Sophronia.
(Suddenly inspired by her beauty to create some poetry)
Sophronia, your name is magic like sweet harmonia, just say it—
Like the music I make, I wanna take—your rhythm and play it.

(SOPHRONIA claps.)

SOPHRONIA: That was beautiful, Willie.

SOFIE: Gorgeous!

WILFREDO: I don't think it rhymed very well…

SOPHRONIA: What would you know about romance, lonely man?

WILFREDO: I've had romances.

SOPHRONIA: In your head maybe.

(WILFREDO turns to SOFIE)

WILFREDO: How about a walk on the beach?

SOFIE: I wouldn't say no.

(SOFIE and WILFREDO leave. SOPHRONIA and WILLIE go to sit on the stools that ROBERT and ROBERTO are occupying. They end up sitting on their laps.)

ROBERTO: This is awkward. She feels good though sitting here.

ROBERT: You got the good one. Willie's a fat ass. Farts all the time. Spends at least two hours a day goin' to the necessary. It's obscene.
(Smiles anyway)
It is kinda good though. Like being on a double-date wid him.

(SOPHRONIA leans forward and gently kisses WILLIE on the lips.)

ROBERTO: That was strange.

ROBERT: I felt it too.

ROBERTO: How long are we supposed sit still like this?

EPIFANI: Till you get tired. Can't stand it anymore.

CORNELIUS: Can't you feel the throbbing in her veins against your leg though?

ROBERT: I had enough.

(HE pushes WILLIE to the floor. SOPHRONIA jumps down from the stool and bends down to see if WILLIE is alright. ROBERT and ROBERTO jump up and run out of the Jook Joint. EPIFANI pours a drink for herself and Cornelius. THEY drink.)

CORNELIUS: Is it working?

EPIFANI: My plans always work.

(Lights cross to ROBERT and ROBERTO on the beach.)

II: SCENE SEVEN

ROBERTO is buried in the sand up to his neck.
HE is looking out to sea. We hear the sound of the sea but there's no water in sight. ROBERT enters and sits beside him.

ROBERT: What's going on.

ROBERTO: Go away.

ROBERT: You know the tide's rolling in?

ROBERTO: I know.
(Silence)
Are you going to sit there and watch?

ROBERT: No. I won' be watchin'. I'm not stayin' here alone.

ROBERTO: There's a lot people here. Too many.

ROBERT: You have a knife. Why not use that?

ROBERTO: The sea was supposed to take me. I shouldn't be here.

(Pause)
Has to be close to high tide by now. My father taught me how to navigate with the tides. We used to row out to an island to gather coconuts. I have scars on my legs from climbing those trees. It was good practice for life on a ship. Pulling myself hand over hand up those scaly coconut trees taught me about balance. Every morning, he'd tell me how many coconuts to collect. And I never failed to get them all. I'd get tired sometimes though, and I'd just take the ones the littler boys had collected. I never threatened them or hurt them. I just told them how many I needed and they handed them over. I never took them all from any one boy. I was fair—about that. About that I was fair. I told myself I wasn't a bully—like my father—I was a leader. They wanted me to have all the coconuts.

(Pause)
I got them all killed. My men. Dead because I couldn't keep them safe. We attacked so many ships. Never once got caught. Until we did.

ROBERT: They all had their own mines to make up about that. You do things, want things, take things...you gotta pay for them too sometimes.

ROBERTO: That's right. You do.
(HE pulls ROBERT into the sand with him.)
Do you really think you can share your stupid philosophy with me and then I'll feel all better because a dumb guitar player thinks he understands my life?! I should kill you!

ROBERT: Again?

(ROBERTO lets go of ROBERT.)

ROBERT: I took things. I paid. Angry husbands. Band mates who stopped playing with me because they thought I was stealing all their light. And their money. Spreading lies about me. I din't care one bit. All those stories just made people more coorious about me. I took what was mine. If it weren't mine, I couldn't take it. Ain't that so? Like the coconuts.

ROBERTO: Like the coconuts. *(Pause)*
The tide won't ever come in here, will it?

(EPIFANI and CORNELIUS watching them from the Jook Joint porch.)

CORNELIUS: What are they doing out there?

EPIFANI: Hoping.
(Lights cross to the side of road in Clarksdale, Mississippi.)

II: SCENE EIGHT-A
A memory. ROBERT and WILLIE on the side of a road in Clarksdale, Mississippi.

WILLIE: You ever notice how the road looks like water in the summer.
It's got a shimmer to it—looks like you're driving across a big dark sea.

ROBERT: I noticed. It's called a hallucination. Like an oasis in a desert. Seeing water where there ain't none.

WILLIE: Ain't you fancy today? Hail-lou-sin-nation.
Damn that's pretty.
(Singing)
"I got a sweet gal who taught me wrong from right.
She gave me a big car and some lovin' through the night.
She left the keys on her yellow kitchen counter.
I knew I could take 'em when the lady let me mount her."

ROBERT: *(Laughing)*
That's jus'plain nasty, Willie. Did any girl ever let you take her car? Did any gal ever let you take her? I don't know any girls sleep that deeply.

WILLIE: I'm working on it.

ROBERT: You don't say. Still never...?

WILLIE: I said I'm working on it.

ROBERT: What's so hard about this? Just find a gal, get her drunk, promise her something and there it is.

WILLIE: Easy for you. You're handsome. Experienced. Cut some records. I'm nobody.

ROBERT: You'll be somebody soon. You already somebody. My best friend.

WILLIE: I do like that Mary May. She's a real sweetheart. She's got the prettiest voice.

ROBERT: You're concentrating on the wrong part of her.

WILLIE: Shush!

ROBERT: She is a pretty gal. She live over near the Stovall plantation don'she?

WILLIE: Yeah, I'm a gonna'take her out after church next week.

ROBERT: Good for you. Take that horn by the bulls.

WILLIE: Thanks, Robert. You a good friend. Thank you for letting me play witch you too. You one tough man to keep up with. Sometimes I look at you playing and it don't even seem like your fingers are attached—they jus'fly.

(ROBERT claps WILLIE on the back and makes wings out of his entwined fingers flying off WILLIE's back, as lights cross to ROBERTO's memory.)

II: SCENE EIGHT-B
ROBERTO and SOPHRONIA are sitting side by side, fishing in Joyuda Bay in Cabo Rojo. SOPHRONIA catches a big one. ROBERTO helps her pull it in.

SOPHRONIA: DON'T HELP ME!

ROBERT: Alright! You don't have to scare all the rest of the fish away.

SOPHRONIA: Sorry. I just—everyone is always helping me. I want to do this myself.
(SHE reels it in finally.)
See? I did it. I'm stronger than I look.

ROBERTO: Marry me! I need a woman who can lift me!

SOPHRONIA: NO!

ROBERTO: *(Whispering)*
Why all the shouting?

SOPHRONIA: Nervous, I guess. I've never been alone with a man before. Without someone watching.

ROBERTO: Well, everybody's staring now, with you carrying on like that.

SOPHRONIA: This fish will feed us for a week. My father will never believe I caught it myself.

ROBERTO: I'll be your witness. And then I'll ask for your hand—

SOPHRONIA: Keep Quiet! I know you're married. I've seen your daughter too. Can't be more than three years old.

ROBERTO: You have a very pretty smile.

SOPHRONIA: I DO?!

ROBERTO: This shouting has to stop, Sophronia. My ears are ringing.

SOPHRONIA: *(Whispering)*
I do?

ROBERTO: Yes. Very pretty.
(HE leans forward to kiss her, SHE puts the fish between them.)
Your chaperone has a strange skin condition. I think she should go to bed immediately.

(SOPHRONIA begins to laugh nervously at the bed remark.)

SOPHRONIA: Do you think you'll be back this way soon, Roberto? How long do you go out to sea for?

ROBERTO: I never know exactly when I'll be back. I do know that when I'm back, I will want to see you first of all. Then I will come see your chaperone and we will fry her in fresh butter.

SOPHRONIA: We never have fresh butter in our house. Oil.

ROBERTO: Oil, then. That chaperone will be tasty. We'll take a knife to her and split her belly open, peel away the scales, cut out the bones, and all the other dark bits of her and then we'll fry her delectable meat. Doesn't that sound like a great evening?

SOPHRONIA: Yes. Oh, yes! Oh, yes. I have to go home now.

ROBERTO: Why?

SOPHRONIA: I have to pee.

ROBERTO: Can't you just go behind a tree or something?

SOPHRONIA: You have to move very far away. Over there.

(ROBERTO obediently moves away. SOPHRONIA begins to pee behind a tree. ROBERTO comes running back.)

SOPHRONIA: Ahh!!! Stop!

ROBERTO: You're beautiful, Sophronia.

SOPHRONIA: Stay back. Goodness. If the priest saw us.

ROBERTO: There's no one here. Lift your skirt. Let me see you.

SOPHRONIA: I can't—
(HE pulls her skirt up and stares at her.)

ROBERTO: Now is when I want you.
(HE pulls SOPHRONIA onto him and they tumble to the ground.)

SOPHRONIA: You're hurting me.

ROBERTO: It won't hurt forever.

(ROBERT and ROBERTO meet in the middle of the sand sea as THEY exit their memories.)

ROBERT: We've got to—

ROBERTO: I know. We have to let them go. *(Pause)*
I never had these thoughts before, Robert. About other people.

ROBERT: Me neither.

(Lights grow to encompass the others as they enter solemnly.)

II: SCENE NINE

A funeral on the beach. A small box being buried in the sand. WILFREDO digs in silence, places the box in the sand and covers it slowly with sand, as the others watch. ROBERT and ROBERTO watch too.

WILFREDO: *(HE is clearly suffering from this loss. A eulogy)*
I bless you, my dear Chirichin. You were a good bird—the best parrot a man could ever dream of having. At least you died of love, gazing at your reflection in the sea.

SOFIE: *(Whispering to the others)*
It's a river. And what happened anyway? Did it drown?

SOPHRONIA: Sea. Why would we be on a river?

WILLIE: A river is what we live near. How could we ever get to the sea?

WILFREDO: Some respect please.
(Stares at the others until they quiet down.)
Thank you…thank you for coming to wish my Chirichin safe passage into the next life. This journey will take him home to fly free with all those angels.

(WILDREDO continues to cover the hole with sand as the others watch.)

WILLIE: *(Starting to leave, HE takes out a flask and drinks)*
That's the kind of funeral I want—short and sweet.

(The others try to leave, but WILFREDO turns back to them and continues his service. Only EPIFANI is crying.)

WILFREDO: I would say the rosary now—

SOFIE: *(under her breath to WILLIE)*
Damn, those are long.

WILFREDO: —but I can't. I lost my rosary in the storm and I don't remember without all the beads.
What I do remember is the last time he spoke. He asked me:
(In a parrot voice)
"Fredito, cantame esa canción que m'encanta."
So, I will sing it for you now. With special words to honor this special bird.

(WILFREDO takes a moment to gather his strength—his composure, before HE sings a modified version of Rafi Escudero's danza "Añoranza", a waltz-like ballad.)

TWO ROBERTS

WILFREDO: *Oye. Quiero cantar una canción cita para el mejor pichón que jamás vivió!, Mi Chirichin.*

Yo quiero ser pan si tienes hambre,
[I want to be bread if you're hungry,]

Ser calor, si acaso tienes frío,
[to be heat, if you're ever cold.]

Yo quiero ser luz si tienes miedo
[I want to the light that shines]

De las sombras que oscurecen a tu pico.
[On the shadows that feed your fear.]

Chirichin, mi amigo con plumas.
[C., my feathered friend,]

Siempre estoy aqui por ti.
[I'll always be here for you.]

Chirichin mi amigo con alas,
[C., my winged friend,]

Siempre estabas allí por mi—
[you were always there for me—]

Chirichin, chirichin, chirichin,
Suena Buena como las lagrimas de los santos...
[Sounds beautiful like Saints' tears]

Chirichin, chirichin, Chirichin,
Buena suena tu nombre sagrada.
[Sounds beautiful, your sacred name.]

I want to be on your shoulder—
for once you were always on mine.
I will not say goodbye, but hello beautiful...

Hello, Chirichin the Divine...

(The others are stunned, by WILFREDO's voice and the passion with which HE sings about his bird.)

WILLIE: That musta been some bird.

WILFREDO: I loved that old fornicator.

SOPHRONIA: How do you get so close to a bird? I've always been afraid of their beaks and their claws.

WILFREDO: That's because you never felt one gliding across the back of your neck at that very moment when you are about to fall asleep. It is like the sweet-soft kiss of your first lover.

WILLIE: Okay. I had about enough of this.

SOFIE: It's true. Birds are real special things. Like they came from something older than we can even understand. I don't mind a bird at all.

*(EPIFANI cries harder. CORNELIUS comforts her.
SOPHRONIA shrugs her shoulders and walks off after WILLIE into the jook joint. SOFIE goes to WILFREDO and comforts him. She runs one long fingernail down his spine. THEY exit into the Jook joint. EPIFANI and CORNELIUS speak.)*

EPIFANI: That was lovely, don't you think?

CORNELIUS: In a way. In a way it was too much. It was just a bird.

EPIFANI: But he truly loved it. It's like he just buried his arm or something. Where do we stop—just at the surface of the skin or inside the viscera of those we love?

CORNELIUS: Maybe we don't stop. Maybe it's one of those perfect seashell spirals. The universe, I mean.

EPIFANI: There it is again. The Fibonacci spiral of the Golden mean—the shape of the universe.

CORNELIUS: Now that Chirichin's soul is off to that place they sometimes go, will there be a crack in our earthly shell?

EPIFANI: Soon.

(Lights cross to the Jook Joint.)
(WILLIE goes to WILFREDO intending to offer comfort.)

WILLIE: Sometimes a drunk's jus'a man whose head's full of poetry. *(Silence)*

WILFREDO: And sometimes a man's poetry drowns in his rum.
"Hablando del Rey de Roma, él a la puerta se asoma."
{Speak of the Devil and he'll appear.}

WILLIE: There was a young gal from Grainger,
who met a mysterious stranger.
This tall handsome fella, knew what'all to tell her,
to keep her a stockin' that manger.
When he fed her some jive, she ate him alive—
Now he knows all about danger.

WILFREDO: Why is there always a girl?

(EPIFANI helps WILFREDO get WILLIE into a chair.)

ROBERTO: Men are so simple. Talking to another man is as restful as a good night's sleep. Even when you're arguing over a chess move or which weapon is most effective on an enemy's skull.

(Pause)
Or the death of a loved one. Somehow the debate is delightful.

(Pause)
Offer them a rum punch.

CORNELIUS: Okey-dokey.
(Offering a rum punch to WILLIE and WILFREDO.)
Here you go. Compliments of the House.

(WILLIE and WILFREDO down their drinks quickly.)

WILLIE: Ooh-weeh, that was sweet and day-lish-oos.

(WILFREDO bursts into tears.)

WILFREDO: It's just like my Captain used to make. As sweet as if he mixed it with his little pinky finger—or that 8th Century dagger he stole from an English lord.

WILLIE: You're a sensitive fella. First the bird. Now the rum. You gotta relax some, son. How about I plays a song for you to calm yer nerves?

(WILLIE takes out his harmonica and begins to blow. Water flies out of the holes. WILLIE chokes on the water. Spits it out.)
Nothing's right here. C'mon, baby-girl. Let's play.

*(ROBERT and ROBERTO cross to the beach.
THEY stumble over Chirichin's grave. It is covered with wildflowers and seashells. They each pick up a seashell and hold it to their ears.)*

ROBERTO: Hear it?

ROBERT: What is that?

ROBERTO: Close your eyes. Stop and listen.

ROBERT: It's a sweet song...

ROBERTO: It's the sea, Robert. She's come back for us.

ROBERT: I know.

ROBERTO: It can take them home.

ROBERT: Without us.

ROBERTO: Without us. We stay here.

ROBERT: That sound...of breaking glass...those ain't angels.

ROBERTO: It's just us.

ROBERT: Without all of them.

ROBERTO: That's all.

ROBERT: They don'need to hear that mess anymore.

ROBERTO: We know what we sound like now. Breaking.

ROBERT: Breaking into pieces fine as sand.

(Lights cross to the deck of the ship.)

II: SCENE TEN
On the deck of the ship that is now in good shape and ready to sail, stand SOFIE, SOPHRONIA, WILLIE, and WILFREDO.

WILFREDO: We have to set sail soon. The wind is picking up. Don't want to get caught in any more storms.

WILLIE: Can't believe we're finally going home.

SOFIE: This here is moving on.

SOPHRONIA: It feels like a dream.

(The boat moves across the sand sea. As it moves, we hear the sounds of the sea. EPIFANI and CORNELIUS wave good-bye until it is out of sight.)

CORNELIUS: What should we do now?

EPIFANI: Play us a song, Robert.

ROBERT: I think I need to write something new. Something about the future. No more old songs.

EPIFANI: Cook us something, Roberto.

ROBERT: No turtles. I still ain't eating no turtles.

ROBERTO: Bacalao and rum punch. *(Pause)*

ROBERT: River Cat.

ROBERTO: Ocean Cod. *(Pause)* What a relief...to finally rest.

(EPIFANI and CORNELIUS, ROBERT and ROBERTO walk together into the Sand Sea. ROBERT and ROBERTO stop walking as two brooms fall from the sky. EPIFANI and CORNELIUS take the brooms and begin to sweep away the sand in front of them. The Jook Joint rolls off. EPIFANI and CORNELIUS stop and watch ROBERT and ROBERTO.
The stage is empty. ROBERT and ROBERTO look around the nothing that is left.)

ROBERT: It happened.

ROBERTO: It's happening.

(Two bottles filled with red liquid fall from the sky. THEY each take one, open it, pour out the liquid and pull out the piece of paper left behind and read it.)

ROBERT: That's it.

ROBERTO: The end. The moment when your eyes close is the only moment when you see yourself clearly—

ROBERT: —when you let yourself mourn all the people you left behind and they go on.

ROBERTO: Without you.

ROBERT: That's it.

ROBERTO and ROBERT: The end.

(As ROBERT and ROBERTO continue to walk into the sand sea, it is replaced by water—a true sea, its sounds and colors fill the space and overtake ROBERT and ROBERTO.)

EPIFANI: You see, Cornelius? There is hope.

(CORNELIUS takes EPIFANI's hand and THEY follow ROBERT and ROBERTO into the churning sand that is becoming the sea, THEY too are overtaken as the lights slowly fade.)

End Of Play For Now...

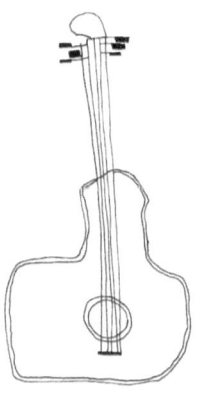

Building a Safe House when No Space is Safe: Your Words are my Home
an afterword by Virginia Grise

Dear Migdalia:
My sister artist friend. I have been thinking a lot lately about legacy and lineage, what we inherit and what we need to let go of, about the world we are born into and the worlds we create with our words. Maybe I have told you this before (I have a tendency to repeat stories) —I stumbled across your plays in a library that no longer exists, next to a river in San Antonio, Texas, many years ago, many miles away from New York City, but really not that far from the Bronx. A city with a 1 in 4 illiteracy rate, I found sanctuary in that library, refuge in those books, home in your words.

But home is not always safe.
I don't have to tell you that.
Your writing has never been safe.

Every word deliberate and intentional.
Fierce and deeply poetic.
You write like the world is on fire—and it is.
But I don't have to tell you that either.

You put it all on the page, sister...

Our hurt.

Building a Safe House when No Space is Safe: Your Words ...

Our rage.
Our pain.
Our secrets,
Our hidden desires.

As a people, a pueblo, a community.
With heart-breaking honesty.

I know I've said that before.

And at a moment when theatre seemed impossible, someone handed me your one act play *Telling Tales* in graduate school, marked with a Post-it Note that said, "there are many ways to tell a story." I can't remember now if I've told you that before—it opened a world of possibility for me as a writer.

Left in pieces, broken open like a piñata, I gather myself again after reading your most recent collection to write this letter.

> *The possible has been tried and failed,*
> *Now it's time to try the impossible.*

—Sun Ra said that.

I see nothing but possibility in this collection of wildly imaginative impossible plays where worlds collide because we were never meant to live inside the frame, the box, the prison of anyone's making, even our own. The breadth of inspiration and influence an endless well, you pull from memory and history, Shirley Chisolm, Martin Luther King and Robert Kennedy play poker with White Jesus and Black Jesus while two Puerto Rican sisters sort through what is left after the death of their parents. You quote from Pol Pot and draw from Fellini to write a dystopian future that feels like a not-so-distant past. You create worlds where people talk to each other across time and place.

At a crossroads.
Betwixt and between.
A liminal space—where anything is possible.

Because you understand the possibility of theatricality, breath, embodiment. The magic of the theatre, the weight of metaphor, the power of story, the perversity of power. I close my eyes after the end of each play and try to listen to the sound of the sea, imagine a room underwater, fish swimming against the walls, wildflowers and seashells in the sand, an animatronic wall of genitalia, a dilapidated jook joint...

I too am overtaken.

You remind us, sister artist friend...
Theatre is about imagination.
Theatre is about the impossible.

I have heard you talk about your dream to create a "safe house for writers—a place for young writers to flee the corporate world of the playwriting/screenwriting establishment, and for old writers to write whatever they damn well please and teach and rest."

You have taught us so much, Migdalia.
Your papers your legacy.
Your books our sanctuary
The impossible possible.

After the Word what's left?
That's it. The end.
For now...

Thanks from Migdalia

Thank you to my husband, Jim, and daughter, Antonia,
My sisters, Gloria, Nancy and Virginia, and my parents,
Pedro and Gregoria, who inspire me every day with their
Laughter and their tears reinforcing my own.

Thank you to my dear friends and colleagues who helped manifest this book:
With Production: Sheila Callaghan, Jacqueline Goldfinger, Daniela Naranjo-Zarate
With Images and Book cover: Christian Potter Drury
With Words of Generous Meditation: Virginia Grise, Morgan Jenness, Todd London
With Etudes of Support: Linda Chapman, Quiara Alegría Hudes, David Henry Hwang,
Caridad de la Luz (La Bruja), and Octavio Solís.

And special thanks to my theatrical family of friends and companies, who along with the ancestors, actors, directors, designers, stage managers, and dramaturgs, have supported my work and my voice and know better than anyone that no one grows without water, sunshine, and a little nutrient-rich dirt.
We all come from some place impossibly beautiful.

ABOUT THE AUTHOR

Migdalia Cruz, the 2023 DGF Legacy Playwright, is a Bronx-born writer, lyricist, translator, and librettist with over 60 works performed in 150 venues across 40 cities in 12 countries. Her awards include the NEA, McKnight, NYSCA, and TCG/Pew, and she was named the 2013 Helen Merrill Distinguished Playwright. Cruz's voice was honed by her mentor, María Irene Fornés at INTAR's playwriting lab, and her residency at Latino Chicago Theater Company. She co-chaired the DGF Playwriting Fellows, mentors the Latinx Playwrights' Circle, was listed on The Kilroys Web 2023, and has taught at Princeton, NYU, IU, and as founding member of the Fornés Institute's Playwriting Workshop. Migdalia is an alumna of New Dramatists, and a member of The Tent, a theater for "Vintage" playwrights. She was featured in: "Fifty Key Figures in Latinx and Latin American Theatre." Her recent essays and interviews appeared in the publications: "Shakespeare And Latinidad," "Diasporic Journeys: Interviews with Puerto Rican Writers in the United States," "A History of Latinx Performing Arts in the U.S.," "The Routledge Companion to Latiné Theatre and Performance," and "Fornés In Context." Among Cruz's touchstone plays: Miriam's Flowers, FUR, Lolita de Lares, SALT, Lucy Loves Me, and El Grito Del Bronx.

tripwireharlot.com

www.ingramcontent.com/pod-product-compliance
Lightning Source LLC
Chambersburg PA
CBHW030226100526
44585CB00012BA/240